Praise for *How We Gather Matters*

How We Gather Matters asks a bold question: Is your event worth... ...provides straight-talk on what makes a purposeful, sustainable event, including honest, practical insights into case studies of hits, misses, and lessons learned. It is a recommended read for event professionals wanting to design their gatherings for socially-conscious, climate-wise attendees and sponsors.

> — Shawna McKinley, Principal, Clear Current Sustainability Consulting

How We Gather Matters is a groundbreaking how-to field guide for the events industry in the 21st century. It skillfully navigates the nexus between impact and sustainable sourcing, offering an insightful and practical blueprint for long-overdue transformative change in a high-profile sector. This should be a mandatory text for any hospitality management course, and bedside reading for corporate event planners.

> — Bob Willard, Founder and Chief Sustainability Champion, Sustainability Advantage

Having spoken at over 2,000 events, I know full well that how we gather matters. But Leor Rotchild's book takes things several steps further, explaining how we can create events that boost the "small but mighty" global movement seeking to ensure that every event and its content is truly future-friendly. He has been there, as they say, and done that.

> — John Elkington, author, *Green Swans and Tickling Sharks*, and
> co-founder, Environmental Data Services (ENDS),
> SustainAbility, and Volans.

Leor has beautifully crafted a page-turner in sustainable event management! Centered on the big issues of circularity, climate change impact, and purchasing, his easy-to-read storytelling approach is thought-provoking and inspiring. After reading this book, event managers will be eager to rush back to work and apply their creative problem-solving skills to sustainability.

> — Meegan Jones, author, *Sustainable Event Management: A Practical Guide*,
> and director, Institute for Sustainable Events

All of us in the sustainability field can recall conferences that preached minimal waste while actually generating tons of garbage and CO_2. If you help plan events or gatherings and are serious about reducing impact, Rotchild's analysis and advice can make an enormous difference in your work.

> — Richard Heinberg, Senior Fellow, Post Carbon Institute,
> and author, *Power: Limits and Prospects for Human Survival*

Leor Rotchild's book *How We Gather Matters* is a must-read for sustainability professionals and event managers around the world. As humanity struggles to forge a sustainable path where all can live well within planetary limits, Leor provides hope for those who bring us together to celebrate and create meaning. His book is a call to action to the global events industry to find its purpose and harness all of its resources, competencies, assets, influence, reach and scale to create a better world. *How We Gather Matters* is engaging, cutting-edge, factual, resource-rich, and evidence-based with an ounce of playful suspense, in other words, a good read. He shows step by step how events can be a greater force for good, setting a new standard for gatherings. Deep within this book is a yearning for all of us as event-goers to play our own part as citizens to make every event count. Thank goodness for Leor's event playbook, which shows us all how.

— Coro Strandberg, President, Strandberg Consulting and Chair, Canadian Purpose Economy Project

How We Gather Matters is a perfectly timed book to help enhance and accelerate a super-power that the global sustainability community has—the ability to collaborate and drive coordinated and systemic change. Leor Rotchild has written a fantastic book that shows why bringing people together in the right way, that walks the talk and helps inspire and stoke more sustainable behaviors, is such a critical piece of the transition to a better future.

— Chris Coulter, CEO, GlobeScan

Most hosts don't take action to make their events sustainable because of the time and expertise required, but Leor has done the work for us. This book needs to be on the desk of anyone considering themselves a professional event producer, or who wants to be sustainable and responsible hosting their next event. A sustainable event is a step in the "everything, everywhere" action called upon by the UN—let this book be your guide to your next step.

— Natalie Lowe, CMM, CRL, owner, Celebrate Niagara;
founder, The Sustainable Events Forum; Events Industry Council winner
for social impact; and Inductee, Canadian Meetings and Events Hall of Fame

In *How We Gather Matters*, Leor Rotchild shows how a well-presented, highly-accessible book can be both practical and inspirational. Drawing on his rich experience in event planning, Rotchild describes how to plan successful events that are good for people and planet. More than this, he explains with examples, that what each of us does and how we do it really matters. I wholeheartedly endorse this fine book.

— Peter A. Victor, Professor Emeritus, York University and
author, *Escape from Overshoot: Economics for a Planet in Peril*

Leor Rotchild has a unique gift for challenging the status quo and making positive change seem not just close at hand, but the only reasonable choice. He has been organizing events and thinking about their role in our lives and in the health of our planet as long as anyone, and his advice on how to make them cleaner and more meaningful makes for a vital handbook for anyone organizing a gathering.

— Chris Turner, author, *How to be a Climate Optimist*

As an event organizer who stewards a 45-year-running, volunteer-driven music festival, the concepts in this book touch on some of the successful strategies that have been the foundation of our longevity. In his book *How We Gather Matters*, Leor Rotchild walks readers through how to design and execute sustainable events that have meaning and purpose. As members of the festival and events ecosystem, the Folk Festival Society of Calgary has a vested interest in other events designing ethical and sustainable gatherings to advance the industry collaboratively. Seasoned event professionals and aspirational event planners alike will gain valuable insights on how to do their best work and make the most of their resources while building community.

— Sarah Leishman, Executive Director, Calgary Folk Music Festival, Block Heater, and Festival Hall

Sustainable event management is now an imperative skill set for event industry professionals, and *How We Gather Matters* teaches you what you need to know. Leor Rotchild describes real-life examples of embedding sustainability into festivals and events, resulting in maximum positive impacts for people and the planet. Readers gain extensive knowledge around reducing greenhouse gas emissions, minimizing waste, avoiding inadvertent greenwashing, and much more. Rotchild's book enables event professionals to better serve their clients, and join the rising sustainable event movement.

— Michele Fox, founder, Members United for Sustainable Events

how we gather matters

SUSTAINABLE EVENT PLANNING
FOR PURPOSE AND IMPACT

LEOR ROTCHILD

Cover design by Diane McIntosh.

Cover images: trees © iStock—Borchee #1257715003;
crowd from above © Shutterstock—Arthimedes #716583703

Interior photos © : pp. 1, 27, 151 IRStone; p. 9 MP Studio;
pp. 67, 89, 101, 127 MVProductions; p. 171 Onchira;
p. 189 annaspoka; p. 211 killykoon; p. 223 Creation Art / Adobe Stock.

Printed in Canada. First printing April, 2024.

Inquiries regarding requests to reprint all or part of *How We Gather Matters* should be addressed
to New Society Publishers at the address below. To order directly from the publishers,
please call 250-247-9737 or order online at www.newsociety.com.

Any other inquiries can be directed by mail to:

New Society Publishers
P.O. Box 189, Gabriola Island, BC V0R 1X0, Canada
(250) 247-9737

LIBRARY AND ARCHIVES CANADA CATALOGUING IN PUBLICATION

Title: How we gather matters : sustainable event planning for purpose and impact / Leor Rotchild.

Names: Rotchild, Leor, author.

Description: Includes bibliographical references and index.

Identifiers: Canadiana (print) 20230596541 | Canadiana (ebook) 2023059655x |
ISBN 9780865719880 (softcover) | ISBN 9781550927818 (PDF) | ISBN 9781771423779 (EPUB)

Subjects: LCSH: Special events—Planning—Environmental aspects. |
LCSH: Special events—Environmental aspects. | LCSH: Sustainability.

Classification: LCC GT3405 .R67 2024 | DDC 394.2068—dc23

New Society Publishers' mission is to publish books that contribute in fundamental ways
to building an ecologically sustainable and just society, and to do so with the least possible impact
on the environment, in a manner that models this vision.

Contents

For Kathryn, Zoey, and Ari.
Thank you for your love and support.

Acknowledgments

I wish to acknowledge Rob West, Judith Brand, Linda Glass, and the whole team at New Society Publishers, as well as Sam Adams and Laura Auna O'Brien for believing in this book and your professionalism throughout the process.

I am honored to have been entrusted with precious stories, resources, and insight from Mark Bannister, David Betke, Jim Button (RIP), Alex Carr, Chris Caners, Mark Cooper, Kalynn Crump (RIP), Gregory Donovan, Frances Edmonds, Tahira Endean, Mercedes Hunt, Suha Jethalal, Lourdes Juan, Sara Leishman, Natalie Lowe, Shawna McKinley, Suzanne Morrell, Hannah Pattison, Mark Rabin, Jose Retana, Andrew Robinson, Brandy Ryan, Elizabeth Shirt, Erika Welch, Bob Willard, and Mayaan Ziv.

Thank you to Kurt Archer, Amanda Langbroek, Marcello Di Cintio, Nehama Horvitz, Denise Hearn, Brandon Klayman, Bob McKenzie, Brenda McKenzie, Kathryn McKenzie, Martin Parnell, Mary Ann Rotchild, Noah Rotchild, Rick Rotchild, and Jason Switzer for your valuable support at critical points in this process.

Shout-out to the Calgary Stampede, Calgary Folk Music Festival and volunteers, Calgary Centre for Newcomers and crew members, Calgary Justice Film Festival, Aga Khan Foundation Canada, Cyclepalooza, Circle Festival, TEDxYYC, Heritage Park and the Innovation Crossing project team, WPC Energy, Rob Ironside, Kelsey McColgan, Bethany Doris, and all the DIG staff and volunteers, my partners Matt Dorma and Chris Dunlap for co-creating many of the projects featured in this book.

While writing this book, I was inspired by Priya Parker, Meegan Jones, Chris Turner, Donna Kennedy Glans, Dave Meslin, Carol Anne Hilton, Annie Korver, Tim Fox, Sophie Jama Malindi, Monica Da Ponte, Abi Skaudis, Julia Zeeman, Julian Zambrano, Aurora Dawn Benton, Colin Smith, Mike Morrison, Nabeel Ramji, Coro Strandberg, Mike Rowlands, and Afdhel Aziz.

Introduction

Each one of us matters, has a role to play, and makes a difference.
Each one of us must take responsibility for our own lives, above all,
show respect and love for living things around us, especially each other.

— Jane Goodall

The sun is out. The beer garden is packed, and flip-flopped music lovers are gyrating to the sound of their new favorite band they don't even know the name of yet. But soon, the roar of the encore will fade and the bright floodlights will mark the conclusion of the festival. For the crew working behind the scenes, this finale signals the start of a long and thankless process known as *strike*. This includes the removal of equipment as well as site cleanup of several tonnes of food waste, packaging, empty water bottles, coffee cups, dirty diapers, and more. These waste items will typically get swept into 20-yard garbage bins headed straight to the local landfill. They will stay there for decades, slowly releasing greenhouse gas emissions into the atmosphere, exacerbating the climate emergency.

New Approach

A new, emerging approach is dramatically changing the events industry not only to address the waste left behind but rather to rethink how it can be a powerful force for good, aligned with the future our world needs.

Whether you're an event planner, service provider, venue owner, or destinations specialist working on festivals, conferences, trade shows, company functions, or weddings, if you work in the events business, you can appreciate

1

how it's the smallest of details that enhance or erode an audience experience. Esthetic appeal, food quality, length of the lineups, available souvenirs—all say something about the culture of the event and the satisfaction of an audience. Now, view each factor through the lens of those who are health-compromised, mobility-challenged, dietary-restricted, or deeply concerned about the climate emergency. How do they view your event?

Inspiring and Welcoming or Wasteful and Part of the Problem?

Many jurisdictions are in the process of changing regulations to achieve net-zero emissions by 2050 to avoid the worst effects of climate change and establish a more circular economy. Since most major events take place in public spaces or buildings serviced by municipalities, planners will be impacted by new local government laws requiring events to have more sophisticated environmental plans in place—and fining organizers not following these rules.

Olympic Legacy

Zero-waste and *sustainable* events have been gaining momentum for some time, but really the ideas became popularized thanks in large part to the 2010 Vancouver Olympic and Paralympic Games, for which the Vancouver Organizing Committee (VANOC) developed best practices for venue design and other infrastructure for legacy use. They demonstrated how mega-events can limit greenhouse gas emissions and landfill burdens. They also benefited socially disadvantaged groups through innovative partnerships and local procurement contracts totaling US$4.3 million. The Vancouver Games also had unprecedented Indigenous participation due to the agreements VANOC signed with the four host First Nations.

The success of the Vancouver Games influenced the zero-waste goals set by the London Games a few years later and net-zero emissions goals that other major sporting organizations have established since, including the Fédération Internationale de Football Association, better known as FIFA.

This welcome trend cannot come soon enough in light of the devastating effects of climate change and biodiversity loss, intensified by the type of runaway consumerism that is celebrated at many popular festivals and events. Audiences are increasingly aware of the significant environmental impacts associated with holding these events. This awareness can be seen either as a risk to event professionals or as an opportunity to wow audiences with a new approach that appeals to their values.

How to Wow

Wowing your audience in this way needs to go far beyond the superficial add-ons that are prone to greenwash accusations. It requires a long-term journey that includes a deeper understanding of the challenges and perspectives. It means prioritizing impact and target-setting with the audience experience in mind. You will also need to invest resources toward making a demonstrable difference to society and the local community, and it should all be grounded in your organizational purpose, which is your fundamental reason for being.

Incorporating social and environmental priorities isn't just the right thing to do. Doing so can attract and retain more investors, partners, staff, and audience members, especially from within younger demographics—who will be your main clients in the years ahead, if they're not already. Millennials and Gen Z are the generations most unafraid of prioritizing their values. In a 2019 survey conducted by Deloitte, roughly half of the Millennials and Gen Z surveyed aspire to have a positive impact in their communities and society.[1] Participating in events that are committed to those same values and aspirations is an important part of engaging younger generations and maintaining their loyalty.

Defining Challenges of Our Time

We find ourselves today in precarious times. Major wars are raging; we're still recovering from a global pandemic; supply chain challenges and inflation are disrupting the economy; an opioid epidemic is claiming lives on urban streets; extreme weather events are causing floods, wildfires, and poor air quality; and systems inequality is limiting justice and economic opportunity for women, Black, Indigenous Peoples, those with disabilities, and other equity-deserving groups.

While these challenges seem daunting, let us not underestimate our ability to effect change. More than a million people are employed in the events industry in the US alone, and the market is expected to grow to nearly US$1.5 billion by 2028.[2] Millions of people attend events each year, which gives our work an out-sized opportunity to influence behaviors and attitudes. No one organizer can possibly address all of the many crises we're facing on their own, so large-scale collective action is required.

Events United

The events industry was once segmented into many isolated areas. Organizers of sporting events and conferences, planners for music festivals and weddings, venue owners, and tourism specialists never met or learned from one another. This is rapidly changing, and the events industry is increasingly acting as one unified sector of society moving toward sustainability. Data from disparate fields is now seen as comparable, and it can be aggregated to track the annual improvements in the industry, both regionally and worldwide.

This evolution of the events industry is reflected in the name change that A Greener Festival made in 2023. After nearly 20 years, the not-for-profit organization is now known as A Greener Future.[3] They help venues and events of all kinds—not just festivals—around the world to reduce their environmental impacts through certifications, training, expertise, and the exchange of best practices. Along with many other wonderful organizations (Net Zero Carbon Events, Vision 2025, and Events Industry Council are a few), they're sharing valuable sector knowledge and driving standards.[4,5,6] There's enough momentum now that audiences are demanding—at an unprecedented level—to see sustainability efforts.

Never before have events been better positioned as a single, powerful industry to meaningfully address climate change, establish a more inspiring and inclusive purpose, and lead change toward zero waste and circularity within the supply chains we all share.

Throughout this book, you will read stories and examples from different types of events. If you work on conferences, it may seem unusual to read about case examples from a music festival and vice versa. I encourage you to see these explorations as universal lessons about change management within the broader high-pressure, deadline-oriented industry you share with those other event organizers.

Your Guide

Allow me to be your guide on a journey toward the future of the events industry. As the CEO of an events services company called Do It Green (DIG), I helped manage the environmental footprint at some of North America's largest festivals and events, diverting more than 300 tonnes of greenhouse gas emissions from our atmosphere and 100 tonnes of waste from landfills. In the process, I became part of a small but mighty movement transforming the events industry toward sustainability and empowerment of marginalized people. In my recent work as executive director for Canada's leading network of sustainable business leaders, known as Canadian Business for Social Responsibility (CBSR), I had the privilege of working closely with several corporate clients of big events on their net zero emissions goals. I still work with some of those companies as a consultant today.

The following chapters are full of practical tips, resources, step-by-step instructions, and personal anecdotes from my experience working with hundreds of event clients. You'll also find stories and case studies entrusted to me through interviews with several sustainable events professionals from around the world—whose shoulders I stand on to bring you this book.

It's my privilege to be your guide on this journey because I love events. I love planning them and attending them. I caught the bug in my early twenties when, along with some friends, I organized an annual 500-person boat cruise party on Lake Ontario that helped me pay my way through college.

Since then, I've been involved behind the scenes at numerous events including the Calgary Stampede, one of North America's largest outdoor events; GLOBE Forum, Canada's largest sustainability conference series; World Petroleum Congress, the world's largest energy conference series, Calgary Justice Film Festival; Calgary Folk Music Festival; Calgary Music Festival; Energy Futures Lab; and a TEDx event series. For a while, I helped produce these events as a side job while climbing the corporate ladder as a sustainability professional in the oil and gas sector. Then a major climate catastrophe put me on a new trajectory.

Climate Catastrophe

The colossal Calgary flood of 2013 was a significant flash point. Sadly, five lives were lost, and there was approximately US$4.5 billion in financial losses and property damage throughout southern Alberta. My then-girlfriend Kate (now my wife) was one of the lucky evacuees, but many people experienced heart-breaking loss and trauma. Office towers were shut for multiple weeks, and Cal-garians, including me and Kate, formed ragtag crews of volunteers that spent every day for three weeks shoveling stinky sewage, pulling drywall apart, and piecing together people's scattered personal property. We did this in several neighborhoods within the city as well as the nearby communities of High River and the Siksika First Nation, which were hit particularly hard.

After weeks of purposeful physical work, I found myself back in the office of a brand-new skyscraper, staring out the window overlooking a beautiful view of downtown Calgary and distant mountains and reflecting on my purpose. I was proud of my time in oil and gas. As a sustainability professional, I effected some positive change from the inside of a major industry driving the economy. I had spoken truth to power, implemented energy transition initiatives, and trained thousands of staff on climate risks, human rights, and the business case for setting ambitious targets. I realized, however, that I no longer felt joy from helping people do less harm.

New Trajectory

I wanted to do something restorative, creative, and 100 percent positive. I began by asking myself what brought me joy. At the time, I was most enjoying my vol-unteer work as environment manager for the Calgary Folk Music Festival. This moment of personal reflection was interrupted, though, when my cell phone rang. On the other end of the line was the organizer of a Flood Aid event to be held at a large sports stadium. They wanted to confirm I was the person respon-sible for the award-winning environmental program at the Folk Fest and asked if I would donate my time to bring the same approach to the 45,000-person fundraising event they were planning.

After hanging up the phone, I called one of my Folk Fest team members to pitch him the idea, and, before we knew it, we were not only planning the envi-ronmental program for Calgary's Flood Aid benefit concert, we were also pre-paring to launch a new social enterprise (DIG) during the event. Three days after that phone call, I wrote my resignation letter and delivered it to my supervisor.

Over the next seven years, as CEO of DIG, I worked with more than fifty event clients in western Canada, helping them plan and execute events that would produce zero-waste and net-zero emissions while also promoting diversity and inclusion. What I observed was that the events organized by people who were pursuing a deeper purpose—beyond profit alone—were more memorable, enjoyable, and ultimately more profitable because they helped people connect to something bigger than just a gathering. They helped attendees feel part of a movement.

My purpose in writing this book is to share my unique approach and lessons learned about creating sustainable events. I hope to equip event organizers with practical tools to do it yourself when it comes to running zero-waste, zero-emissions events that are inclusive and accessible to all, and I want to inspire more people to join the sustainability movement and revolutionize the future of events.

While writing, I was introduced to so many wonderful and supportive leaders in the sustainable events ecosystem who took the time to provide great content, feedback, and encouragement for the creation of this book. Many of them shared with me why they got into sustainable events.

Natalie Lowe of the Sustainable Events Forum in Canada made the connection between climate change and the wildfire that devastated her hometown of Slave Lake, Alberta, in 2011 and vowed to use her platform as an events and destinations spokesperson to advocate for climate-smart events. "I don't like to mince words," she told me in one of our epic conversations. "I want event organizers to feel the urgency we need to solve the climate emergency now." [7]

Suzanne Morrell, of Creating Environments and the Sustainable Event Alliance, grew up in Florida where people painstakingly grow orange trees then harvest and transport the delicious fruits to markets around the world. When she first witnessed gallons of unconsumed orange juice poured down the drain at the end of an event, she felt a great sense of shock and anger. "It was like uncovering a colossal scam with major implications affecting laborers, supply chains, and capitalism itself," she told me. "I made it my mission to meaningfully address overconsumption of the events industry." [8]

Mercedes Hunt, Director of Energy and Sustainability for Marriott International, was motivated to join the sustainable events industry because of all the unsightly waste left behind at the end of events she attended during her early days in the tourism business. "I don't come to your house and leave all my garbage behind," she said to me with overflowing passion, "but events culture has somehow evolved to normalize mass amounts of wasted food, materials, and infrastructure transported from all over the world to die in the host city's local version of a landfill."[9]

Mark Bannister, Production and Operations Director for COP26, came to sustainability through one of his large event clients, Google, who required it as part of their event contracts.[10] "Seeing that client-led desire for sustainability was quite a key moment for me," said Mark. "Some clients tell me 'it has to be exactly that and this, even if you have to make it from scratch,' but Google's approach to events and sustainability required us to do *less*, to adapt to the rough guidelines rather than exact specifications when it can lower the footprint." He added that "seeing a giant, very image-conscious brand like Google come to the agencies with the willingness to compromise in return for sustainability wins" made him believe any event client could and should do so.

I'm so grateful to these and many other events industry leaders for sharing their stories and diverse perspectives with me. Each of them inspired me with their passion for this industry, and if you're reading this book, I suspect you share that passion too.

What Purpose Do You Serve?

This book is an invitation to reimagine the events industry—not just to do less harm but to re-emerge post pandemic to become the world's most powerful vehicle to reach large numbers of people and inspire profound change.

Doing this with a specific set of tools, which I have laid out in these chapters, will unleash the full potential of events to reach larger audiences, enrich our lives, empower people to live according to their true values, and meaningfully contribute to a more purposeful, inclusive, waste- and emissions-free society.

The future of events is going to look different than it does today. Entertaining people, making memorable experiences, or driving tourism spending are not unworthy objectives in themselves, but they fail to answer much bigger, more important questions:

Why does your event exist in the first place? How can it be used to drive the positive change we need to see in our world?

1

Start with Purpose

The purpose of your gathering is more than an inspiring concept.
It is a tool, a filter that helps you determine all the details,
grand and trivial.

— Priya Parker, *The Art of Gathering*

As a Jewish kid growing up in Toronto, it was not obvious I would one day work closely with a church group to create a successful film festival in Calgary, but working on that event for several years was how I came to learn about the importance of *purpose*.

I was on the board of directors for a nonprofit organization in the process of establishing an environmental and human rights-themed film festival. While waiting for a taxi in a trendy Calgary coffee shop, I happened to pick up a community newsletter calling for volunteers to help plan the inaugural Marda Loop Justice Film Festival. Was this an opportunity to combine efforts? After sending an email, I was invited to attend a meeting in a church with the six founding organizers, a few of them in their senior years.

They laid out their plans to share great documentaries with the community, and I asked them why. They seemed surprised by the question, so I explained, "You could design other types of events. Why a film festival?" I was met with stunned silence.

It felt rude to ask directly, but I wanted to know if they were trying to leverage the film festival as a way to introduce their religion to new audiences. I was considering whether to recommend that my board colleagues should pool their resources with this church group. I couldn't figure out if this was going to be a small community church group gathered around a screen with a potluck or a major opportunity to reach a wide mainstream audience and encourage them to act on important causes. Inspiring change through film would be the defining purpose my colleagues and I would rally around.

What Is Purpose?

Your purpose defines *why* your event and organization exist, beyond financial gain. Establishing an overarching and inspiring purpose ensures that the well-being of people and the planet is not consigned to programs or add-ons that fluctuate as you react to competing priorities and irregular levels of funding. A clear and effective purpose drives every aspect of event strategy and execution, including staffing, training, budgeting, format, logistics, supply contracts, partnerships, and communications.

This should not be confused with your vision, which describes *where* you want to arrive, or a future state. Purpose and vision are not always referred to by name even when they exist. They are often buried in long-winded mission statements. I strongly encourage making your purpose, vision, mission and values statements separate, distinct, and concise.

An effective mission statement communicates *what* you will do to arrive at your vision, including specific initiatives or tactics. Your mission can change several times as your event grows and evolves, but your purpose should remain constant.

Your values represent *how* you want to behave in order to achieve your mission.

In combination, your purpose, vision, mission, and values should articulate the positive impact your event aims to make for society.

Does My Event Need a Purpose?

What if it's just a concert or music festival? Can't it just be about the music? That status quo thinking is on its way out. There are risks to using outdated thinking as an event organizer and plenty of lost opportunities to have a positive impact in the local community.

Taylor Swift's record-breaking Eras Tour, for example, was a smashing success by every measure, but it's the local economic impact she had that may be most profoundly remembered and admired years after her catchy songs fade into the background.

Swift donated to food banks in every stop she made on the tour and employed various local businesses for her and the touring crew's daily requirements. She also awarded unprecedented bonus payments totaling over US$55 million to her entire US touring crew, including $100,000 to each of the fifty truck divers involved in transporting the tour's production equipment.[1] The local impacts she left behind were positively life-changing for many people struggling during a difficult time of inflation and pandemic recovery.

After two devastating years of COVID-19 and social isolation, we are all hungry to reconnect with community, celebrate traditions, learn, and be entertained, but let's not default to old conventional patterns. Instead, let's reimagine the way we gather to be more purposeful, inclusive, and waste- and emissions-free. Doing this with a specific formula in mind will unleash the full potential of events to reach larger audiences, enrich our lives, and empower people to live their true values and meaningfully contribute to a better world.

Events Matter

If you're in the events business and you made it through the COVID-19 pandemic, I congratulate you for your resilience. Not only was it a financially devastating period for event planners, service providers, suppliers, and venues, it was also physically, mentally, and emotionally traumatic for almost everyone.

Many events professionals who saw their revenue disappear turned to other industries and side hustles to get by. Some of them are never coming back. For those of you that made it through and are still here in the events industry, you need to know that *your work matters*. In fact, events matter much more than we previously realized.

Recent research out of the UK shows that loneliness and social isolation are directly linked to increased inflammation, which can lead to dementia, depression, and cardiovascular disease, which is the leading cause of death globally.[2] Conversely, in-person, face-to-face meetings stimulate the brain, help form strong bonds, and offer surprising health benefits, according to additional research published in the *Journal of Neuroscience*.[3] Events can serve as valuable community reconnection points with positive health outcomes.

We've all likely attended various kinds of events for personal and professional reasons. Every sector has them, therefore events affect each of us and every segment of the economy.

Events connect us to our community and to each other. They stimulate our senses through music that makes us move, spectacular sights that spark imagination, and scents reminiscent of days long past. We mark major milestones, express cultural traditions, meet new people, learn new skills, and communicate inspiring ideas through events. We also celebrate the triumph of the human spirit through competitions and sporting events.

As an event organizer, you are the conductor of an orchestra, full of moving parts that come together to entertain and delight. The environment you create can serve as an escape from everyday pressures and challenges, and it can make space for connection, reflection, and epiphanies.

However, too often, events take the form of wasteful, resource-intensive gatherings that glorify excess and exclusivity. Municipal landfills serve as graveyards to past events with single-use signs, swag, water bottles, coffee cups, and food waste compressed under decades of unnecessary junk—all of it slowly releasing harmful methane gases into the atmosphere. Events themselves generate significant greenhouse gas emissions, especially when you factor in all the travel required and energy expended. The plastic waste from those events has very likely traveled thousands of miles, and it will eventually leach its way into the food we eat and water we drink.

Instead of being beneficial, events are threatening our lives.

> The purpose of business is not to produce profits. The purpose of business is to produce profitable solutions to the problems of people and planet.
> — Colin Mayer, Future of the Corporation Program Lead at the British Academy

Your Purpose Should Lead to Change

In my experience, it's always better to be a driver of change than be a victim of it.

With your next event, you have an important opportunity right in front of you. You can join a movement with momentum and help determine the future of the events industry. The benefits for doing so are many.

Moving beyond status quo thinking requires an honest assessment of your organization's core purpose, which should be a clear, concise, and aspirational statement about why you exist and what impact you want to have.

According to Priya Parker, author of *The Art of Gathering* (and the inspiration for the title of this book), people often begin event planning with a *format* in mind. They might say, "I like TED Talks, so let's plan a series of eighteen-minute speaker presentations." But this is a misguided approach that will result in a less meaningful event.[4] To make your event matter, you need a clear understanding of how it connects to an overall purpose and helps all involved arrive at a solution to a problem.

Purpose Is Not CSR or ESG

Purpose is often conflated with corporate social responsibility (CSR) or programs designed to invest in local communities, increase transparency, and/or address stakeholder concerns. CSR is often used as a way to secure a social license to operate. Purpose can also be confused with environment, social, and governance (ESG) practices, which aim to quantify non-financial risks for business decisions and investors. Both CSR and ESG are inward-looking and competitive; neither inherently seeks to make a positive impact in the world.

Purpose is a more holistic framework built right into an organization's mandate, which is inherently outward focused, collaborative, and solutions oriented. When deeply integrated, that purpose will guide your organizational culture, strategy, relationships, and event operations. When difficult business decisions are faced, those most aligned with your purpose will be prioritized—even when it's the more expensive option. Your purpose becomes your *do it anyway* factor because it's a commitment to stakeholders and the foundation upon which everything else is built.

Purpose Determines Partnerships

When I met those aspiring organizers of the Marda Loop Justice Film Festival at their church and asked about their intentions, after their stunned silence, they eventually summarized it this way: "We want to welcome people into our church and share great documentaries." Then I asked the *elephant-in-the-room questions*: "Why your church? Are you trying to introduce the audience to your religion?" To my relief, a number of them responded in unison, "No!"

Table 1.1. Evolution from CSR to Purpose

	Past—CSR Leadership By Example	Forward—Purpose Catalyzing Collective Action	Examples
Intent	Build profile, reputation and differentiation	Accelerate change and mobilize networks, collaborations, and partnerships to build a better world	Energy Futures Lab[5] was established as a safe and brave space for unlikely suspects from industry, government, academia, NGOs, and Indigenous communities to collectively chart Canada's energy transition.
Focus	Our organizational strategy	Our shared human challenges	GLOBE Forum[6] completely sold out in 2022 for the first time in 30 years by creating a platform for participants to co-create the road map for Canada to achieve net zero in the next decade.
Goals	Be less bad—subjective and difficult to measure	Be restorative—reversing, reusing, improving in a way that is clearly measured and communicated	Calgary Folk Fest[7] went from incrementally increasing recycling to decreasing its total waste volume and diverting 95% of it within 5 yrs.
Relationships	Stakeholders are "recipients"	Stakeholders are active partners in a social movement, recognizing partnerships may require support and capacity building along the way	GLOBE nurtures a national youth network, which plays an active role in the design and execution of the event, and subsidizes youth leaders to attend and actively participate.
Champion	Manager or advisor	Everyone from the CEO to the contract workers	Calgary Folk Fest trains every volunteer on its sustainability milestones in the onboarding process, regardless of role.
Benefits	Unclear	Tangible—new investment opportunities, attraction of top talent, clients, partners, long-term viability, and reduction in risks, costs	Heritage Park[8] opened the new Innovation Crossing to engage visitors on energy transition, unlocking new partnerships, capital, and transformed the tourist attraction into a dynamic events space.

Source: Rotchild, Leor (based on work from Junxion Strategy).

"Then why is it so important to you to hold this film festival and do it in your church?" I asked. "Well, the church is free," they responded, and I had to agree—a free venue was a pretty good reason to select it. The Riverside Church in Calgary is also a beautiful wheelchair-accessible space with top-notch audio-visual capabilities.

Jenny Krabbe, the de facto leader and the strongest personality of the church group, finally articulated what I was waiting to hear: "We are trying to use film as a way to inform people about important moral issues in the world." That was more consistent with why I was there. I asked why one more time and was rewarded with: "So they will get involved and take some action." Bingo! There it was, the purpose of the event: to inspire people to get involved and take action.

Once our common purpose was clearly established, we were able to move from *why* to *how*. We agreed some documentaries could be depressing, and the challenges depicted might seem too daunting and hopeless to motivate audiences into action. I proposed highlighting heroic people and organizations already tackling big challenges. We planned to focus on the issues themselves and invite speakers who would inform audiences about constructive ways to get involved and further the causes explored in the documentaries.

We also established a nongovernmental organization (NGO) village (now known as Peace Fair), an area devoted to people learning more, uncovering meaningful volunteer opportunities, and supporting charitable causes through donations or purchases of baked goods and holiday gifts.

Together, we grew the Marda Loop Justice Film Festival (now known as the Calgary Justice Film Festival) into an annual 4,500-person event showcasing dozens of social justice and environmental documentaries and causes. The festival's success led to a year-round quarterly film screening series as well as expansion into multiple venues and satellite locations—in Red Deer, Canmore, and Fort MacLeod in Alberta, and Sarnia, Ontario.[9]

Lead with Purpose to Land Your Dream Partner

Dream big for a moment and think of the ideal client you'd like to work with. Your purpose and theirs will ultimately determine whether you fit as partners. For me, as an ambitious new entrepreneur running a sustainable events business based in Calgary, it was a no-brainer who my dream client was: The Calgary Stampede, also known as "The Greatest Outdoor Show on Earth."

Each year, the Stampede welcomes a million visitors through its gates in the very heart of a city that is itself populated by just a little over a million people. It encompasses numerous attractions including a parade, a rodeo, art and agricultural exhibitions, an amusement park, Indigenous cultural celebrations and competitive pow-wow, a food and music festival, and a fireworks display—for ten days straight.

I was often asked how I landed the Calgary Stampede as a major client in my first year of business—and how I maintained them as a loyal and trusting partner each year after that. The answer is simple: I led with purpose. I sought to demonstrate how my company's purpose, which was to "make our communities more livable and sustainable for everyone, one event at a time," could help advance the Stampede's purpose "to preserve and celebrate our western heritage, cultures, and community spirit." [10]

In our first meeting, I suggested they reframe the negative stereotype of "Cowboys VS. Indians" with the more accurate narrative of rural agriculturalists and Indigenous Peoples as "the greatest environmental caretakers the world has ever known," and I connected each of our environmental service offerings back to their purpose around preservation and community. I expressed my genuine belief that doing this could help heal our community, one event at a time.

I was asked to deliver that exact same presentation four times to different teams at the Calgary Stampede and was told by one of the people who saw it each time that environmentalists like me don't usually speak to them that way. "Usually, people want to point out what's wrong with us and how they can fix us, but your approach is all about helping us become who we're striving to be."

I understood what he was getting at. Focusing on the Stampede's *purpose* helped me secure their business, but reframing the Stampede was a key motivator for the top talent we were able to attract.

> Putting in long hours for a corporation is hard. Putting in long hours for a cause is easy.
>
> — Elon Musk

Recruit Top Talent

A strong and inspiring purpose helps to attract top talent, motivated volunteers, and a generally more engaged staff, which results in decreased turnover and burnout and increased innovation stemming from a greater sense of buy-in. Team members are more motivated to bring forward new ideas to increase efficiency and maximize impact when they have a very clear idea of the overall purpose.

We were very fortunate at DIG because we were able to attract top collaborators: operations managers coming out of an extremely well-paid oil industry; event managers with large-scale, high-profile events experience; and municipal waste and recycling specialists willing to sort through trash and compost for hours on end. DIG certainly did not lure these professionals with competitive compensation; in fact, some of them volunteered their valuable time. One benefit of the job was access to free music festival tickets and other events, but many of our most talented and experienced team members never took advantage of such perks. They showed up and worked hard because they felt they were part of a community of like-minded people, passionate about the environment, effecting positive change *"one event at a time."*

Purpose, Vision, Mission, and Values

Your purpose statement is a sentence or two defining *why* your organization and event exist. It's not about financial gain. It's not a tagline, program, or marketing campaign, and it's not the same as your vision, mission, and values.

> Social purpose is a "North Star"— an ongoing quest, forever pursued.
> — Social Purpose Institute, United Way

The well-known Burning Man event serves as a good example to highlight the difference between these four elements. Since its inception in 1986, Burning Man has inspired a global cultural movement and loyal community. Each year more than seventy thousand people gather in the Nevada desert for the annual nine-day festival that includes art installations, spontaneous performances, wild costumes, and celebrations. Burning Man is organized by a nonprofit called the Burning Man Project. Its reason for existing—its *purpose*—is to *"produce positive spiritual change in the world."*[11]

Unfortunately, Burning Man's purpose is buried in its long and wordy mission statement, and they would do well to separate and highlight it. Similarly, their vision is embedded in the same statement. An effective vision statement describes a future state or destination which is *where* they want to arrive. For Burning Man, it seems that destination is an active and creative society connected to the environment: *"A society that connects each individual to his or her creative powers, to participation in community to the larger realm of civic life, and to the even greater world of nature that exists beyond society."*

Your *mission* is *what* you will do to arrive at your vision. There could be several missions that show up as specific initiatives or tactics within your event operations, strategies, or communications describing what you will or won't do for a specific audience.

Simplicity of TED

TED has produced one of the most impressive global event brands in history. Originally focused on technology, entertainment, and design—hence the name, TED—it is now responsible for countless viral TED Talk videos that advance its more general purpose to *"foster the spread of great ideas."* TED aims to "provide a platform for thinkers, visionaries, and teachers, so that people around the globe can gain a better understanding of the biggest issues faced by the world, and feed a desire to help create a better future." Most TED admirers know this purpose through the popular tagline that summarizes it: *Ideas Worth Spreading.*

So succinct and consistent is TED's purpose, that, through a radical decentralization of their business model, TEDx events have proliferated around the world, making the event series fundamentally more inclusive—while adding rocket fuel to the spread of ideas. While TED's tagline may come across more like a mission statement, it's important to note their mission has actually changed multiple times, but it was all in service of their purpose to spread ideas as widely and rapidly as possible.

As an organizer of one of those TEDx events in Calgary, I cornered TED staff at a TED Active event, which gathered TEDx organizers from around the world, and I pressed them about how to get our TEDxYYC Talks picked up by TED.com (YYC is the airport code for Calgary). I was told that sound quality mattered a lot and visual quality, too, to some degree, but it was really all about the quality of the ideas and their potential to change people's minds or behaviors.

Burning Man's mission is to *"nurture and protect the community created by Burning Man and its culture."* What they developed in connection with this mission was the Ten Principles as guidelines for the worldwide network of "Burners" who connect with each other to foster Burning Man's values through local community events and other year-round activities. All these efforts are geared toward the ultimate purpose of producing positive spiritual change.

That clear purpose and consistent approach enabled us to sell out our TEDxYYC events to 1,600 people each year, create an innovative learning environment for people to connect with one another, and recruit world-class speakers—more than 30 of which were featured on TED.com and streamed over 3.5 million times.

It was through local TEDx events like ours that unknown speakers such as Brené Brown and Simon Sinek catapulted to stardom. Theirs are some of the most widely watched talks in TED's history. Had TED not innovated their business model to make it more accessible, the world may never have known about Brené Brown or Simon Sinek, who are household names in some circles today.

Perhaps unsurprisingly, Sinek's TEDx Talk, the most viral of all time, introduced mainstream audiences to the topic of purpose. He introduced us to his *Golden Circle* and explained that, too often, people lead with what they *do*, while people are more attracted to *why you do it*.

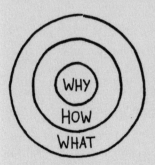

Why = The Purpose
What is your cause? What do you believe?
APPLE: We believe in challenging the status quo and doing things differently

How = The Process
Specific actions taken to realize the Why.
APPLE: Our products are beautifully designed and easy to use

What = The Result
What do you do? The result of Why. Proof.
APPLE: We make computers

FIGURE 1.1. The Golden Circle. Credit: Simon Sinek.

An organization's values will shape *how* you want to act to achieve your vision. They describe the ethos and culture you are developing for your team, your supply chain, and your audience.

Burning Man's values are captured in its Ten Principles:

- Radical Inclusion
- Gifting
- Decommodification
- Radical Self-reliance
- Radical Self-expression
- Communal Effort
- Civic Responsibility
- Leaving No Trace
- Participation
- Immediacy

These values serve as a guide to shape the actions of the Burning Man community as well as the organizers, who should nurture these behaviors by example. These are the attributes they believe will lead them to be successful in their mission to achieve their vision in service of their ultimate purpose to produce positive spiritual change in the world.

How to Craft Your Purpose Statement

A great purpose statement is first **found**, then **lived**, and, finally, **communicated**. It may be tempting to jump right to the communication of your new purpose statement, but that carries the risk of coming across as inauthentic—a form of *purpose-washing*—if it is misaligned with a clear demonstration of that purpose in action.

Look Back

The right place to begin, regardless of event type or scale, is a *look back*. Ask yourself: *Why am I doing this?* Is there a particular problem you want to solve? What passion or motivation draws you to this event? I encourage you to reflect on your initial intention, especially if you are someone who has been planning events—or this particular event—for many years.

We often begin a major endeavor with one type of experience in mind, but through the steep learning curve of practicality, time constraints,

> Gathering is a form of leadership, it's not a form of logistics.
>
> — Priya Parker

and financial reality, we too often come out the other end with something feasible but fairly conventional compared with the original vision. This is a natural part of any process, so it's not necessarily negative, but if we completely lose sight of that initial Big Idea, we run the risk of spending our precious time and resources only to deliver an event for a limited number of people who will find your event unremarkable, uninspiring, and forgettable.

A look back may involve revisiting your origin story. When I was invited to advise on Heritage Park's Innovation Crossing project in Calgary, for example, there was a lot of confusion about what they were trying to achieve with their beautiful new space. When I came on board, it was a static, museum-like experience attempting to tell a convoluted narrative about how innovative the oil and gas industry is, but there was nothing at all innovative about the experience.

It was helpful to take a few steps back and work with the leadership team at Heritage Park on why they had pursued this project in the first place. It brought us right back to the origins of Heritage Park, which was established in 1963 to *"preserve the history of the West and educate guests of all ages"* about the transitions that took place over a long span of time.

Look Out

After looking back, the next step in developing a project's purpose is a *look out*. It requires a full assessment of the key risks and challenges in the world most relevant to your business and the future of your industry. How do you determine which issues are most relevant? Consider your values and build out from there. Why values, as opposed to your mission or strategy? Because missions are fluid and strategies can fail. Values tend to be long-lasting. Ask yourself and other team members:

- What do we all care deeply about?
- How can we amplify that to make the world better?
- What concerns or frustrations do we have about our industry?
- How can we change what frustrates us most?
- What are the best practices in our industry?
- Who are the key influencers?
- Can we collaborate or establish partnerships with those influencers?

Whether you're at the early stages of establishing your event's purpose or reviewing an existing one, I invite you to think big and draw inspiration from the UN's 17 Sustainable Development Goals (SDGs).[12] They will prompt you to reflect on the world's most urgent to-do list and connect your event to a bigger movement for change. The SDGs were unanimously adopted by all 193 UN member nations in 2015. There are 169 targets summarized under the 17 broad goals, which you can see in figure 1.2. As you review these Sustainable Development Goals, ask yourself the following questions:

- Which SDGs could we contribute to if we were wildly successful?
- Which SDGs could we credibly align with our purpose and values?
- How would we measure performance progress in these areas?
- What partnerships make sense for us to establish to address those SDGs?

FIGURE 1.2. The United Nation's 17 Sustainable Development Goals. Credit: United Nations.

Look to Stakeholders

Speaking to your stakeholders is another important part of the process to determine what's most material to them. In the process, you may discover in what way you are uniquely qualified to make a significant positive impact.

On the Heritage Park project, for example, we spoke to a number of stakeholders. We all agreed the most urgent and relevant topic to address was energy *transition*. We arrived at the idea that transition stories throughout history could be the perfect backdrop to engage visitors on what navigating this current energy transition might require of us. This process led to interesting conversations and new relationships with key influencers in, as well as outside, the energy industry, which Heritage Park had no previous exposure to.

Look Within

The final step in the process of finding your event's purpose is to **look within**. This should include an honest assessment of your strengths, culture, assets, brand, reputation, and track record. Talk to your staff, suppliers, clients, sponsors, partners, and guests, and ask them:

- What makes you proud to be working with our organization?
- How would you describe our culture?
- What are we really good at?
- What makes our events memorable?
- Where are the areas we can improve?
- What are we uniquely positioned to contribute?
- What existing programs can we leverage?
- What might we need to stop doing?
- How can we incentivize the behavior we want and the change that we need?
- What new opportunities might open up as a result of pursuing a grand ambition?

When Heritage Park leaned into the idea of using historical artifacts, anecdotes, and interactive displays to engage visitors on the challenges and opportunities surrounding energy transition, they knew it could be a divisive topic for some. After all, they are situated in Calgary, the very heart of Canada's fossil fuel industry, and many of Heritage Park's largest donors were active or retired senior oil and gas leaders.

As Priya Parker notes in her book, having the right kind of controversy provides a level of tension that can make gatherings more energetic, more lively, and ultimately more memorable. That tension, when channeled effectively, can lead to greater understanding and breakthrough solutions.

Heritage Park's strong reputation as an educator positioned it perfectly to offer a safe space for disparate groups to explore ideas, have important conversations, break bread, and find solutions to common challenges. This realization influenced the design of the space. Instead of having bulky, immovable artifacts taking up a lot of the available space, a flexible design was developed to accommodate flowing crowds as well as convert into an event space for gatherings and meal service.

By understanding the key differences between purpose, vision, mission, and values; integrating the *look back, look out, and look within* approach; and collecting feedback from your various stakeholders, you will have all the tools you need to define a compelling purpose for your event or organization.

Once you find your purpose, conduct a simple self-assessment of it through the free Social Purpose Assessment tool available from the Social Purpose Institute at the United Way.[13] See the Tools and Resources section of this book for the link.

Going through this process and finding your organizational purpose will help elevate your event from yet another gathering to something truly inspirational, important, and good for the world.

Build a Better Future

The events business is a deadline-focused, high-pressure profession with myriad small and large variables that can determine the difference between wild success and economic ruin. It helps to be reminded that your event can be so much more than just another conference, tourist attraction, or client gig. Events help us connect with and expand our community. They can expose us to new perspectives, cultures, and ideas. They can be personal or professional opportunities to learn, grow, and explore.

After many years of working with hundreds of major music festivals, sporting events, and conferences, I was surprised by the low number of purpose-driven event organizers and their notoriously poor articulation of a compelling purpose.

I was fortunate that an early experience with the Justice Film Festival helped me see how important it was to establish a purpose as a way to establish trust, find space to collaborate, and build for the future. A new generation of organizers now runs the Marda Loop Justice Film Festival. They changed the name to the Calgary Justice Film Festival, but the purpose remains: *"To influence positive behavioral change by sharing environmental and social justice films that inspire and engage neighbors to become global citizens."*

I met my wife at the Calgary Justice Film Fest. We were both drawn to the event based on our common values and sense of purpose, and our virtual baby shower was attended by some of the people who were part of that purpose-driven community we helped to nurture.

If the events industry is going to exist in the future, it will not be because we have a human right to live music, networking, or sporting events. It will be because, for the short time that these events take place, we can connect to something bigger than ourselves, something meaningful, and catch a glimpse of the future we need and want to live in and the community we want to be part of.

2

Grow Your Audience
through Inclusion

Inclusion is not a matter of political correctness. It's the key to growth.

—Rev. Jesse Jackson

"How can we? We're fasting!"

That was the question and challenge presented to the organizers of an infamous breakfast event for approximately seven thousand people during the Calgary Stampede in Alberta, Canada.

It's difficult to describe to someone who has never been to the Calgary Stampede how completely the ten-day festival permeates its host city—and even surrounding areas. One way Calgarians partake in the festivities is to attend the free pancake breakfasts offered throughout the city. They are so abundant, you need to download an app to keep track of them all. No joke.

Arguably the best of these Stampede breakfasts is the one hosted by the Ismaili Muslim community at the city's largest *jamatkhana* (a religious Ismaili Muslim prayer hall). The Stampede's outreach committee usually has a booth and visible presence at this breakfast, and the Ismaili community enjoys being embraced wholeheartedly by one of Canada's largest and most enduring entertainment institutions.

The Ismaili Stampede breakfast is extremely popular. In part, this is because it fuses two cultural traditions in an interesting way, but it's also because the components of the meal are all freshly prepared by a team of 250 volunteers who also serve bottomless cups of delicious chai, a sweet treat called *jalebi*, and *bharazi*—a protein-rich East African dish made with pigeon peas in a coconut milk sauce.

In 2014, the Calgary Stampede took place during the holy month of Ramadan. The religious holiday always takes place in the ninth month of the Islamic calendar, but, since it's a lunar calendar, the timing fluctuates on our Western calendar. During Ramadan, Muslims traditionally fast from dawn to dusk, so a Stampede breakfast during Ramadan would exclude all those observing the holiday—including the hundreds of volunteers needed to pull off the event. In order to enable the Ismaili community to feel included in the culture of one of North America's largest festivals, the breakfast event organizers had to get creative.

Why Be Inclusive?

Including diverse communities in your events is not just the right thing to do, it's an important way to grow your audience and enhance the experience for everyone. Inclusion is not inevitable. It requires a focused effort because there are usually significant barriers that prevent certain demographics from fully participating or recommending your event to others in their community. Understanding those barriers and finding creative solutions is really the key to scaling your event, growing into diverse communities, deepening your potential impact, and building your future audience.

One of the most basic objectives for any event organizer is to make people feel welcome. Chances are, you've felt out of place at some point in your life when you walked through the door into some new environment. Perhaps you didn't know anyone. Maybe you felt younger or older than the rest of the crowd. Maybe people looked different, spoke another language, or wore very different clothing than what you showed up in. This feeling is common, especially for anyone visibly identified with a particular culture, religion, ethnicity, race, gender, sexual orientation, or physical ability.

As humans, we all want to feel safe and belong, but feeling that way can be easily taken for granted by those who have never experienced discrimination, microaggressions, verbal abuse, physical violence, or generational trauma.

The steps you take to make your event accessible to diverse audiences can grow your event, but that growth won't be sustained if you don't do the up-front planning required to create a safe and welcoming space where diverse voices are respected, represented, and heard.

If your event does not already have a strategy in place for engaging immigrant communities, Black, Indigenous, people of color (BIPOC), lesbian, gay, bisexual, transgender, queer, questioning, intersex, asexual, two-spirited (LGBTQIA2S+), and people with mixed physical and cognitive abilities, then you're writing off millions of potential audience members at your events.

Events can be the world's most powerful vehicle to reach large numbers of people and inspire profound change. Events also celebrate, protect, and advance culture in our society. We often think of weddings, births, coming-of-age celebrations, holidays, and memorials as cultural events. However, sporting events, festivals, and even conferences are also types of cultural gatherings full of rituals and traditions, including what we wear and how we greet each other.

Culture is the territory of the events industry, more so than any other sector, and experienced event professionals know the traditions you alter, content you curate, speakers, performers, and music that you feature all affect the overall experience in significant ways, not just for the audience, but for everyone behind the scenes too.

This book is my medium, and I'm using it to elevate diversity, equity, and inclusion because I've come to understand how systems and norms established long ago affect our everyday interactions and gatherings today. *We can end vicious cycles or perpetuate harmful stereotypes with the language we use and the environment we create.*

I understand some of the topics addressed here are provocative. It would certainly be easier to ignore them and jump straight into the environmental issues associated with events. There are many with more lived experience of these sensitive issues, and I recognize as I write these words that my perspectives may seem outdated or archaic even a few short years from now. I choose to share them, though, because I believe it's impossible to meaningfully address our greatest environmental challenges without an appreciation for the social impacts and opportunities associated with the decisions we make.

However, I'm still learning, myself. It's thanks to my interactions with justice, equity, diversity, and inclusion (JEDI) masters that I have a clearer understanding of how inclusion can be a conscious change from systems designed for power *over* others, which fuel human suffering in the name of economic growth, toward an approach that creates power *with* others that recognizes the strengths and potential of a diverse ecosystem of perspectives, contexts, skills, experiences, and ways of knowing.

Your event is *your* medium. It's important that you recognize the responsibility you have in creating something that uplifts rather than divides participants. The message you deliver through your event should not perpetuate stereotypes, historic injustice, or exclusion. You can completely flip the common narratives by introducing inclusive language and perspectives that highlight more voices, enable reflection, and update old paradigms. Doing so will make your event more dynamic, memorable, and relevant for your current and your future audiences.

This approach is the secret to growth and longevity.

You could design an event like others you've done before, or you could think of your event as a "pop-up" experience—a temporary alternative world that borrows the Burning Man principles of Radical Inclusion and Leaving No Trace Behind. Or you could use the Passover principle that Priya Parker writes about in *The Art of Gathering*. On Passover each year, we're encouraged to ask: *"How is this night different from all other nights?"* [1] The answer could be: *"Tonight, we welcome and celebrate those who still long for freedom from oppression."*

> The medium is the message.
> —Marshall McLuhan

There are some who will view any attempt to create safe and accessible spaces for those that have been historically marginalized as pandering to left-wing "cancel culture" or flavor-of-the-month "woke-ism." Tune that out. Those arguments are caricatures of the human rights struggles that have endured through generations of antiquated and suppressive power structures enabled through ignorance and apathy.

Break the Fast

Faced with the possibility of canceling the Ismailli Stampede breakfast, event organizers rallied together with their stakeholders to consider their options. Together, they solved the challenge by reimagining the breakfast event to be a *Break the Fast* sunset event. This not only ensured that the Ismaili Muslim community could fully participate in the beloved Stampede tradition, but it also tied beautifully to the common Islamic practice known as *Iftar*, which involves breaking the day's fast at sunset with family, friends, and community members.

In the 100-plus years of the Calgary Stampede, there had never been a pancake breakfast held in the evening. But why not? The idea captured people's imaginations, and the non-alcoholic, family-oriented evening event resulted in one of the most successful Stampede events ever. It demonstrated how combining the holy traditions of a cultural community with the festive traditions of a local events institution can result in something altogether new, and farther reaching than either one could have imagined on their own.

Newcomers Make It Sweeter

The Ismaili Stampede event reminds me of an old story I heard long ago about a group of Zoroastrians who fled Persia to escape religious persecution. They arrived on the port of Gujarat in India during a major cultural festival. King Jadhav Rana, not wanting outsiders to disrupt the festivities, sent an emissary to greet the strangers. Since they did not speak the same language, the emissary was sent with a full glass of milk to communicate symbolically that the festival and community were already full to the brim and could not accommodate the weary group. The Zoroastrians immediately got the message.

However, one particularly astute Zoroastrian priest responded by pulling out a sack of sugar the group brought with them on their harrowing journey and poured some of its contents into the glass of milk, asking the emissary to deliver it back to the King. He understood the gesture to mean that just as the full glass does not overflow with the addition of sugar, so too can the festival and community be made richer and sweeter with the inclusion of these strangers. King Rana was so impressed that he granted asylum to the group and made them his honored guests during the festival.

The Calgary Stampede was recently made sweeter thanks to the addition of a new community partner. When the Stampede emerged from a devastating two-year hiatus due to COVID-19, they had to work quickly to rehire and replace thousands of staff and contractors. When the Stampede contacted me for help with their compost programs, the timing was difficult. After two years on the sidelines, the team I had groomed over several years to deliver an efficient Stampede program had all gone in separate directions. I really wanted to support the continuation of the environmental programs I helped initiate at the Calgary Stampede, but where could we possibly find the staff needed to manage the project on such short notice?

Through a chance conversation resulting in an innovative partnership with the Centre for Newcomers, a Calgary-based social services agency, we were able to source, vet, and train a new team of 40 newcomers to Canada in record time. The team included refugees from Ukraine, Afghanistan, and Syria. For most of them, it was their first-ever Canadian work experience. Their work ethic, enthusiasm, and gratitude for the well-paying, meaningful work was nothing short of inspiring. This was by far the most rewarding and stress-free project I have enjoyed over a decade of collaboration with the Calgary Stampede. The Stampede staff agreed; they hired four of the crew members as permanent staff. And, based on the success of the collaboration, the Centre for Newcomers set up a revenue-generating social enterprise to take over project management of the annual festival compost program.

Creative supplier partnerships like the refugee-powered compost program at the Calgary Stampede enable all kinds of positive social impacts. The program generated meaningful employment for marginalized populations, which made them better equipped to support their families and facilitated a quicker and more fulsome integration into their newly adopted community. The experience engendered an emotional connection and long-term loyalty for all those involved. It was also very inspiring for the event staff, especially those that went on to work with the four new staff members; over time, staff learned much more about the refugee experience. This purpose-driven success story could have sweet ripple effects on many levels, for years to come. It has the potential to motivate many more creative supplier partnerships and innovative ideas in several other areas.

Pursuing Inclusion Means Addressing Injustice

The negative ripple effects of the COVID-19 pandemic have been especially devastating for the most vulnerable members of society. Socioeconomic pressures caused by the war in Ukraine and the rising costs of food, energy, and housing have only exacerbated the situation. Recent social and political movements have pushed these issues into mainstream consciousness—with calls for meaningful action by all sectors of society.

As a result, conversations about diversity, equity, and inclusion have become common, and corporate priorities have shifted to address the issues. Too often, though, the results show up as headcount statistics and tokenistic gestures. Actual inclusion is most successful when it aims to address inequalities, injustices, and barriers or to create safe and welcoming environments for those historically marginalized, excluded, or colonized.

If your audience is apathetic toward justice, equity, diversity, and inclusion, it's up to you to find ways to meaningfully engage and inspire them toward behavior consistent with your purpose, values, and the impact you aspire to make. There are times when you may have to go further than engagement. You may have to implement policies that specify positive behavior that shapes the kind of culture you want at your event and protects people from abuse or psychological harm.

> Environmentalism without class struggle is just gardening.
>
> —Chico Mendes, Brazilian rubber tapper, trade union leader, environmentalist, and human rights activist

Give the Headdress a Rest

In 2014, as Indigenous headdresses were becoming a popular fashion trend at music festivals, a boutique music and arts festival called Bass Coast, taking place in interior British Columbia, Canada, became the first festival to ban non-Indigenous people from wearing them. It was a controversial move at the time with security crews responsible for enforcing the ban. It was about showing respect, according to Paul Brooks, the festival's communications manager. He was quoted as saying, "There are many Indian bands in the area, many reservations, so we want to be good neighbors." The headdresses are a sacred symbol of strength, bravery, respect, and responsibility in Indigenous cultures. They're typically worn during ceremonies, powwows, and other formal occasions. For a non-Indigenous person to wear the symbol without understanding the meaning or earning the privilege to wear it is demeaning.

For generations, Indigenous Peoples around the world have fought for acknowledgement of the violence done to them through colonization and the ongoing harms of settler colonialism. Appropriating sacred symbols without any understanding or acknowledgment for where they came from is an act of disrespect. It's especially insensitive in light of recent discoveries of more than 1,000 children's remains in unmarked graves at former residential school sites in Canada. Those discoveries provided the impetus for Pope Francis to visit Canada in 2022 and eventually issue an apology for the Roman Catholic Church's role in the spiritual, cultural, emotional, physical, and sexual abuse of First Nations, Inuit, and Métis children in the church-run, government-funded schools—schools that had been designed to convert and assimilate Indigenous children while eradicating their languages and cultures. Residential "boarding schools" with similar culture-erasure goals were instituted in the US, Australia, New Zealand, South Africa, Ireland, and Sweden.

As the grandson of Holocaust survivors, I can't help but see parallels with what my family went through and empathize with the invisible, multigenerational trauma that so many carry today. I don't know firsthand how painful it must be to see pictures of drunk festivalgoers dancing in Indigenous headdresses, but I imagine it to be something like seeing neo-Nazis wearing yarmulkes to a costume party.

Policies like the one initiated by Bass Coast can help people feel physically and psychologically safe and welcome. They can also move us closer toward healing and equality. Bass Coast's policy was widely celebrated, and it attracted international media attention. More importantly, it sparked a global conversation about cultural appropriation and the responsibility festival organizers have to address it. Several other festivals across Canada have passed similar policies regarding the Indigenous headdresses, but curiously, many of the notable ones such as Burning Man and Coachella, where such offenses have been common, have yet to take a firm public position on the matter.

Black Lives Matter

One of the keys to creating safe spaces is to recognize and acknowledge how power was lorded over those perceived to be "different" and reform the ecosystems where we have influence to be more powerful and enduring because of the inclusion of diverse people.

> The opposite of racist isn't "not racist." It is "anti-racist."
> — Ibram X. Kendi, *How To Be an Antiracist*

In his seminal book, *The Color of Law: A Forgotten History of How Our Government Segregated America*, Richard Rothstein writes, "We have created a caste system in this country, with African Americans kept exploited and geographically separate by racially explicit government policies.

Although most of these policies are now off the books, they have never been remedied and their effects endure."[2]

Many parts of our everyday lives, such as the suburbs where we live and the sports leagues our children play in, were originally designed with exclusionary intent.

Sports offer interesting case studies as many sporting event organizers choose not to market to diverse demographics because it's believed that people in white, affluent communities are more likely to be physically active and therefore a better fit for their events. It's worth taking a look at some of the factors that contribute to that perception. According to a 2015 literature review from Arizona State University, fears of violence, unleashed dogs, and lack of sidewalks were cited as some of the main barriers preventing people of color from more physical activity.[3] So, access to local sports and physical activities are really key justice and accessibility issues that your sporting event may be in a unique position to help address.

Looking beyond the literature and into the world around us, we see it has changed significantly since 2020, when the world woke up to the COVID-19 pandemic and a 25-year-old Black athlete named Ahmaud Arbery was shot to death by a former police officer and his son, while out for a jog near his home on a Sunday afternoon in Brunswick, Georgia. To mark what would have been his birthday, hundreds of thousands of runners around the globe took part in the 2.23 mile (a nod to the date of Ahmaud's murder) virtual run and documented it using the hashtag *#IRUNWITHMAUD*.

Arbery's senseless murder occurred just one month before the murder of another Black man named George Floyd. This time the tragic final moments under the knee of a Minneapolis police officer, and Floyd's last words—"I can't breathe"—were captured in a now infamous nine-minute-and-29-second viral video. His death exploded into mass protests across the US—more than 15 million Americans took part—as well as an international movement to end white supremacy once and for all.

When the Black Lives Matters movement hit a tipping point, many event organizers posted black squares on their social media channels and released generic public statements about standing in solidarity with the Black community. However, moments of intense social unrest should not be used to redirect attention to ourselves or drown out the marginalized voices screaming to be heard. Those voices are calling for action and meaningful change, not empty gestures of support. When emotions are raw and people are mobilizing, words can feel performative and aggravating.

Your role as an event organizer in such volatile moments should be to listen with an open heart to the key figures engrossed in the struggle. Amplify their voices in your social media channels rather than your own. Seek opportunities to learn more about the context, plan to take meaningful action, reflect on your organizational purpose and who you need to engage, and talk to others around you about the issues.

Check in with your team and encourage internal dialogue about how people are feeling. Some may be triggered by what's happening and need a safe space to share what's coming up for them. If you have team members with contrary views, provide a safe space for them to express themselves, but set some boundaries about respectful language and criticism of systems, institutions, or outcomes, rather than individuals.

When contrarians counter the "Black Lives Matter" mantra with "All Lives Matter," they're refusing to acknowledge the unfortunate truth that not all lives are valued in the same way. Ignoring this reality reduces the ongoing challenge of inequality to just a rare and archaic individual prejudice as opposed to something systemic, institutionalized, and solvable.

As an event organizer, you have the power to leverage your immense platform— your medium—to amplify marginalized voices and promote powerful ideas that expand access to equality.

Addressing the great challenges of our time as solvable, rather than hopeless, places the responsibility for change on us all. It empowers participants to be actively anti-racist, establishes a sense of community, and can inspire incredible loyalty toward your event and you as an event organizer.

What's in a Name?

In 2020, Dan Snyder, National Football League (NFL) owner of the (now former) Washington Redskins, finally walked back his infamous comments from 2013 published in *USA Today*, in which he proclaimed that the team would never change its name. Never say never. Holding onto old rigid ideas is stifling in a world of shifting societal values.

The name change from the Redskins to the Washington Commanders finally occurred when a social movement succeeded in changing the economics of the situation. Eighty-seven financial firms and shareholder groups wrote letters to the team's three main sponsors urging them to end their relationship with the sports team unless they reconsidered the name change. The three sponsors were Nike, PepsiCo, and FedEx. FedEx has been the naming rights sponsor of the team's stadium since 1998 and "official delivery service sponsor" of the NFL since 2000. FedEx Chairman and CEO Fred Smith was also a minority owner of the team, and he threatened to sell off his shares. All three sponsors vowed to end their relationship with the team, which ultimately forced the name change.

Inspired by the name change in Washington and moved to action following the discovery of the unmarked children's graves at former residential schools, Belairdirect, a national insurance provider in Canada, announced it was rethinking its relationship with the Edmonton Eskimos—a major Canadian Football League (CFL) team. *Eskimo* is a colonial term imposed on the Indigenous Peoples of the Arctic, who largely refer to themselves as *Inuit*. The team changed their name soon after to the Edmonton Elks.

In both sports examples, despite many years of grassroots activism, it was the investors who ultimately created the impetus for change—but it's not always about the money.

> We'll never change the name. It's that simple. NEVER—You can use caps.
>
> — Dan Snyder, NFL Owner, Washington Commanders (formerly Washington Redskins)

Diversity Has a Significant Return on Investment

A 2018 study by the *Harvard Business Review* found that the most diverse organizations also tended to be the most innovative, giving them the capacity to market to a broader range of people and consumer segments.

Organizations that are diverse themselves tend to perform significantly better than their industry peers. Figure 2.1 shows the results of a study conducted by McKinsey & Co in 2014. It estimates that organizations that have both gender and ethnic diversity can financially perform up to 25 percent better than the national industry median. Organizations in the top quartile for racial and ethnic diversity were also 35 percent more likely to have financial returns above their respective national industry medians.

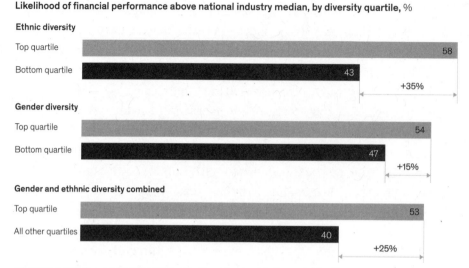

Likelihood of financial performance above national industry median, by diversity quartile, %

Ethnic diversity

Top quartile — 58

Bottom quartile — 43

+35%

Gender diversity

Top quartile — 54

Bottom quartile — 47

+15%

Gender and ethhnic diversity combined

Top quartile — 53

All other quartiles — 40

+25%

FIGURE 2.1. Ethnic and Gender Diversity Correlates with Financial Performance. Source: McKinsey Diversity Database.

Finally, organizations in the top quartile for gender diversity are 15 percent more likely to have financial returns above their respective national industry medians.

According to Innovation, Science and Economic Development Canada, adopting diversity and inclusion (JEDI) strategies can help organizations advance their organizational targets. Many have shown that leveraging these strategies can have the following beneficial effects:

- Attract and retain the best and the brightest to broaden the talent pool and help overcome skill gaps in a rapidly evolving and increasingly volatile economy
- Gain access to more diverse markets
- Increase employee satisfaction, engagement, and overall performance
- Catalyze innovation by bringing multiple perspectives and experiences together to solve complex problems

Why Are We So Behind?

Although diverse organizations are more profitable, it seems the events industry has a serious representation problem to overcome. In the UK, 82 percent of the events industry is White. Only 3 percent of event organizers identify as Black, and another 3 percent identify as having a disability of any kind. These were the findings from a 2020 study by BCD Meetings and Events, in partnership with Leeds Beckett University, and Worldwide Exhibition for Incentive Travel, Meetings, and Events (more commonly known as IMEX).

While women make up approximately 80 percent of the events industry, just 27 percent hold executive roles, and they get paid roughly 11 percent less than men in the same or similar roles, according to a Meetings & Conventions 2018 salary survey. Although that pay equity gap has been closing since 2015, it seems to have stagnated since the start of the pandemic.

> Privilege isn't about what you've gone through; it's about what you haven't had to go through.
>
> —Janaya "Future" Khan

Nearly 70 percent of the respondents in the BCD study felt that *traditional bias* was a key reason that women are underrepresented at senior levels. Issues concerning work/life balance and maternity leave also polled highly, suggesting that the industry must find better ways to support working mothers through incentives such as childcare vouchers and enhanced paternity pay to encourage more dads to be primary caregivers and support their partners to reenter the workforce. Having taken parental leave twice myself, I highly recommend it.

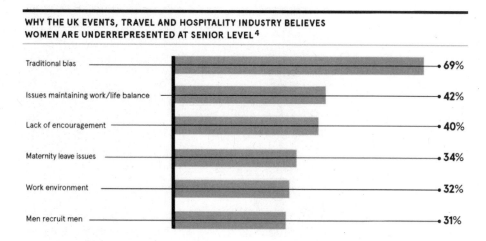

WHY THE UK EVENTS, TRAVEL AND HOSPITALITY INDUSTRY BELIEVES WOMEN ARE UNDERREPRESENTED AT SENIOR LEVEL[4]

Traditional bias	69%
Issues maintaining work/life balance	42%
Lack of encouragement	40%
Maternity leave issues	34%
Work environment	32%
Men recruit men	31%

FIGURE 2.2. Why Are Women Underrepresented in Senior Event Roles?
Source: BCD Meetings and Events 2018.

Which opportunities are currently being left on the table? What risks and limitations are you not addressing by working in an industry where the majority of us are White and a small percentage of women hold leadership positions.

It's imperative for event professionals to actively work to change these demographics by seeking out third parties, new partnerships, and diverse team members to help close a major gap limiting future growth potential.

#MeetingsToo

The problematic demographics are showing up in all kinds of ways that cause significant risks to event professionals. Sixty percent of women event planners report having endured sexual harassment at some stage of their careers, according to Prevue Meetings & Incentives and the Society for Incentive Travel Excellence.[5]

The #MeToo movement, originally started by American activist Tarana Burke to help women stand up for themselves in the face of sexual harassment and assault, has found footing in the events industry with the #MeetingsToo and #MeTooMeetings hashtags being used to call out gross misconduct in the events industry and during events themselves.

Conferences and conventions are particularly vulnerable to inappropriate behavior. Travelers often stay in swanky hotel rooms paid for by their employers, and alcohol may be free-flowing and complimentary. The whole experience can feel a little like a paid vacation with too little thought given to accountability.

Cool It with the Brews

Some events are providing alternatives to alcohol beyond bottled water. Social Venture Institute in Canada, for example, chose to change the nature of their social gatherings being centered around alcohol to one that highlighted the non-alcoholic beer brand, Partake. That brand's purpose is "to provide a craft brew that allows all people to celebrate together and to change the narrative that alcohol has a monopoly on good times."

In addition to disrupting the culture around intoxication, establishing a code of conduct for meetings and events, with clearly communicated procedures for addressing sexual harassment and assault, should be a top priority across the events industry.[6] *"That includes providing event staff and security with specific instructions on how to handle reports of harassment,"* explains Annette Naif, founder of Naif Productions, a New York City-based event production firm.[7]

In 2019, a high-profile example of sexual assault was uncovered by a *Financial Times* investigation that found evidence of a men's-only event where hostesses were propositioned, groped, and abused at the annual Presidents Club Charity Dinner. The event has been a mainstay of the London social calendar for 33 years. Hundreds of businessmen and financiers attend.[8]

The event organizer was forced out of his job with the Department for Education's board of directors, and the Presidents Club was later disbanded altogether in the wake of public outrage. However, soon after the Presidents Club scandal, and despite a warning by the chief executive of the UK Gambling Commission, the three-day International Casino Exhibition (ICE), Totally Gaming conference, took place, complete with a Playboy-themed strip show, pole dancing, and scantily clad women.[9]

Outrageous examples like these are a stain on the events industry, and we have a responsibility as events professionals to nurture a culture where women and those identifying as women can feel safe, not sexualized, and equally represented.

Tech-tonic Shifts Required

Even a future-focused industry like the tech sector is notoriously archaic when it comes to addressing gender equity and safe spaces for women. And the gaming industry in particular has been notably ineffectual in addressing these issues. Gamergate was a misogynistic harassment campaign launched in response to efforts at promoting more women and diversity in the sector. Women in the industry were targeted with death threats and threats of rape.

At tech and gaming expos, there's a common practice of hiring provocatively dressed models and colloquially referring to them as "booth babes." Exhibitors claim it works to attract more people to their booths, especially introverted young men. However, it can discourage women and others across the gender spectrum. In my interview with David Betke, President of GreenShows and Do Better Marketing, he referred to the practice of booth babes as *"just another example of lazy marketing where a business considers the number of people who came to their booth the most critical metric."* [10]

Some evidence, including a 2013 controlled experiment by Spencer Chen of Frontback Marketing, concludes that staffing people at booths without deep knowledge of the product does very little to drive actual sales.[11] *"A solid strategy includes attention, connection, follow-up, and conversion strategies,"* says Betke. He added, *"While 'booth babes' can attract attention, the wrong type of attention can often lead to negative consequences such as the avoidance of your booth and, ultimately, the sanctioning of your brand."*[12]

In 2020, just before many large events were canceled due to COVID-19, the world's biggest technology convention—the Consumer Electronics Show (CES)—announced a ban on the use of booth babes. They stated that exhibition staff "may not wear clothing that is sexually revealing or that could be interpreted as undergarments."[13] However, some booth babes were reported to have been seen anyway. It may take time for the ban to shift the culture of the event. More exhibitions should adopt the ban, be fearless in enforcing it, and put an end once and for all to the practice.

Be Family Inclusive

You can enhance gender equity by establishing programs and amenities that make it possible for parents with young children to participate.

In 2023, for example, Canada's longest running marathon—the Calgary Marathon—announced the addition of three new amenities for race day, with the goal of increasing family inclusivity and reducing barriers to entry. These new programs include:

An on-site camp for kids aged 4 to 12, which provides an opportunity for parents and guardians to race.

Four freely accessible infant feeding stations were added for use by any participants, volunteers, or attendees who require a private space to breastfeed, pump, or bottle-feed. Two of the stations were located on-course, and two stations were located near the marathon start and finish areas.

A pregnant and postpartum deferral option was introduced at the same time for pregnant or postpartum individuals to defer their registration to the following year with the understanding that some may need to step back from running and walking. This deferral encourages people to register for the event and strive for their physical fitness goal despite a potential life curveball.[14]

What Does Diversity Even Mean?

Here is where things get complicated—there is no consensus on what defines "enough" diversity or even what diversity means.

> Diversity is being invited to the party; inclusion is being asked to dance.
>
> —Verna Myers, *What If I Say the Wrong Thing? 25 Habits for Culturally Effective People*

Research from Deloitte Consulting indicates a generational gap in these perspectives. Older generations tend to view diversity only through the lens of representation, focusing on categories like gender, race, and religion while younger generations tend to view cognitive diversity, or the diversity of thoughts, ideas, and skills, as equally important.[15]

If you already attract a diverse audience to your event, then congratulations—your event officially reflects the reality of what exists in the world, rather than the artificial monoculture that we're often presented with. Reflecting reality, however, is not enough. We need to take the difficult next steps of expanding access to voices that were previously silenced and repairing the harm that has been caused to members of our community.

Let's go beyond empty words and help people feel they belong through actions that reflect their actual needs, rather than what we perceive. We need to be willing to be changed through new perspectives and cultural ways of knowing. This will enable you to create something greater, altogether new, and farther reaching than you could have done otherwise.

Events with inflexible cultures diminish the value of diversity and cause those who bring uniqueness to your event to shoulder the burden of fitting into an existing culture. To ensure inclusion at your event, you must practice it yourself. This means getting out of the autopilot mode that often happens with event planning and looking at your event through fresh eyes to achieve your desired purpose. You don't have to sacrifice the culture, traditions, or esthetics important to you. Your event can reach its full potential as a modern, innovative medium and an intentionally welcoming environment. Inclusion at events is all

> The world isn't designed for everyone in mind. Millions of places all around the world are still inaccessible to people with disabilities.
>
> —Maayan Ziv, Founder, AccessNow

about the environment you create for diversity to flourish. That means enabling people from a wide range of diverse backgrounds not only to feel safe and welcome but also to be their most authentic selves. Only then can you create an overall sense of belonging.

In addition to being a successful entrepreneur and in-demand public speaker, Maayan Ziv has emerged as an important disability rights advocate; in particular, she has brought to light the way airlines treat people with wheelchairs. Maayan's emotional video went viral. After landing in Tel Aviv to speak at a high-profile disability tech conference, she was mortified to discover the Canadian airline she arrived on was negligent with her electric wheelchair: it was damaged beyond use or repair.

"Imagine someone basically chopping off your legs when you arrive somewhere," Maayan said in the video. "That's the equivalent of what this feels like," she added. Maayan said that her wheelchair is an extension of her body, and when it's taken away, it strips her of her independence, mobility, health, and comfort. She called for an end to this kind of discrimination that is a reality for many people with disabilities.

If we want to see more audience members and conference speakers with disabilities at events, we need to consider the challenges they face during air travel as well as local travel and how venue logistics might be limiting.

Maayan's business venture, AccessNow, is an app that connects people with accessibility challenges to venues that welcome them around the world. In 2019, when Maayan was invited to her alma mater to speak about her global success, the trip didn't require air travel, but it did require the organizers to move the event to a different building so their star graduate could access the space in her electric wheelchair.

The organizers at Toronto Metropolitan University had the wherewithal to know that Maayan sits tall in her wheelchair, and they asked her about how high they should seat other speakers so they could be at a similar height when together on stage. Bar stools did the trick, and Maayan said she appreciated the gesture.

Such accommodations are necessary to include more diverse speakers at your events. They help make people with disabilities feel equally valued, which also puts the other speakers and panelists at ease.

(Coincidentally, her alma mater [and mine], Toronto Metropolitan University, recently changed its name from Ryerson University—a name associated with the architect of Canada's residential school system, the same system designed to assimilate and convert Indigenous children.)

Typically, when we think of mobility challenges, we think of those in a wheelchair like Maayan, but there is a wide range of abilities to consider, including those with vision or hearing loss, missing digits, seniors with hip and knee joint problems, and even young families trying to maneuver through your event with baby carriages.

The more scenarios you test and design for ahead of time, the more barriers you can uncover and overcome. Eliminating barriers for a wide range of people enables them to not only physically participate, but also be able to show up in a way that makes them feel at their best and ready to meaningfully contribute to the success of your event.

World Cup Leans In

The world's largest sporting event, FIFA, was held in the Middle East for the first time in 2022. While there were some controversies, several precedent-setting initiatives were implemented during that tournament.

Mobility assistance, accessible transport, parking, facilities, and five ticket types for people with limited mobility were available.

Audio-descriptive commentary in English and (for the first time) Arabic was made available for people with blindness and vision loss to enjoy matches in the live stadium atmosphere.

For the first time at a FIFA World Cup, sensory rooms were also offered to enable people with sensory access requirements to attend a match without becoming overwhelmed by the sounds and stimuli of match day.

Improving accessibility is a key first step toward building diversity; however, if we limit ourselves to *just* the first steps, our actions can be viewed through the lens of tokenism.

It's not enough to fly a pride flag at your event as an act of allyship without also providing gender-neutral bathrooms for LGBTQIA2S+ people who may not feel comfortable in a binary-gendered facility.

The solution may be as simple as removing the common silhouetted figure of a man or woman from the bathroom doors, or you may need to redesign your space to accommodate individual stalls with a shared hand-washing area. The upfront costs to create gender-neutral bathrooms may be a barrier, but I encourage you to consider the long-term economic benefits of growing your audience. The strong message you will send to all your guests about your commitment to inclusion and your ultimate purpose should be your "do it anyway" factor.

A simple and inexpensive way to make people feel welcome is to include a space for pronouns on name tags and to encourage online participants to rename themselves using pronouns. It helps to avoid embarrassments and normalizes the ability to identify by their chosen gender in social and professional settings.

> I hope as people celebrate Pride this year if they go to the parade or they go to any events, they have conversations with themselves and with their family and friends about how they want to contribute to the protest and the idea of equality year-round.
>
> —Mike Morrison, Activist, Blogger and Founder of the SocialNext digital marketing conference series

Avoid Performative Actions

Too often, event organizers resort to performative acts to demonstrate *allyship* rather than taking the necessary actions to actually address issues of inequality, racial injustice, and systemic discrimination.

On social media, don't aim to establish your credibility as an ally or draw attention to how you are following the basics to ensure representation. Instead, amplify others who are on the front lines of the struggle and demonstrate who you're listening to and what you're learning from them.

We need to reach out to those most impacted with a willingness to learn and without preconditions to establish relationships and community partnerships. Creating access means recognizing our unconscious biases, removing barriers, and building capacity.

Diversity is not tokenism. Different perspectives are important. When audience members can relate to the speakers and performers and feel that the logistics enable their full participation, they are more deeply invested in the subject matter and a successful outcome.

What a Drag

Events specifically designed to desensitize engagement with members of the LGBTQIA2S+ community can go a long way. Reading with Royalty for example, is an event that takes place at the Calgary Public Library, introducing children up to the age of eight to drag queens who will read them a story.

Unfortunately, Reading with Royalty did attract some controversy after a local pastor disrupted multiple readings and even pulled a fire alarm at one event to evacuate the library to protest the family-friendly event. His actions caused the need for increased security at public libraries and for the City Council to pass its new Safe and Inclusive Access Bylaw, which prohibits protests within 100 meters of entrances to recreation facilities or libraries. Calgary Mayor Jyoti Gondek said at the time: "There's no banning of protests. It is simply removing protesters from the entrance so that people can have a safe experience inside those buildings."

The Reading with Royalty protest was not an isolated incident. Libraries across Canada have faced demonstrations over similar events. There have also been anti-drag protests outside the Tate Britain art gallery in London, as well as several bookstores and libraries in the US.

Across the US, conservative activists and politicians have complained, without any evidence, that drag contributes to the "sexualization" or "grooming" of children; these baseless complaints were used as context for a recent Tennessee law banning drag shows in public spaces.

This all underscores the fact that, all over the world, spaces normalizing LGBTQIA2S+ people have disappeared at a rapid pace. In the US between 2007 and 2019, the number of gay bars fell by 36.6 percent, with a drop of 59 percent in bars serving "LGBTQIA2S+" people of color, and 52 percent for lesbian venues over this same period.[16]

Opportunities for self-expression are increasingly difficult for many communities—including those that identify as LGBTQIA2S+—and your next event could play a critical role in providing safe spaces for people to fully participate as they are and build human connection.

Steps for Building an Effective Diversity and Inclusion Program

Establish or Revisit Your Purpose

If part of your purpose aims to improve society, then leveraging your medium to amplify typically underrepresented and underengaged communities is an important way for you to achieve that purpose.

Assess

Perform a thorough and realistic assessment of your existing diversity scenario. Collect data and set a baseline. It's important to take stock of existing realities before you can set targets for continued growth. This is not a checkbox exercise where you can say "yes, we have that," like you do with other event logistics. The goalpost is continuously changing, and the key to not falling far behind is to renew relationships and remain engaged in the ecosystem of people working on these issues.

Outcomes to consider measuring:

- Representation among specific demographics
- Stakeholder survey results from staff, contractors, suppliers, volunteers, and audience members
- Staff and volunteer retention rates
- Public recognition

Measure and benchmark the diversity of your current team to identify areas of concern and track trends over time. Categories for data collection could include demographics such as gender, race, and ethnicity, as well as learning styles, personality types, and life experiences. Be thoughtful about this, though. Some staff, volunteers, and suppliers may feel uncomfortable self-identifying and sharing private information, especially if it's not well communicated how the data will be collected, used, and shared. Pay particular attention to privacy protection, and be sure you're able to produce aggregated results. Anonymous data collection is best.

Perhaps there's nothing urgent driving such an assessment, and/or there's a feeling that no problem exists. Prove yourself right. Engage your stakeholders. Bring in outside experts to guide you through an assessment process. It might make sense to have them speak to a subset of your stakeholders. Enter the assessment process with an open mind in the spirit of continuous improvement. Doing this will enable you to identify risks and opportunities that may not have been previously apparent to you.

> [We] have long been trained to see the deficiencies of people rather than policy.
> —Ibram X. Kendi, *How To Be an Antiracist* [17]

Ultimately, inclusion is the result of policies that are designed to enable diverse voices to have full participation; they need to be informed by relationships and deep understanding.

Armed with data about your team, suppliers, audience, and event culture, you can now begin to identify areas for improvement and develop meaningful diversity and inclusion initiatives.[18] Outline your diversity and inclusion road map. This could be something as simple as committing to hire women for a certain percentage of leadership roles or creating safe spaces and environments for minorities to air their grievances.

The Calgary Folk Music Festival has a *safer spaces policy* that acknowledges "sexualized and gender-based violence is a pervasive and widespread issue within the music community."[19] The Festival partnered with local community organizations, Calgary Communities Against Sexual Abuse and Sagesse, a domestic abuse education and prevention agency, to nurture a nonthreatening, harassment-free environment for everyone.

The Folk Festival has put its policy into practice with the help of reporting mechanisms that include an online form that can be submitted anonymously or at an on-site safer spaces tent supervised by trained volunteers. The festival also has a safer spaces committee to investigate all reported incidents; enforcement may include ejection and a ban of any individuals who have violated the policy.

The Festival's executive director, Sara Leishman, told me that "complaints are not something to be feared but rather valuable information." She added, "At times they might serve as an early indicator of a potentially larger risk and an opportunity to find a remedy and improve processes and policies."

The Calgary Folk Fest lists the behaviors that are not acceptable as part of the registration process and requires all festivalgoers to sign off on their adherence. Inappropriate behaviors include:

- Offensive, derogatory, threatening, aggressive, or silencing comments related to gender, gender identity + expression, sexual orientation, disability,

physical appearance, age, language, body size, race, ethnicity, nationality, religion, and socioeconomic standing
- Violence, intimidation, stalking, or unwanted following of a person
- Persistent micro-aggressions in the form of comments, jokes, or otherwise
- Inappropriate physical contact without consent
- Unwelcome sexual attention
- Advocating or encouraging any of the above behavior

If any discriminatory behavior arises before, during, or after your event, make sure to call it out. Clearly state the actions you will take and the what the consequences of this behavior will be.

Sarah told me that her Festival's safer spaces policy "is an important part of our commitment to create inclusive events for the many diverse communities that we are proud to welcome to the Calgary Folk Music Festival."

Set Targets
Organizational Targets
The targets you set for diversity and inclusion should be measurable indicators of the change you are effecting. Without targeted key performance indicators, you can't learn whether or not your program achieved its intended purpose.

One strong move you can make to bake diversity and inclusion into your events is to integrate that objective into your recruitment process at the board and all staff levels of your organization. Doing so will help grow the internal capacity of your team to speak knowledgeably about justice, equity, diversity, and inclusion; establish partnerships; and expand access to underrepresented groups at your events.

> It doesn't make sense to hire smart people and tell them what to do; we hire smart people so they can tell us what to do.
>
> —Steve Jobs, Founder, Apple Inc.

Don't make the common mistake of placing your new team member in a position where they're expected to act as the sole voice on behalf of a wide spectrum of perspectives within each specific demographic. Instead, empower them to build partnerships that lead you closer to understanding your market. Partners may not have all the answers, but they can save you time by pointing you in the right direction. Remain open to having your business culture changed as a result of more diverse ways of knowing.

Recruiting diverse candidates may require you to look outside your conventional channels for new talent. If you're dependent on tools like LinkedIn to find candidates, recognize that those you seek may not be on that platform. Using the same channels you've used in the past will likely produce a talent pool similar to the one you've already seen. If you use a recruitment agency, find out if they have any experience reaching your target demographics. If they don't, you should challenge them to build more capacity. Consider partnering with local universities and colleges, community groups, or internship programs.

Recognize that unconscious bias in the hiring process is incredibly common. It could take place in the form of exclusionary job descriptions, filtering for prestigious colleges or companies, or using homogenous interview panels.[20] Get advice from partners and experts to ensure the language within your job descriptions is welcoming and clear about who you're looking for.

About Live Nation

Live Nation is a US-headquartered events promotion, venue operations, and artist management firm. In 2010, they merged with Ticketmaster to form one of the world's largest entertainment conglomerates. In one of their recent job postings (for a National Sustainability Coordinator), the company included language that was well-informed and demonstrates a commitment to inclusion:

> Live Nation strongly supports equal employment opportunity for all applicants regardless of age, ancestry, color, religious creed (including religious dress and grooming practices), family and medical care leave or the denial of family and medical care leave, mental or physical disability (including HIV and AIDS), marital status, domestic partner status, medical condition (including cancer and genetic characteristics), genetic information, military and veteran status, political affiliation, national origin (including language-use restrictions), citizenship, race, sex (including pregnancy, childbirth, breastfeeding and medical

conditions related to pregnancy, childbirth or breastfeeding),
gender, gender identity, and gender expression, sexual orientation, or any other basis protected by applicable federal, state or
local law, rule, ordinance or regulation.

It goes on to state:

> We will consider qualified applicants with criminal histories in
> a manner consistent with the requirements of the Los Angeles
> Fair Chance Ordinance, San Francisco Fair Chance Ordinance
> and the California Fair Chance Act and consistent with other
> similar and/or applicable laws in other areas.
>
> We also afford equal employment opportunities to qualified
> individuals with a disability. For this reason, Live Nation will make
> reasonable accommodations for the known physical or mental
> limitations of an otherwise qualified individual with a disability
> who is an applicant consistent with its legal obligations to do so,
> including reasonable accommodations related to pregnancy.

Using language like this in your job description is putting your best foot
forward; but don't just assume the right candidate will appear. It may
take a concerted effort to reach out to targeted communities, utilizing
community partner newsletters and local ethnic media websites.

Increasing the diversity of your team will help you access different
perspectives, make better decisions, and capitalize on new opportunities to grow your event. It will also make your team more attractive
to top talent. According to Glassdoor, 67 percent of active and passive
job seekers *consider workplace diversity an important factor* when
considering employment opportunities.[21] At the same time, more than
50 percent of employees want their workplace to do more to improve
diversity.

> As the leader in live music, we have an opportunity and a
> responsibility to amplify the conversation around anti-racism
> and Black Lives Matter in order to be a part of the solution.
>
> — Michael Rapino, CEO, Live Nation

In 2020, Live Nation released a plan to increase its diversity and impact by 2025. Some highlights of the plan include:

- $10M over two years to develop, promote, and hire Black and underrepresented talent
- Achieving 30 percent diversity of their board and senior leadership
- 50 percent gender diversity and 40 percent racial and ethnic diversity in staff overall

They also committed to anti-bias education training, tracking diversity data globally, tying their goals to leadership compensation, and establishing an Equity Accountability Board led by leaders from across the business spectrum to maintain momentum and accountability toward the goals.

All this is definitely to be commended, and it sets a strong example for the rest of the events and entertainment industries. However, it

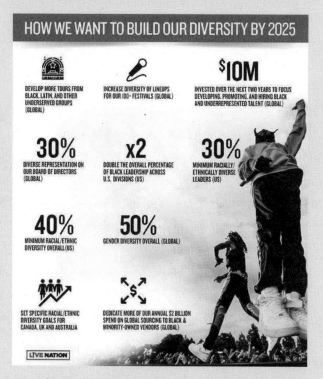

FIGURE 2.3. Live Nation Diversity and Inclusion Goals. Source: Live Nation.

could have gone even further. For example, there is no mention of closing the gender pay gap that commonly exists.

Live Nation does seem to understand their immense responsibility and significant ability to influence change through the massive media they have conglomerated. At first glance, $10M seems like an impressive investment toward grooming diverse talent, but more metrics are required to understand whether this would be 1 percent, 5 percent, or 10 percent of what they currently spend on overrepresented talent. The company aims to increase the diversity of musical lineups and develop tours by more underrepresented groups, but these are the parts of their 2025 targets with the fewest metrics.

Live Nation made a wonderful commitment to amplify social justice issues, such as voter registration on-site at venues and registration online through the Ticketmaster experience, as well as causes championed by the artists they represent. The company recently matched Lizzo's $500,000 donation to Planned Parenthood in response to the US Supreme Court decision to overturn Roe v. Wade and the associated rights to safe abortion. However, no targets were listed as part of the 2025 goal. A best practice would have been to announce a multiple-million-dollar fund that correlates to a percentage of their overall revenue, allocated to addressing urgent social concerns.

One big miss is not having a target associated with arguably the most material concern for most of Live Nation's stakeholders—the outrageous and exclusive surge pricing for some of the most sought-after shows through Ticketmaster.

However, as Michael Rapino wrote in an open letter to his employees:

> This is a movement, not a moment. Rest assured these actions will continue to expand and evolve over time.... Racism and inequality are systemic problems, and we must make this an ongoing dialogue in order to drive real, lasting change.... The core of our business is promoting, and we are committed to improving our promotion of diversity within our company and the world at large.

Kudos and best of luck to Live Nation on their efforts.

Audience Targets

Who are your current and future target audiences? This is an important question to consider because it's not inevitable that they'll find you or find relevance in your offerings.

The GLOBE Series has a primary purpose "to create a sustainable, prosperous, socially just future in a generation."[22] Their signature event, GLOBE Forum, is a three-thousand-person conference taking place every two years in Vancouver. It brings together a North American community of sustainability leaders, policymakers, and environment, social, and governance investors transforming the economy around a plan to achieve net-zero emissions by 2050.

However, the thirty-plus-year-old conference organization recognized many years ago that young professionals will be moving into leadership roles in the coming years—and most of them have never been to a GLOBE event. GLOBE began nurturing a national youth network called Leading Change,[23] whose leadership team plays an active role in the planning and execution of the GLOBE event. It includes a forum the day before the main event for young professionals from across the Canada to meet, network, and learn together. Delegates receive free tickets to participate in the rest of the conference. Many Leading Change alumni return as speakers, sponsors, exhibitors, and delegates. The dynamic of GLOBE has changed as a result of the influx of young professionals. The questions asked in each session are tougher, and the after-parties are a lot livelier.

Attracting certain demographics requires ambassadors within those communities to help promote your event through their personal and professional networks. Reaching out to local ethnic media outlets can also be an effective way to target the demographics you want to attract to your event. In addition to their youth development program, GLOBE also targets local Indigenous communities and leaders and invites them to attend with free tickets to events.

Getting targeted demographics to your event is one matter. Getting them to return and encourage others in their community to do so is another. For audience members to feel a sense of inclusion, they need to see other people who look like them not only in the audience but also on the stage. However, many events are lagging behind with respect to diversity. According

> Breakthrough ideas are rarely generated among like-minded people.
>
> —Nicol Turner Lee, The Brookings Institution

to a 2020 study by Skift Meetings, 35 to 40 percent of the 150 conferences evaluated—mostly in the US—did not have a single Black speaker on any of their panels.[24]

"The issue of systemic racism is front and center," said Keneisha Williams, founder of the Black in Events Network. She added, "The event industry must do better, and speaker selection is an easy but essential first step."[25]

Planning for diverse speakers and panel discussions is not tokenism. Elevating different perspectives is important to have any kind of impact. When audience members see themselves in the speakers, they're more invested in the subject matter.

The most memorable events are ones where the content is provocative, the speakers or performers are relatable, and the networking opportunities are full of unexpected possibilities. All of these depend on designing for diversity. When you have the power to do something important through the curation of speakers and performers, why bother booking the same old speakers parroting the same predictable points that others on the same panel have already made? Panels where the speakers all agree are boring.

In the previous chapter, I tried to channel my inner Priya Parker when I wrote that having the right kind of controversy provides a level of tension that can make gatherings more energetic, more lively, and ultimately more meaningful. That tension should not diminish hope or cause cynicism. When channeled effectively, the difficult conversations you curate can lead to greater understanding and breakthrough outcomes. Everyone has different lived experiences, but when your presenters have had to overcome enormous obstacles to arrive at that moment, their message tends to carry significant weight.

The challenge often cited is that high-profile speakers with truly diverse backgrounds are notoriously in demand and difficult to secure. So, start early. Be sure to communicate to any speakers' bureaus you work with that you are looking for more diverse speakers. It will encourage them to add more underrepresented speakers to their roster. Engaging diverse communities and partner organizations can help uncover new speaker names, and recruiting team members who bring a wealth of contacts from diverse communities should be prioritized during your hiring process.

Increasingly, experienced speakers are declining invitations based on the organizer's inability to recruit for diversity. I recently did just that with a speaking invitation I received to join a panel discussion at a sustainability-themed event. When I asked about the other speakers, I was given two names, which I quickly looked up on LinkedIn. Both were Caucasian men. I politely declined and explained it would be a reputation risk for me and possibly the other speakers as well, to appear on stage as a panel of three white, middle-aged men. I recommended some other speakers they might choose to pursue and offered that if those did not work out, I could help with a few more contacts once I had the chance to reflect on it.

It can be difficult to turn down speaking invitations, especially when prestige and money are involved, but as soon as I asked about the diversity of the panel, the person who invited me said, "You're right, I completely forgot to consider that," and thanked me for helping them avoid an awkward mistake.

Speakers Who Are Sponsors

Sometimes, companies sponsor an event, and part of the sponsorship agreement involves positioning their senior leaders as speakers. However, those senior leaders may not represent much diversity. If you include too many speakers who are sponsors, you'll lose the ability to curate large sections of the medium you control. When encountering this challenge, try encouraging the sponsor to identify additional potential speakers—maybe people the company would like to groom as effective spokespeople for their brand. If any of them seem like a better fit with the diversity you're curating, let your sponsor know that. Doing so will reduce reputation risks for you and your sponsors who wouldn't want to be photographed as part of a panel under the caption: "pale, male, and stale."

The lack of representation and inclusion of diverse communities is depriving audiences of valuable insights and perspectives. People learn through exposure to new points of view, so seek out those with diverse backgrounds and perspectives that make your events more memorable and impactful.

Outreach

Circle This

In 2013, successful entrepreneur and recently departed community leader Jim Button and his partners founded Circle the Wagons—a traveling food, beer, and music carnival with a purpose to inspire community consciousness and engage diverse communities across Calgary. The name for the event was a clever play on the fact that all three main organizers owned stylized "wagons" (the BassBus, Village Brewery beer truck, and YYCFoodTrucks) at a time when Calgary was beginning to embrace an exploding food truck scene.

After four years, the unique event tripled in size, traveled to several neighborhoods around the city, and garnered a tremendous amount of attention—not all of it positive. A comment was made on the event's social media channel complaining that "circling the wagons" was a racist throwback to early colonialists waging war against Indigenous Peoples. The comment quickly went viral.

"It took us by surprise," Jim Button told me. "We didn't realize the name would offend anyone," he explained. Ideally, it should not take something going wrong before we examine how the words we use might affect others, but the reality is we all have blind spots. Our unconscious biases can be so subtle that we're often not aware of how language we regularly use might reinforce systems and institutions that privilege some, hold others back, or trigger emotional responses.

After consulting some Indigenous community members that were referred to him, and with only a few weeks left until their next big event, Jim and the other organizers addressed the issue head-on and announced from the stage they were dropping the name, effective immediately. They later announced *Circle Carnival* as their new name. The following year, they attracted their biggest crowd ever—more than seven thousand people.

The controversy Jim faced regarding Circle the Wagons served as a valuable lesson for him and his team at Village Brewery years later when they secured the rights from Molson Breweries to revive a legendary brand known as Calgary Beer, first produced in 1892 and discontinued in 1994. Jim and the team returned to consult with Indigenous Elders to determine whether the Calgary Beer logo, which has always been a buffalo, could be triggering. Historically, the tens of millions of buffalo in North America sustained a traditional way of life for Indigenous Peoples; they used the animal as a major food source, its bones for tools, and its hides in clothing, teepees, and ceremonies. Tragically, this traditional way of life was severely disrupted when millions of buffalo were slaughtered by early settlers of North America.[26]

The Village team found no consensus among the Elders they spoke to, and the delayed rollout cost them precious time and money, but they nevertheless decided to quietly replace the 130-year-old buffalo logo with a Black Angus cow.

When asked if he was happy with the decision, Jim responded assuredly: "*I have no regrets. Once you know something is hurtful and exclusionary to some, you can't unknow it. It's always going to be there.*"

Responding to controversy is never easy. Reaching out to those most affected when our blind spots are uncovered and defaulting to our event's core purpose can help us course-correct quickly and expand our audience. Jim's story also demonstrates that establishing trusted relationships based on positive intentions and a genuine effort to learn and incorporate diverse perspectives can help us grow as professionals and proactively avoid future controversies, which can negatively affect events as well as the brands featured within them.

Test-drive

If you're human, you can't help but hold unconscious beliefs about various groups of people. However, you do not need to be limited by these beliefs. Working with trusted advisors and attracting team and board members deeply engaged in the communities you seek to build relationships with are essential to overcoming unconscious biases, managing risk, and growing your audience.

The people you actively reach out to may bring some of those valuable relationships with them and act as effective spokespeople. You can also leverage those relationships to help you test-drive your complete user experience—including navigating your website, the language you use in your opening remarks, the logistics of your event, and the sensitivity training you provide to your staff and volunteers.

Be mindful if you remain resistant to change; be aware of whether your process is too opaque, rushed, or inauthentic, or your advisors and diverse team members feel unheard and possibly exploited or tokenized. They may turn into your most vocal critics. It's important that we accept any feedback we get, not as criticism but as opportunities for continuous improvement. Acknowledging people's concerns and lived experiences as valid and worthy of reflection goes a long way in earning their trust and support. Then we must do the work to reflect and incorporate that input in meaningful ways and keep testing to confirm and measure the desired outcomes.

When we successfully harness a greater diversity of thinking, we can uncover new revenue opportunities and innovative approaches to overcome some of society's greatest challenges.

Train

After you've identified your gaps and once you've established targets and policies, it's time to increase the capacity of your team to identify unconscious bias, speak knowledgeably about justice and inequality, and act with empathy toward unlocking growth and inclusion for those who may have felt excluded, ignored, or subjugated in the past.

Diversity and inclusion training should aim to equip your staff and contractors with increased awareness, tools, and education against sexist, racist, homophobic, or transphobic language.

> If a training session is like a vaccine, you're going to need booster shots to keep it effective.
>
> —Katerina Bezrukova, Professor, University of Buffalo

You can leverage the training to gain feedback and buy-in for your targets and policies. You can also distribute guides to inclusive language among your team, speakers, and attendees. The training could be used to develop or retain diverse talent and nurture an inclusive culture. It's most effective when it addresses your specific areas of concern and aligns with your business objectives and purpose. See the American Psychological Association for a terrific resource on inclusive language.[27] You can find a link in the Tools and Resources section and my website, leor.ca.

Engage an expert to get started. Begin with your leadership team, go through all staff, volunteers, and suppliers, ensuring everyone from the cleanup crew to the bartenders and security guards are committed to upholding your values. This should be enshrined in the onboarding process, and repercussions for not acting accordingly should be clearly communicated and carried out consistently.

Don't just depend on a single diversity point person or human resources department for accountability on these important matters.

Make diversity and inclusion the business of every team member through smaller, simpler initiatives, and statements in their job descriptions and service contracts.

A Remesh study with more than one hundred professionals to understand the state of diversity and inclusion programs broadly found that, while 77 percent believed in the importance of diversity and inclusion programs, almost all respondents indicated that there was a lack of formal training within their organization.[28]

Another, more comprehensive research paper published in 2016 found that short single-day training sessions are not very effective compared with longer frequent sessions focused on building awareness about biases as well as skills for interaction.[29] Interactive training where people from different backgrounds work together garners far better results than lectures. The biggest takeaway from the study was that the skills and information from diversity training are quickly forgotten, so frequent updates are necessary.

Learning with Ethnic Cuisine

Programs like lunch-and-learns on diversity and inclusion topics can complement an initial training and help continue the momentum necessary to enact meaningful long-term change.[30] Hire a social enterprise like Ethnicity Catering, which provides Canadian work experience and training to immigrants in transition to Canada, while utilizing their traditional home cooking to offer a unique and delicious international menu to all types of clients.[31,32] You can also hire a talented chef from a local cultural community. Better yet, why not make it a potluck and have your workers bring in some of their favorite ethnic dishes for colleagues to sample? Food and the traditions associated with different cuisines can be a fun and creative starting point toward a meaningful and educational cultural exchange.

Continuous Learning

Identify opportunities for continuous learning about your country and region's history as well as contemporary perspectives regarding human rights. These could include a team visit to the Jim Crow Museum in Big Rapids, Michigan, or online courses such as Indigenous Canada—the 12-lesson MOOC (Massive Open Online Course) offered free through Coursera.

The Truth and Reconciliation Commission produced a report in 2015 that every Canadian should read. Its 94 Calls to Action provide guidance on restoring justice for, and acting in allyship with, the Indigenous Peoples of Canada. Some of these Calls to Action may be especially relevant to your event and audience.

Regardless of geography, all event professionals should educate themselves about the Indigenous traditional territories they live, work, and play on. Native-land.ca is a terrific online resource to help you identify the traditional territory your event will take place on—anywhere in the world.

Land Acknowledgments

Opening events with a land acknowledgment is increasingly common in Australia, Canada, New Zealand, and parts of the US.

In 2023, the Calgary Flames became the last National Hockey League (NHL) team to include a land acknowledgment before game time. Arriving at that historic puck drop with Chiefs and Elders from the Treaty 7 Nations took several months of discussion between the Flames hockey team and First Nations representatives.[33]

"We've created this safe space," said Dr. Tyler White, CEO of Siksika Health Services, who consulted on the special celebration event that kicked off the hockey team's first-ever land acknowledgment. He added, "We've created this platform to really showcase the beauty of our culture."

The tradition of land acknowledgments dates back hundreds of years, to when Indigenous Peoples visited other territories. It was (and still is) customary to respect and acknowledge the traditional custodians of the land. When done well, land acknowledgments can be a moving and respectful gesture of welcome, inclusion, and reconciliation.

However, too often land acknowledgments are performative or rushed, as though they're an unpleasant formality that we must suffer through to get to what we actually want to say. Not only can this be deeply offensive, but it misses the opportunity to anchor land acknowledgments as an opportunity to start with the "whys." Why we're all gathered here, why it's important to acknowledge inequality at this moment in time, and why it connects with the purpose of your event.

An effective land acknowledgment involves preparation and should be informed by some type of training that you and your team receive. It will involve identifying the traditional tribes who have called this land home, so learn to pronounce them correctly in advance. It should be authentic and include your own personal connection to the land.

Leverage the opportunity to reach out to the local Indigenous community and establish a relationship or communication channel. You may also choose to invite an Elder from this community to acknowledge the land, welcome guests, and provide a prayer. Be prepared to present them with a culturally appropriate token such as tobacco, sage, cedar, or Indigenous-made art, as well as an honorarium for their time. Note their opening prayer may be longer than you expect, so remain flexible and factor in extra time or bump an agenda item if you need to. At no point should you cut the Elder short or ask them to "move it along."

Here is an example of a land acknowledgment in Toronto, Ontario:

> We are grateful to be gathered here in T'karonto, the Ancestral Wendat territory and the shared territory of the Anishinaabeg and the Haudeno-saunee, covered by The Dish With One Spoon Wampum Belt Covenant, an agreement between the Haudenosaunee and Anishinaabeg and allied Nations to peaceably share and care for the resources around the Great Lakes. Later, Treaty 13 was signed with the Mississaugas of the Credit, and the Williams Treaties were signed with multiple Mississaugas and Chippewa bands. Beyond T'karonto, we acknowledge that the lands on which we gather and collaborate with other community leaders are the traditional gathering places for many Indigenous Peoples. We honor and respect the history, languages, ceremonies, and culture of the First Nations, Métis, and Inuit who call this territory home.

The acknowledgment could be followed with a call to action for the audience to help further your commitments toward strengthening justice, equity, diversity, and inclusion. If these commitments are not yet in place, be humble and call it out publicly as an area for improvement.

Beginning with land acknowledgments sets the tone that respectful gestures and language are important and acts like a warm seat being opened at the table in anticipation of someone who has not yet arrived.

Deepening our learning, using inclusive language, and acting in allyship with others in our community strengthens our collective values, makes your event more accessible, and helps to build the future we want to live in.

Communicate

There is no such thing as over-communicating or too much outreach when you are undergoing transformation. Ongoing communication about diversity and inclusion initiatives propels understanding and increases audience engagement. However, inauthentic communication or one-way announcements can damage relationships and cause distrust.

Authentic communication begins by acknowledging the problem, owning any past mistakes, committing to a tangible solution, amplifying the partnerships you've established, and acknowledging that there's a long journey ahead.

If the "medium is the message," then the message you're sending when you choose to use local and ethnocultural media is: "You're important to us, and we value what you value."

It's important to effectively communicate the level of importance that diversity and inclusion have within your organization and at your event. You should aim to inspire your team and your suppliers to make sustained commitments, and you should pilot and support diversity and inclusion efforts to help you achieve your goals and live your values.

Measure Progress and Adapt as Needed

Measuring and communicating the results of diversity initiatives demonstrates your organization's commitment to diversity in the workplace and can help to bridge the gap between implementation and impact.[34]

Designate a single point of contact for all diversity-related questions, matters, and complaints.

Don't get stuck doing something simply because it's what you committed to. If it's not working and doesn't add value, pivot and reinvest in programs that deliver strong and meaningful results to you and your partners.

It's okay to iterate, fail fast, assess, and course-correct when you discover a better way to achieve your desired outcome. Just be sure to effectively communicate and explain your decisions.

Default to transparency wherever possible. It's one thing to boldly proclaim that you're inclusive and another to publicly display the numbers that back your claim. Displaying a diversity dashboard on your website for all stakeholders to track your progress is a powerful way to demonstrate you take it seriously.

Having specific targets, measuring results for diversity and inclusion initiatives, and effectively communicating your progress makes the difference between theory and action, ideology versus results.

Questions to Ask

As you build your JEDI program ask yourself and your team the following questions:

- In what ways are we integrating diverse recruitment, retention, and advancement practices into our organization?
- What kinds of policies do we have in place to ensure diversity in our leadership positions?
- Do we have an Indigenous board member or advisor to help engage Indigenous communities and invite them to participate?
- How many Black, Indigenous, and/or people of color do we have on staff?
- What type of parental leave policy do we have in place?
- Are we effectively incentivizing men on the team to take parental leave?
- What types of accommodations are we making available for those with physical barriers to accessing our event?
- What percentage of diversity are we striving for in our team, with our suppliers and contractors, and audience members?
- Has the whole team read the 94 Calls to Action in the Truth and Reconciliation Commission Report published in 2015?
- Are we including a meaningful land acknowledgment at the start of our events to signal the safe space we're trying to create?
- Which third parties can we engage or partnerships can we establish to advise us?
- What key stakeholder groups will we engage to receive training and give supplier recommendations to widen our network, promote job postings, and identify potential candidates?
- What kind of training would help our staff, contractors, and/or volunteers be sensitive to diverse needs?
- How much budget can we make available for sensitivity training and capacity building for our team?

Make Waves

Your one event may not change the world on its own, but as part of a broader effort to effect change, reform the events industry, and address the most critical challenges of our time, you and your event can join a significant global movement that is already transforming the way we live, work, and play with regard to greater equity, justice, and balance with nature.

3

Produce Zero Waste

If it can't be reduced, reused, repaired, rebuilt, refurbished,
refinished, resold, recycled, or composted, then it should be restricted,
redesigned, or removed from production.

— Pete Seeger

First Time Viral

The picture went viral. In it, I was holding up the one and only bag of trash from the 1,200-person pancake breakfast event hosted by the Premier of Alberta. Most of what was in that bag was other crumpled-up garbage bags, small cups, and packaging brought into the event from elsewhere.

Events typically generate one pound of waste per attendee per meal.[1] That means that a one-thousand-person event serving one meal will generate about one-thousand pounds of waste—which is equivalent to the weight of a horse or grand piano. Producing a virtually weightless amount of waste from a 1,200-person event shouldn't be that uncommon. Especially because it's not very difficult to execute a zero-waste event—*if* you plan for it in the procurement process and account for natural audience flow and waste disposal points.

Your next event could realistically produce zero waste or close to it. Better yet, it could contribute to a more restorative, circular economy through the purchasing choices you make, the physical environment you create, and the culture you nurture. Pursuing zero waste will save you money, especially with respect to storage and disposal, as well as generate positive brand equity, audience loyalty, and greater demand for zero-waste events.

Waste has become so normalized in our society that we barely think about the impact it's having on our waterways, soils, and skies. When I look back,

I'm amazed at the ingenuity that enabled human advancement through the invention of modern sewer systems, landfills, recycling facilities, and efficient combustion technologies, but it seems those stopgaps were designed for a world that no longer exists today. Those systems have become overwhelmed and incapable of preventing or eliminating plastic in the natural world and greenhouse gas emissions in the atmosphere.

Going forward, we need not only to *reduce*, but to design waste *out* of our products and processes and rapidly decarbonize our society—at scale—while opening new opportunities for millions of people currently shut out from full economic participation. No small feat, I know.

Our Recycling System Is Broken

"Reduce, reuse, and recycle" was a mantra I was brought up with in grade school. It sounds good in principle, but in reality, the system is broken. Mass consumerism is widely promoted as a sign of economic health; disposable goods are cheaper than long-lasting products; it's cheaper to produce new plastics than recycle existing plastics; and the recycling system is not resilient enough to withstand the discontinuation of China as a dumping ground for the world's junk.

In late 2017, the Chinese government announced a ban on the import of *foreign garbage*, which everyone is still adapting to. In that same year (according to the Census Bureau), the US exported approximately 157,000 twenty-foot shipping containers full of plastic waste (about 429 per day). Most went to China. Some went to countries (including Canada and South Korea) that typically reexport the waste to Asian and African countries with poor waste management practices. According to the Plastic Pollution Coalition, it's these final destinations that are primarily responsible for the vast amount of plastic pollution in our oceans.

Worldwide, waste generated per person per day averages about 1.5 pounds, but it can be up to ten pounds in high-income countries such as the US and Canada, which generate about 34 percent, or 683 million tonnes, of the world's roughly 2 billion tonnes of municipal solid waste each year.[2]

Most of the world's waste is either dumped or disposed of in some form of a landfill; 37 percent is sent to landfills, and only 8 percent of that amount ends up in landfills equipped with gas collection technology. Open dumping accounts for about 30 percent of waste; nearly 20 percent of that is recovered through recycling and composting, and approximately 10 percent is incinerated. To give you an idea of what that means, in a single year (2021), the US incinerated enough waste to generate roughly 30,000 tonnes of toxic ash, air pollution, and greenhouse gas (GHG) emissions.

Emissions from Waste

Waste management and climate change may feel disconnected, but they are intricately tied. It's been estimated that 7 percent of GHGs produced globally are due to preventable food waste. Recent scientific studies have also shown that, of the world's total GHG emissions, plastic is responsible for nearly 4 percent and paper generates 1.3 percent. These, along with construction-related waste, are the bulk of what is in our landfills.

Waste management was an important part of the net-zero strategy for COP26. They calculated that diverting 53 percent of all their venue-related waste from the landfill saved approximately 50 tonnes of CO_2 from being released into the atmosphere.

Decomposing material in landfills releases gasses that are roughly 50 percent CO_2 and 50 percent methane. This is distressing because, while methane has a short lifetime, it's a potent GHG—twenty-eight to thirty-six times more

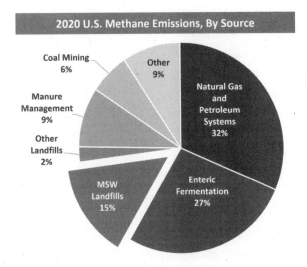

FIGURE 3.1. 2020 US Methane Emissions.
Source: US Environmental Protection Agency

effective than CO_2 at trapping heat in the atmosphere over a one-hundred-year period, according to the Intergovernmental Panel on Climate Change's Fifth Assessment Report (AR5).[3] Landfill waste is responsible for 15 percent of US methane emissions and about 11 percent of methane emissions globally.

Offset Your Waste

Several jurisdictions throughout North America have established GHG quantification protocols for aerobic composting. These establish parameters for buying and selling voluntary offsets based on the diversion of waste to an eligible composting facility compared with sending the same volume to a landfill. This means if you produce enough compost volume to generate offset credits, you may be able to sell those credits to a motivated buyer—perhaps one of your sponsors or clients. The downside is that verification of those credits may require significant upfront costs, especially in the initial setup of the program.

Protecting Nature from Plastic

I know it can be annoying to hear so much noise about single-use plastics (and straws, in particular), but plastic pollution has become a serious global threat to nature and the survival of various birds, fish, turtles, dolphins, sharks, and whales.

According to the United Nations, at least eight hundred species worldwide are affected by marine debris, and as much as 80 percent of that litter is plastic. It's estimated that up to 13 million metric tonnes of plastic ends up in the ocean each year—the equivalent of one garbage truck load's worth every minute.[4,5] Only 9 percent of the planet's plastic has ever been recycled.[6]

All this is the context that contributed to the development of the Kunming-Montreal Global Biodiversity Framework, which 190 countries agreed to at the 15th Conference of the Parties (COP15) to the UN Convention on Biological Diversity in Montreal in 2022. The framework is like the Paris Agreement on climate change, but instead of emission reductions, it measures restoration of land and sea habitats. The agreement targets the protection of 30 percent of the world's land and seas by 2030 and a ten-fold reduction in the species extinction rate by 2050.

Plastic Threatens Human Health Too

The problem has become so dire that microplastic pollution now shows up in the food we eat, the water we drink, and the air we breathe.[7, 8, 9] Microplastics are found in the feces of babies and adults, and in 2022, microplastics were detected in human blood for the first time.[10] In fact, scientists found the tiny particles in almost 80 percent of the people tested.[11] Half the samples contained polyethylene terephthalate (PET) plastic, which is commonly used in drink bottles, while a third contained polystyrene, used for packaging food and other products. A quarter of the blood samples contained polyethylene, from which plastic bags are made.

The long-term impact on health is as yet unknown, but we know that microplastics cause damage to human cells in the laboratory, and air pollution particles are already known to enter the body and cause millions of early deaths every year.[12, 13] The particles can also travel around the body and lodge in organs.

Disney's Approach to Waste

The iconic visionary Walt Disney used to sit on a bench at his Disneyland theme park to watch visitors and count how many steps they would take before getting impatient enough with the trash in their hands to put it down somewhere, anywhere. He declared: "Thirty is the magic number," and to this day, Disney theme parks have waste bins every thirty feet. Frontierland alone has over 120 trash bins.

Other theme parks and special events the world over have emulated the Disney approach, including the Calgary Stampede, but what was novel back in 1955 needs innovation today. Locating waste bins everywhere sends the message that garbage belongs everywhere rather than in specifically designated spaces.

The Disney approach aims to blend waste bins into their surroundings, which is why you might find them decorated with Avengers or Star Wars insignias.[14] The Stampede traditionally used disused oil barrels as garbage bins, and a few covered wagons doubled as waste collection points. These are commendable for their on-brand subtle touches. However, my recommendation is to abandon this approach in favor of a more uniform look that taps into the psychology of your visitors' behavior.

Audiences are used to equating blue with recycling and black with garbage, so using consistent colors helps them know they've done the right thing. Using colors and symbols is another way to increase accessibility since it means you are not relying on language alone, but on universal icons and colors.

Science of Waste Collection

A 2019 experiment at Nanyang Technological University in Singapore found that manipulating the configuration of trash bins to make them less convenient to access than recycling bins significantly increased the rate of recycling.[15] In Singapore, rinsing recyclables before disposal is important, so simple visual instructions were used in combination with strategic positioning near sinks and water fountains—with extremely positive results. On the other hand, when bins were less strategically placed and when more informational messaging was used, for example, text explaining why rinsing was important, the results were far less successful. What the Singapore University experiment shows is that designing the physical environment to make trash bins less convenient than other bins, in combination with simple and effective messaging, can steer behavior toward pro-environmental actions.

Confusion in the Market

In addition to the recycling system being broken, it's also inconsistent across jurisdictions. Take pizza boxes, for example; some municipalities want you to recycle them, others to compost them, and many ask that the boxes be sent to landfill because of the cheese residue mixed with cardboard.

Consumers often try to do the right thing by ordering foodware that's labeled *biodegradable*, but the term is misleading. The breaking-down process can take *one hundred years*, and it can even be detrimental to the environment because many items biodegrade into harmful chemicals or gases. *Compostable* is the preferred designation; it describes a product made from organic materials that can *disintegrate* into nontoxic water, soil, or biomass. This may be moot, however, because compostable materials need to be processed in specialized facilities; in a landfill, the process releases methane into the atmosphere.

Each city employs different technologies at its composting and recycling facilities. Frustratingly, many composting facilities cannot accept compostable cups, cutlery, and foodware because they're usually made from corn, sugar beets, seaweed, and other plants. If a facility is attempting to decompose food waste into soil and fertilizer, they have to use anaerobic processes, and these don't generate the kind of intense heat required to break down those types of cups, cutlery, etc.

In 2018, Keurig Dr. Pepper rolled out their recyclable K-Cup pods across Canada after successful trials in which the new pods made it all the way through recycling facilities in Montreal and Vancouver. Three years later, the Competition Bureau fined the company for claiming the pods were recyclable in their advertising because many jurisdictions still couldn't process the pods.

A good service provider can help you mine through these complexities, but don't just take their word for it. Ask them for copies of their waybills and receipts from the facilities they haul your waste to. If they're a service provider dedicated to educating their market, they will welcome this. If you find them obfuscating the details, ask yourself: Am I practicing effective procurement practices by working with this contractor or can I do better in selecting a partner committed to our overall purpose and objectives?

Recycling Is the New Last Resort

The Premier's Pancake Breakfast event was a great example of a strategic approach to bin placement and procurement control. Because my team placed all the orders for plates, cutlery, cups, and more, we were able to ensure all the waste materials were completely compostable. This kept the audience messaging simple and meant that we could largely circumvent the broken recycling system.

The only other trash originated from outside the event, and small black waste bins were stationed at two natural entrance/exit points of the outdoor venue. Some large city bins were scattered throughout the perimeter of the event site, but we sealed them all up with fitted canvas bags that were difficult for participants to remove without some effort.

It helped that we arrived at the event early enough to help with food preparations; this allowed us to recycle all the food packaging and set up compost bins to capture runaway sausages or pancakes that were flipped in the air too ambitiously by the cooking team.

The main waste stations were located adjacent to the primary food service and eating areas. The bins were well-signed and colored blue for recycling and green for compost. However, we still staffed the bins to reinforce the message that nearly everything was indeed compostable—as well as answer the most frequently asked question: Where's the trash bin?

PlanetPossible

The approach we took for the pancake breakfast was very different from Disney's, but Disneyland itself is in a transition to encourage more composting with new separated waste stream bins slowly being introduced to parts of the park with a more typical color scheme for compost, recycling, and trash.[16] This is in part to support their new PlanetPossible initiative.[17]

As part of PlanetPossible, Disney World in Florida sent 15 million pounds of food waste to an off-site commercial composting facility where it was converted to soil, some of which came back to the park to fertilize plants and gardens. That same year, Disneyland Paris recovered more than 2,000 tonnes of food waste to produce biogas equivalent to roughly 745 megawatts of power, or the annual consumption of 230 families.

Don't Poop on My Parade

Parades can be a wonderful celebration of inclusivity. They can also be an opportunity to expand social impact. When the Calgary Stampede asked if we could help them clean up the horse manure left behind by the parade, we took the challenge to a local homeless shelter known as the Calgary Drop-In Centre. They helped us source a number of able-bodied folks who worked hard to clean up the streets and shovel horse manure into compost bins, which we delivered to a local compost facility.

We were glad to be able to provide good-paying jobs to vulnerable people who needed it, but I've since learned that composting was only one of the options we had available. We could have used that manure to generate power. The Helsinki International Horse Show has been doing it since 2015.

In 2019, the electricity needs during the International Federation for Equestrian Sports (FEI) World Cup Jumping qualifiers were covered entirely from manure. More than 100 tonnes from 370 horses was used to create 150 megawatt hours of energy. That was not only enough to power all the lights, scoreboards, and charging stations during the four-day event, it also added electricity to the national power grid, enabling Helsinki residents to heat their homes.

The manure-to-energy technology used was developed by Fortum Horse-Power. Anssi Paalanen, their vice president, said, "It's possible to charge a phone with only 0.2 decilitres of horse manure, and the manure produced daily by two horses can generate heat for a single-family home for a year."

Since the system was installed in 2015, more than 100,000 tonnes of manure have been put to use, providing heat to more than 2,000 homeowners.

Outstanding

The Calgary Folk Music Festival definitely does not subscribe to the Disney approach. They don't want to send the message that garbage belongs everywhere throughout the pristine island park venue. People often purchase their food and beverages in one area and take it to one of the picnic areas or outdoor stages to watch a show. When they're done and need to dispose of what's left, they can see a strategically placed waste station marked with a tall banner flag. It may be more than thirty feet away, but there is no ambiguity about where it is. The stations are not designed to blend into the background. They're designed to stand out. Once there, a trained and friendly attendant will guide audience members to separate their waste and reinforce the message that the cutlery, plates, food shells, and beer cups are all compostable.

Having a trained attendant at every waste station may seem very people-intensive, but it's even more resource-intensive to keep the entire site clean. It's simpler to have waste stations that stand out with friendly attendants who can monitor cleanliness and overflow at fewer waste collection points.

The Calgary Folk Fest is a warm, inclusive community that excels in recruiting and retaining a large team of volunteers; some celebrate ten- and twenty-year volunteer anniversaries with the festival. Attendants have micro-moments with audience members, yet those moments translate into significant opportunities for behavior change. It is so satisfying when an audience member transforms from proclaiming, "This is too complicated" then turns to their family member to help them with their waste separation. Those micro-moments happen hundreds of times during a typical Folk Fest weekend.

Challenges

Waste stations with clear signage and trained attendants work very well in the daytime, but they are more challenging at night, especially if audience members are intoxicated—which can also lead to intimidation and harassment of station volunteers. Well-lit stations that stand out from other booths are important. Ensuring everything on-site is compostable also helps to keep waste sorting simple to compensate for impaired cognitive abilities. By all means, take good care of your front-line staff. Make sure anyone working night shifts is of an age and maturity level to understand the risks. Partner them up with someone so they are never alone and check in on them frequently to cover bathroom breaks as well as reinforce safety and hygiene practices including proper bending and lifting, use of gloves, and effective handwashing.

Tips for Getting Started

Revisit your Purpose

Find out what waste reduction initiatives are already underway and determine whether these meet the standard you've set with your intended purpose.

1. Follow the Data

Weigh Your Waste

Don't only rely on your waste hauler to measure the volume of your waste. Some haulers don't like to share this information because the tipping fees they've built into the service contract may be inflated, and they don't want you to see the math. Others may be combining waste from your event with other pickups, so they won't have accurate numbers. In my experience, it's rare to get these numbers at all and even more rare to obtain them on a per-day basis.

It's a good idea to establish your own weighing process or have a sustainable events service provider measure the volume of your waste daily. It will give you baseline data to work with and enable you to compare against tipping fees so you can get a realistic snapshot of how much waste diversion can save your bottom line.

Having your own daily waste results also provides great content to engage your audience. It's very empowering and "shareable" to communicate that you "diverted 70 percent of all the waste from Day 1, and we need your help to get us to 80 percent on Day 2. Here are some tips...."

Know What's in Your Waste Stream

What is the most material waste item produced from your event? If you don't know, you should conduct a *waste audit*.

When I first started working with the Calgary Stampede, I was asked to conduct a waste audit. It was very glamorous. Let me tell you about it. My team and I took several bags of garbage from two different twelve-yard bins during a major indoor event. We dumped out all the contents and began sorting them into different piles and weighed each one to determine the percentage of total waste each subcategory represented. Food waste and refundable beverage containers made up a significant portion of the total waste. Ketchup packages and other unused condiments made up a shocking amount. These could be easily eliminated.

Notably, spending time with kitchen staff uncovered a poor practice needing corrective action. We observed the disposal of used cooking oil directly into the drainage sink. Not only was this an environmental hazard, it was a financial risk to the organization because the city could issue a fine for this. Fortunately, the action was corrected shortly thereafter. But it led us to a new understanding of what was possible. There's a viable market for used cooking oil to be used as a biofuel. Finding a service provider that will pick up used oil for resale is one way to contribute to the growth of a circular economy.

2. Engage Your Team

Attracting passionate and committed talent is a large part of the success or failure of any event, and it's no different with a zero-waste event.

Listen to Your People

Obtaining buy-in from your teams is critical to the success of any new programs; oftentimes, the most innovative ideas come from those on the front lines of your event. Such was the case with the stackable beer cup sleeve—developed by Lillian Bertha, a long-time volunteer with the Calgary Folk Music Festival's environment team. She found that the compostable festival beer cups were overflowing from compost bins and getting crushed under crowds of festival-goers. She took it upon herself to prototype a new sleeve and placed a number of them in a few high-traffic waste bins. People immediately recognized the logic of stacking their cups in the sleeves, instead of tossing them into full compost bins. The stackable sleeves were such a successful and popular feature of the festival that the main beer provider decided to develop their own sturdier version, sponsor and brand them, and roll them out at several other festivals where their beer was available on tap.

Ensure Consistent Training

Whether it takes place over one hour, a whole day, or several weeks, proper training of your staff and volunteers can mean the difference between a negative and an extraordinary audience experience.

Trainings and orientations often focus heavily on health, safety, run of the show, and logistics. They should also include an equal amount of attention to the purpose and values of your event. Find a way to turn words on a page into a clear understanding of your sustainability ambition and empower the trainees to contribute in making a positive difference for people and the planet.

Mercedes Hunt, the Director of Energy and Sustainability for Marriott International, said, "To do any sustainable event effectively, you have to start with the people, not the programs." She points out that the events industry has historically been so dependent on temporary workers—workers who, for the most part, are not coming back after the COVID-19 pandemic forced them into other, more stable lines of work. Therefore, the events industry has struggled to come back to its full capacity. But this is an opportunity to train up a whole new generation of event professionals to understand and deliver on sustainability objectives.

The spinoff effects of doing so are immense. "I was a researcher in a past life," Mercedes shared with me. "I conducted interviews with employees at convention centers. People said they learned about sustainability at work and took it home and shared it with their families. The research confirmed that practices people learned in the workplace were largely their practice at home regarding waste, energy use, or safety culture—people bring it home with them. It's an amazing multiplier effect."[18]

During my time with the Calgary Folk Festival, we developed a partnership with the local municipality's waste and recycling department; they provided experts to help train our volunteers and waste station attendants to give accurate and consistent instructions to festivalgoers at each waste station. Volunteers also went on trips to the local landfill and recycling facility to increase their learning and to bond as a team.

3. Engage Your Vendors

The key factor for working with food vendors is to contact them *in advance* and communicate your purpose and intentions clearly. Ask questions to understand their key challenges and present your program features as a solution.

For example, food vendors at the Calgary Stampede loved the compost program we provided because if they didn't have the compost bins, they would have to dump their donut batter, corn husks, pressed lemons, fruit skins, and onion peels into the garbage bins; these would fill up quickly, requiring staff to take time out of cooking and selling food to hungry rodeogoers to move heavy bags of garbage a long distance. Nobody was picking up their garbage bins for them, so the pickup program we offered for their compost waste was valuable and made it more favorable to compost over using the trash bins. This understanding of an important key attribute of our program gave us the authority we required to communicate with vendors that were not using the compost bins properly. When we simply told them that we would not be providing any more green bins or picking them up, they doubled down on training their staff to compost properly.

Putting your expectations in writing and constantly reinforcing messages is important. You should do this through the agreement they sign, the main communication you send them, and the orientation meeting you provide. Leave yourself an enforcement mechanism for any serious laggards. One example, used by the Calgary Folk Fest, was a power and water supply shutdown for any vendor that ignored multiple warnings about a lack of compostable cutlery.

Greenest Vendor Recognition

It's human nature to have some people who are open to change and new ideas and others who wait on the sidelines to see how things materialize. For any process of change, you need to have successes, and you need to have an ecosystem of people who believe in what you are doing. In a system of change, you need to identify who the leaders are and praise them with carrots and who the laggards are who might react better to sticks. You want to reward your leaders because they are the ones who set the example for everybody.

It's good practice to establish and publicize the existence of a reward for early action. One way to celebrate early adopters is to have a *Greenest Vendor Award*. The winner(s) receive a physical prize and recognition—ideally in some sort of awards ceremony. Winners can then display this recognition at their booth or food truck for customers to see. Although not all customers will care, it does create a competitive advantage because specific demographics will be drawn to it. Seeing environmental best practices at work during your event may spur your audience to develop loyalty to particular food vendors and even become defenders of your event. An award for best practices also provides vendors and the event with a natural opportunity for increased media attention.

4. Engage Your Audience

Race events (such as the Vancouver Marathon) require two separate waste reduction strategies: one for the participating athletes, and one for the spectators they bring with them.

For these events, much of the waste is produced before it even begins, often even days prior to the event—when people pick up their bibs and go through a gauntlet of free samples and promotional material from sponsors and exhibitors and participate in other races and activities. Those free samples are a problem to be solved. They typically come in nonrecyclable wrapping. In fact, many of the wrappings we thought to be recyclable are not at all (such as those on Clif Bars and most protein bars).

The Vancouver Marathon organizers took the opportunity to reach both racers and attendees. Their clothing donations program they facilitate for both audiences has been so successful that they actually have a net positive waste diversion rate because of the amount of clothing and shoes they receive.

Invest in Effective Signage

In addition to the trained friendly volunteers staffing waste stations at the Calgary Folk Fest, signage played a major role in effectively communicating and transferring waste separation knowledge to audience members.

Large reusable vinyl signs zip-tied to fencing (which could be seen at eye level and from afar) conveyed which items belonged in which bins. Black garbage bins were labeled "LANDFILL" to indicate that waste streams should be avoided when possible. Samples of common waste items were also pasted to the bins to clearly indicate where they belonged.

Signage should be simple, concise, and instructive without a lot of context or other messaging, such as listing other sustainability initiatives. The more focused the message is, the more it will influence that split-second decision of where to toss that food item.

5. Consider Your Impact on Nature

Many races occur in urban environments where runoff from pavement to streams is common, but even more heartbreaking is watching this play out in lush natural spaces such as forests and mountainous areas where wildlife can be immediately and severely impacted by waste pollution.

The 24 Hours of Adrenaline was an endurance biking event in Canmore, Alberta. The province pressured the tournament to shut down because of its significant impact on bears, cougars, and other local wildlife populations in the heart of the pristine Rocky Mountains.

From setup to cleanup—the event generated a significant volume of waste over several days, particularly from attendees camping and cooking on-site in tents and camper vans. Many competitors took turns sleeping between relay shifts, and their campsites became all-night parties.

A new iteration of the event called Canadian Rockies 24 is emerging to replace the shutdown 24 Hours of Adrenalin event. Let's hope they establish a nature-first approach that's aligned with a strong social purpose such as the 5 Peaks Trail Running series, which describes itself as a *celebration of nature*.

6. Address Low-Hanging Fruit

It's important to start with the items that your staff, vendors, and audience interact with most when deciding where to target your zero-waste efforts. Regardless of the action you take, it will be met with cynicism if people can point to a ubiquitous poor practice. Single-use plastic items such as straws may feel trivial, but leaving them in place while you make other changes sends a signal that you can't be trusted to address the little things; as a result, the bigger, more complex, or expensive interventions can come across as less credible. From my point of view, the most important low-hanging fruit to address first is Styrofoam.

Eliminate Styrofoam
Research has shown that when Styrofoam is burned it releases toxic chemicals and smoke that can damage the nervous system and lungs.[19] The US produces about 3 million tonnes of Styrofoam every year, releasing approximately 21 million tonnes of CO_2 equivalent into the atmosphere every year.

The Award Goes To...
In the Olympics, only those that make it to the podium receive a medal, but in most race events, all participants receive one. These are all typically made in China, where environmental and labor standards are substandard and transparent emissions data is difficult to obtain. The medals are then transported a long distance in nonrecyclable packaging so they can adorn everyone pushing themselves to the limit.

The 5 Peaks Trail Running series, which takes place in various locations across Canada, provides a unique wall-mountable trophy created by local artists instead of a medal.

Trail runners have a particular responsibility to protect nature paths and wildlife. Fortunately, more federal conservation laws are becoming common as are Leave No Trace outdoor ethics—the seven principles that help guide backcountry etiquette.[20] Trail runners should be discouraged from taking disposable cups on the course and encouraged to carry their own hydration bottles. They can also wear running belts to hold trash, such as empty gel packets and wrappers, some of which are recyclable.

7. Scrap the Tees
Yes, t-shirts offer promotion of the race and allow events to fulfill sponsor requirements by displaying logos, but if a race is looking to be more environmentally friendly, the t-shirt is a place to cut back.

We're now seeing some events charge extra for a race t-shirt, which can make runners really think about whether they want yet another to add to their collection. Other events have done away with them altogether.

A UK-based program called Trees Not Tees (TNT), organized by the Future Forest Company, develops reforestation projects on degraded land to protect biodiversity and remove carbon from the atmosphere.[21, 22] They work with race organizers to give runners the option of planting a tree instead of receiving a race t-shirt.

Many participants only want the tees for one day as a way to provide photographic evidence they completed a major milestone. Creating more Instagrammable backgrounds and offering pre- and post-race photo opportunities could have the same desired effect without the supply chain headaches.

8. Address Your Food Footprint

According to Feeding America, 119 billion pounds of food is thrown away each year. That equates to 130 billion meals, more than $408 billion worth of food—and nearly 40 percent of all food produced in the US! In Canada, 58 percent of all food grown goes to waste, largely because misshapen or esthetically imperfect-looking food is rejected by major grocery chains and restaurants.

This is especially egregious given that nearly 924 million people in the world faced extreme levels of food insecurity in 2021, according to the World Health Organization. Those numbers have increased by 207 million since before the outbreak of the COVID-19 pandemic in 2020.

Nice and Smoothie

A company called Trendi in Canada works with growers around the world, buying their misshapen food products to make gourmet smoothies that they distribute through their vending machines in airports and transit stations, which are available for rent at your next event.

Phase Out Meat

The Scope 3 emissions for food include the greenhouse gases associated with the production and transportation of their ingredients, as well as emissions associated with the packaging and transportation of the finished product. Emissions associated with disposing of any food waste generated by the company could also be considered Scope 3 emissions.

In addition to the associated GHG impacts, meat is difficult to manage from a waste perspective. The countdown starts quickly before leftover meat becomes too rotten to donate. Even traces of meat contamination require the disposal of an entire load of recyclable material, whereas most vegetable residue on recyclable products is generally forgivable at most facilities.

Psychology of Food

It's not uncommon for event organizers to have nightmares about guests running out of food. But usually, instead of running out of food, we have heaps left over after an event due to no-shows and ambitious over-ordering. The environmental consequences of producing and wasting all that is immense.

An event hack I've used for ordering food that will be displayed buffet-style is to always ensure a beautiful fruit display is included. Ideally, it should be different kinds of fruit with a peel (and appeal) and local—or as close to local as you can get. They typically go uneaten at the beginning of an event because most people gravitate to hot food, but the fruit display ensures the food area never looks bare. Even if your food order is stretched over staggered replenishments, there are always options available, even for latecomers. Plus, leftover fruit is a great, healthy snack for staff and vendors at the end of a long event day. It's also easy to donate. Fruit with peels is especially attractive as donations because it lasts longer and is less likely to be mishandled or contaminated.

> A lot of the food that we view as waste, is actually not waste at all.
>
> — Lourdes Juan,
> founder of Leftovers Foundation

Lourdes Juan is the founder of the Leftovers Foundation, Alberta's first food rescue program, which started in 2012. They work with volunteers, donors, and service agencies across Canada to reduce waste and increase access by rescuing and redirecting food to those most vulnerable.

"*Leftovers* is seen as a pejorative term when it doesn't have to be," Lourdes told me during our conversation. The idea for Leftovers first came to Lourdes when her cousin was picking up bread for his church from a local bakery. She was helping him get the bread to the homeless Drop-In Centre in Calgary when she learned the bakery had excess bread at the end of every day. She began to wonder how many other bakeries had food left over. "The gears started turning that night, and I began researching food waste at the retail level," Lourdes said.[23] What she found was a food waste problem global in scope. She asked at her local coffee shop what they were doing with their leftover baked goods at the end of the day…and the Leftovers Foundation was born.

Their first big break came at the Calgary International Film Festival when the festival screened a film about food waste. Lourdes and the Leftovers team were invited to participate in the event and leveraged the opportunity to raise awareness about what they were doing locally.

Part of the problem with food access, Lourdes explains, is "our cities were not designed with marginalized people in mind. A lot of these families and senior citizens don't have the privilege of being able to travel twenty minutes to a grocery store." As she points out, many of the people in marginalized communities are able to pay for their food; they just can't always afford the premium prices for fresh, healthy food. This is why, she says, "We need to think about these things more innovatively and more creatively."

Her creativity led to significant expansions: Leftovers started operating in four other nearby cities; a separate social enterprise called Fresh Routes was established to bring fresh, healthy, and local food to remote communities; and an app was launched that connects donors of leftover food with people and agencies most in need all across the country. The app was recently spun out as a new company called Knead Technologies, with sales across Canada, the US, and plans for global expansion.

In 2022, Leftovers redirected more than 1 million pounds of food to those in need, resulting in roughly 865,000 pounds of CO_2 diverted and over US\$2.5 million saved.

9. Repurpose Everything You Can

Repurpose Lanyards

How many lanyards do you have from previous conferences? Very few people need another lanyard that's just going to hang in their office.

I love lanyard libraries consisting of reused lanyards collected on the final day of previous events. They can be laundered and used again. I have seen a lot of success in these programs when they're used. The barrier is that many events still have the lanyard "sponsorship" built into their model, so they produce new lanyards every year to serve that sponsorship need.

Repurpose Your Flowers

Source locally if you have flowers at your event, and find a partner like ReBLOOM to repurpose them. ReBLOOM is Canada's first floral recycler and composter, servicing the entire country. Since 2014, the social enterprise has repurposed event florals, partnering with anyone wanting to make a difference—corporate clients, global conferences, fundraisers, hotels, and galas. ReBLOOM converts florals that would otherwise be thrown out into little bouquets of happiness, donating them to a charity of your choice, in your name. Often the donated flowers end up in a halfway home, senior citizen center, or hospital.

"Honestly, you just have to give flowers once, once to someone who feels truly forgotten or who has no family, and it will break your heart open," Kalynn Crump, founder of ReBLOOM told me. "I always get a little choked up because it truly is this emotion that you feel."[24]

Kalynn got the idea for ReBLOOM after seeing so many gorgeous gala florals going to waste. After one event ended, the florists walked in, picked up the arrangement, removed the vase for reuse, and just left the flowers on the table for disposal. Kalynn was mortified! "That beautiful single-use lasted six hours after traveling a minimum of four thousand miles and then straight to landfill," she said. "So, I took them." After a few similar experiences, Kalynn's mom came over and said, "Your home looks like a funeral parlor."

So, Kalynn showered a family member with the flowers who was in the hospital at the time. "It was such an emotional boost—that little bit of love to feel like there's something more outside those windows, that there's just a little bit of something else."

ReBLOOM started in Calgary, but it is now national. Team members will go and collect the flowers after your event is over, almost anywhere in the country. They will repurpose the flowers into smaller table arrangements and donate them to a charity of your choice in your event's name or someone else's name. ReBLOOM will personalize the tags and add the company logo on one side if desired. Finally, they come back a week later to recollect the flowers for compost.

"I can't tell you how many people have said, "No, no. You must have me mistaken for someone else. No one would send me flowers," and we're like, "No, these are for you. They're actually for you. There's a personalized little note on there. It's amazing," Kalynn shares, very animatedly.

In Calgary, ReBLOOM partners with a halfway house where the people are trying to get back on their feet and demonstrate they've been gainfully employed and consistently showing up. "They do the recollection for us," she told me. Since the program began, Kalynn has provided references to more than ten of the participants, who have gone on to secure full-time jobs because of their experience with ReBLOOM.

ReBLOOM has also partnered with the Toronto International Film Festival, Fashion Week, the Canadian Opera Company, and many more organizations.

10 Report Results
Folk Fest Results

I was incredibly proud to lead the Calgary Folk Fest environment team for a number of years before joining the festival's Board of Directors. At the beginning of my time with the festival, we set a baseline goal of 50 percent waste diversion from the landfill. We obtained third-party audits as we added new environmental programs each year, and—after only four years—we achieved a 92 percent diversion rate! At the same time, we decreased our overall waste footprint, mainly through the elimination of disposable water bottles. See chapter 4 for more information about the water bottle phaseout.

Normalize Zero Waste

My picture from that Premier's Stampede Breakfast went viral because many people simply couldn't believe or had never heard about the possibility of a zero-waste event. It's still a relatively new idea to most people. By reporting your progress, even when it's imperfect or incomplete, you are creating awareness about the possibility of moving in this direction and normalizing zero-waste events.

Producing zero-waste events doesn't just address the unsightliness of overflowing garbage, it can promote the reuse of materials, reduce greenhouse gases such as methane, protect nature and endangered species from toxic materials, and save human lives.

4

Ban Bottled Water without Causing a Meltdown

> If there is magic on this planet, it is contained in water.
>
> — Loren Eiseley

"Are you crazy?!"

That was the response I received from crew members when I presented the idea of banning bottled water from the fifty-thousand-person Calgary Folk Music Festival.

Actually, the full reaction was: "You're going to dehydrate the audience with your reckless plan, but you're really crazy if you think we can deny water bottles to performers! These are people who can't even remember where they put their guitars, much less a reusable bottle of water!"

I would soon learn an important lesson about change management: uncover the area of greatest resistance, start there, and then co-create solutions and reinforce.

The Calgary Folk Fest was where I cut my teeth producing sustainable events. It's a truly special event taking place over four days annually in a pristine island park nestled between two flowing rivers that cut through the heart of downtown Calgary. For many, Folk Fest is much more than just a music festival. It's an institution with more than forty years of history.

While a small but mighty team of paid staff leads the Calgary Folk Music Festival year-round, it's largely executed by more than 1,200 dedicated volunteers who clean the site, provide security, serve the beer, and manage sound and power at each of the seven stages. The Festival enjoys a loyal following. Some audience members camp overnight, rain or shine, outside the entrance gates on the beautiful Prince's Island Park just to be among the first to skip across the park—that's right skip, no running allowed—and lay down their tarps right in front of the main outdoor stage to claim the real estate where they'll be lounging, eating, reading, chatting, and dancing well into the evening.

I served as the Folk Festival's Environment Manager, and then I was a member of the Board of Directors for seven years. My team and I had a valuable opportunity to teach city staff how to support outdoor venues. This meant we got access to city infrastructure for the large volume of recycling and compost that we were collecting. Partnering with the city was a key ingredient in going from the 50 to the 95 percent waste diversion rate we achieved over that seven-year period.

Ecosystem

As we launched and scaled new environmental programs at the Folk Festival, an ecosystem of complementary initiatives emerged. As we grew and trained all 1,200 volunteers including our 80-person environment team, we also hired several service providers. Some of those businesses eventually hired volunteers from our environment team. Some team members went on to work for the City of Calgary or other municipalities, and others even started their own environmental businesses. This inspired me to do the same in partnership with two other veterans of the Folk Fest environment team.

What we created was not just a great environmental program at a much-beloved music festival. We also lit the fuse that exploded into a spectacular environmental ecosystem, which has truly changed the face of Calgary and beyond. It felt like we were part of a movement.

Canada's folk music festival organizers maintain a close relationship with one another, and I was honored to be invited to deliver workshops at their annual gatherings. (I can't say, however, whether my zero-waste session was more interesting than the one on how to source good pot for performers and whether or not to pre-roll.)

The invitation to share lessons learned with many other folk festivals made me feel I had really earned the confidence of senior event staff. This allowed me to innovate and make even more sweeping environmental changes at the Calgary Folk Festival. Of these, none was more controversial than the plan to ban plastic water bottles.

Bottled Water Is a Scam

Bottled water is so prolific, and it's staggering to think that more people in North America drink bottled water than milk or beer approximately—42.6 billion bottles each year. The average American drinks more than thirty gallons of bottled water in a year. At an average price of $1.50 per bottle, that is nearly US$300 spent by almost every American on something that comes out of the tap for free.

I've never really understood the mass appeal of bottled water. Most of it is just municipal tap water that's filtered, packaged, and sold back to us—with a 4,000 percent markup, according to Readers Digest.[1] (And this is *in addition* to the tax dollars we're paying to subsidize the infrastructure that large soft drink makers are incentivized to exploit through volume discounts.)

Having spent time in developing countries where access to safe potable water is unaffordable and out of reach for millions of people, I struggle with the ethics of commoditizing something required for basic survival. I'm astonished and concerned that water is now openly traded on some stock exchanges along with gold and consumer goods.

Environmental and Human Health Catastrophe

The carbon footprint of a bottle of water is very high when you factor in the impact of shipping, distribution, and manufacturing. If you were to fill a plastic water bottle a quarter-full with oil, that's roughly the amount needed *to make* that bottle.

In Canada, plastic has been classified under the Canadian Environmental Protection Act as a *toxic substance*, and there are proposed amendments to the Act that would prohibit the export of plastics as a means of disposal.

More than a decade before the government called plastic a toxic substance, I brought the idea forward to ban single-use water bottles from the Calgary

Folk Music Festival. I quickly learned that in addition to the ethical and environmental considerations, there was an important economic issue that required discussion, too.

Economics of Donated Bottled Water

One of the Folk Festival's sponsors was PepsiCo, and they supplied multiple pallets of their bottled water brand (Aquafina) as an in-kind donation. The festival then sold the water to its food vendors, who in turn sold them to the audience—with a significant markup. The remaining pallets of bottles were stockpiled in case vendors sold out and needed more product, and any left over at the end of the festival were stored in a warehouse until the following year's event. It was all an elaborate product placement scheme for the sponsor and not an insignificant revenue source for both the Folk Fest and the food vendors. For the environment team, however, the water bottles meant countless hours fishing plastic pollution out of the rivers, constantly managing hundreds of large bins of overflowing bottles, and a daily cleanup of crushed bottles from every square inch of the park.

To their credit, it was not a hard sell to get the Calgary Folk Fest staff to agree to walk away from the PepsiCo sponsorship. The staff saw it as an opportunity to reclaim their position as an environmental leader and suspected the move would be well received by their audience. I felt fortunate that my main contact on that team, Talia Potter, was a passionate and influential environmental champion who committed to making it happen.

We agreed that the remaining supply of bottled water from the legacy PepsiCo sponsorship would be phased out over time and that the festival would not be accepting an offer to replenish the supply after that, which effectively concluded that partnership.

Move in Stages

The feeling of elation I had after maneuvering the water sponsor issue distracted me from foreseeing that it would be other volunteer crew members who would voice the strongest objections. Volunteer managers have a lot of influence in the planning and execution of the Calgary Folk Festival, and some of them had been in their role for decades. They knew the event logistics inside and out, and some of them placed an oversized emphasis on their identity as an authority within their area of the festival. That was especially true for those responsible for sound. That is understandable, I suppose. After all, who wants to go to a music-less music festival?

It was from the Stages managers that I received the "Are you crazy?!" reaction. They wanted an exemption from the bottled water phase-out. I told them it would send the wrong message if plastic water bottles were available only to performers. "We should go all the way or not at all," I said. One Stages team member posed the following scenario: "Say one of the artists knocks over the bottles and shorts out the sound equipment? It would cut the sound for the whole festival." However, this was no more likely than it had long been with unsealed half-drunk plastic water bottles littering the stage. Because they were long-time volunteers and experienced musicians themselves, I asked them, "How was live music performed before the days we were inundated with water bottles?" They could not remember, and in fairness, most of us can't.

It became very clear that, in order to successfully eliminate bottled water from the Calgary Folk Music Festival, I would need to earn the trust and support of the Stages crews. So, I worked closely with them over several months to address their concerns, which I found to be very reasonable once we talked them through. I realized that they mostly wanted to be heard, and their deepest fears were actually not that the sound would be negatively affected but rather that the relationships that they enjoyed developing with the artists would be negatively affected by denying them water.

We agreed to co-create a focused pilot project to begin the bottled water phase-out focused first on the artists. It involved placing water refill stations at staging areas that were designated *for performers only* and having our teams share responsibility for regular cleaning, sanitizing, and replacing the large Culligan water jugs throughout the four days of the event. We agreed that if it did not work, we would abandon the plan entirely.

Make It Memorable

One of the Festival sponsors, TD Bank, funded the purchase of a large number of high-quality reusable water bottles; these were then branded with the loveable cow that was part of the Folk Festival's vintage logo. They were distributed to musical performers in their welcome package. We had a plan in place to collect all the disused or half-drunk bottles for washing and redistribution—but we didn't need it. In fact, the artists loved their reusable bottles so much that they clipped them to their belts or bags and raved about them onstage.

One of the main headliners, Michael Franti, announced from the stage that he would be taking his souvenir Calgary Folk Fest bottle on tour with him around the world. His announcement generated demand for the reusable bottles, and audience members went into the merch tent to purchase their own. The pilot program was an unmitigated success, and the Stages team was unreserved in their support going forward.

The following year, we rolled out the water program audience-wide. We hired a company called H2O Buggy to supply several large mobile water stations with built-in filtration systems that could be wheeled in prefilled with potable water or set up in areas where they could be plugged right into municipal water systems underground. The H2O Buggies enabled audience members to access the equipment from either side; there were multiple taps for filling reusable bottles, as well as taps to drink from directly, like a water fountain.

Our water bottle sponsor expanded their support of the water program with one of the most innovative corporate sponsor activations I've ever been a part of. TD Bank event staff filled up specialized backpacks using the H2O Buggies and then walked around the site offering to refill reusable water bottles for festivalgoers. Thus, clean and safe potable water was made available free and on demand—without lineups anywhere in the venue. The program was incredibly well received by the public and the mainstream media, and that year the Calgary Folk Music Festival was recognized with an international Greener Festival Award (now known as A Greener Future) alongside Bonaroo and many other well-known international music festivals.[2,3]

Not All Sunshine and Rainbows

Some of the food vendors were unhappy about losing water as a revenue source. The other group negatively impacted by the elimination of bottled water was our refundable bottle partner, Vecova. They are a local social enterprise that manages a bottle depot employing people of all physical and mental abilities facing barriers to employment. Vecova also provides various critical programs, services, and facilities to people with a wide range of disabilities.

For many years, Vecova used to park their semi-trailer backstage during the Calgary Folk Music Festival to store all the empty soda cans, beer, and water bottles. The semi was driven to the depot and back several times throughout the four-day event to unload and make room for more.

On the first evening of the festival, during the year we stopped selling bottled water completely, I answered a call from someone at Vecova who informed me that a large load of bottles had been stolen from the semitrailer. I asked if he remembered that we no longer have bottled water for sale, and we both laughed after some stunned silence. The difference it made was enormous, and we soon realized the semi-truck was no longer necessary; this opened up a significant amount of available space backstage.

Eliminating bottled water did mean less bottle revenue for this wonderful community organization, but they were supportive of the change. In subsequent discussions with Ron Meeres, the twenty-two-year veteran manager of the Vecova bottle depot (now with the Alberta Bottle Depot Association), he explained that while Folk Fest was an early mover, the whole recycling industry is scrambling in light of the disruption caused when China—the world's largest importer of plastic waste—decided in 2018 to block imports of metal, steel, and plastic. If typical plastic recycling rates were below 30 percent before China's move, they certainly are far below that now.

Taking Water on the Road

My experience at the Calgary Folk Music Festival was a rewarding opportunity to make a positive impact while listening to some great music, connecting with a diverse community, and further developing my leadership skills. It was also like a living laboratory that served as an incubator for me and my co-founders, Matt Dorma and Chris Dunlap, to launch our own social enterprise called Do It Green (DIG), which was our vehicle to bring zero-waste, net-zero emissions, and water-bottle-free programs to many other events.

Some jurisdictions have a legal requirement for event organizers to ensure a specific number of water refill stations, usually based on audience size. I view this as a growing trend, especially given the frequency of heat exhaustion that's exacerbated by drug use at many major outdoor events. That was why DIG purchased the assets of H2O Buggy (later sold to Quench Buggy) and rolled out the mobile water stations alongside other environmental services.

Over the next few years, DIG secured partnerships with the city of Calgary, which awarded subsidies to public events that wanted to hire our H2O Buggies but did not have it in their budgets. Shortly afterward, we secured a partnership with the country's largest bank, Royal Bank of Canada (RBC), that helped us expand that subsidy program throughout Alberta. This enabled DIG and our clients to displace a total of more than *one million bottles of water* from hundreds of events over a period of seven years.

We also partnered with a wonderful international charity, the Center for Affordable Water and Sanitation Technology (CAWST), that provided fun and engaging water education-related activities for kids and adults at events utilizing our mobile stations. CAWST volunteers also helped to monitor and sanitize the equipment, and DIG donated 1 percent of its pretax revenues to the charity each year.

Water Bottles and Sports

Having worked at more events than I can remember, I've observed that each has its own culture, which is shaped by myriad factors including venue, visuals, leadership, and messaging. It's easier for some events (like the Calgary Folk Fest) to ban bottled water and much more challenging for others—but it's almost never impossible.

> Culture eats strategy for breakfast.
> — Peter Drucker

Sporting events have some of the most challenging cultures to transform regarding water. That may be because athletes are very health conscious and bottled water has been so effectively marketed as a healthy and convenient status symbol to this demographic. I can understand the convenience argument, but the health claims do not stand up to scrutiny. While bottled water companies are increasingly using BPA-free plastic, other potentially harmful chemicals are still commonly present in plastic bottles, and these can leach into the water if the bottles are exposed to heat or left to sit for long periods of time.[4]

Competitive athletes (along with the rest of us!) should note that some of those chemicals are possible endocrine disruptors that could mess with hormone levels and affect athletic performance.[5] Over the years, traces of phthalates, mold, trihalomethanes, and arsenic have all been found in bottled water, and only relatively recently did the US Food & Drug Agency even start to regulate bottled water for *E. coli*.[6, 7, 8, 9]

Whether it's a mountain bike endurance race, marathon, or Spartan race, each event caters to a community with its own very distinct way of being in the world. Even those with an acute sensitivity to the evils of bottled water and the degradation of natural spaces become uber-wasteful when they're breaking barriers in their extra-steep trail training or gasping for just a sip of water at the finish line after a particularly grueling race.

The Calgary Marathon developed a recycling and composting program and provided mobile water stations for the 11,000-person crowd, but there were plastic water bottles available for the runners as they crossed the finish line. What I observed was that many of them experienced significantly limited cognitive abilities in those first few minutes, due to the severe mental and physical exhaustion of pushing their bodies to run 42.2 kilometers in extreme heat.

I was astonished the first time I saw firsthand how many people grabbed a water bottle seconds after crossing the finish line only to pour some of it over their head or take a gentle sip before irrationally smashing the nearly full bottle and cap to the ground. When I first saw it happen, I thought the runner was unwell and silently wished them a speedy recovery, but after two thousand people repeated this action, I realized I was witnessing a regular part of marathon culture. The crushed Gatorade cups that pave the marathon route are also emblematic of this cultural behavior. Changing culture can take time, but it can happen through bold leadership backed by continuous reinforcement.

The Calgary Marathon does collect all the cups along the route in clear plastic bags and recycles them. This works well in Calgary, but the wax coating on those standard Gatorade cups means they are not recyclable in every jurisdiction. The Marathon also has an interesting initiative called the *3Rs Challenge* to encourage runners to walk, bike, carpool, or take public transit to the event as well as to reuse water bottles and forgo those waxed-paper cups. "Green Athletes" are then awarded prizes and recognized online for their leadership.

Reusable Cups at Water Stations

Kristina Smithe was so appalled at the volume of cups on the ground while running a marathon in California in 2019 that she launched her own company called Hiccup Earth. The rental service provides reusable eight-ounce silicone cups for running events across the US. Since the company's debut in 2020, more than thirty races have used the bright blue vessels, saving thousands of cups from landfills and recycling centers.

The St. Pete Run Fest in St. Petersburg, Florida, rented 26,000 reusable Hiccup Earth cups to serve water to six thousand race participants during the two-day, four-distance event.[10] (The race still used the Gatorade-branded bamboo compostable cups to serve the sports drink.[11]) Many of the participants wrote notes of gratitude for the sustainable upgrade.

"We had a 65 percent reduction of compost cups, which takes time to deliver post-race and decomposes slowly," St. Pete Run Fest co-founder Ryan Jordan told *Runner's World*. "Renting reusable cups was operationally, efficiently beneficial for us. It made our lives easier, and the change was financially neutral."[12]

Use Compostable Cups

When reusable cups are unavailable, compostable cups are another option for lessening environmental impact. However, this is only effective if you have a program in place to transport the cups to a proper commercial composting facility for processing. Not all race host sites have access to such centers.

The California International Marathon (CIM) offers compostable cups on the course to more than eight thousand runners and provides hydration stations at all aid stops along the course. They also provide bins for TerraCycle collection and partnered with GU Energy Labs to enable gel packet recycling.[13] CIM received Gold-level certification from the Council for Responsible Sport in 2017 and 2019.[14]

"CIM diverts over seven thousand pounds (about 75 percent) of waste from landfills at our event through our sophisticated and systematic sustainability practices," said Scott Abbott, executive director for CIM. "We spend tens of thousands of dollars not only to purchase compostable cups but also to ship those cups to a facility that can compost them, as our region does not have the infrastructure to compost such cups."[15]

No Cups at All

Some runners participate in the Calgary Marathon to qualify for Boston, but if they succeed, they'll find themselves cut off from water when they arrive at the Boston Marathon because they no longer hand out bottled water at the finish line. They also recently switched all their cups to compostable for their thirty thousand registered participants.

A handful of races simply don't offer cups of any kind on the course. The High Lonesome 100 for example, a one-hundred-mile high-altitude ultramarathon with 23,500 feet of vertical gain in Colorado, has been cup and disposable water-bottle-free since they began the race series in 2017. "I understand the desire to fall back on disposable cups, whether they're recyclable or compostable," said Caleb Efta, the race director, founder, and co-owner of the High Lonesome 100, "but going cupless is not a hard behavior to ask volunteers or racers to do."[16]

When Bottled Water Is Necessary

Some elite competitive athletes regularly get tested for banned substances, and they may have been conditioned to only drink from sealed plastic water. In such cases, I would recommend sourcing bottled water through the Earth Group, a social enterprise that supports the UN World Food Programme to provide school meals to children. Their aluminum packaging is more sustainable and safer than plastic in terms of the chemical leaching concerns.

Before rushing out to source Earth Water bottles for your next sporting event, ask yourself this: Could it be that the athletes are kind of like performers at a music festival? Perhaps you need to uncover your area of greatest resistance and start there. Then you can offer clear guidance and support to make it an exciting and memorable experience. Identify the champions and influencers on your events team and empower them with good information as I did with Talia at the Folk Fest. Start with a pilot project and consider what a phased approach might look like. Communicate frequently and get people to see how it all connects to a desired state that you are working toward.

If you target the biggest challenge first—like the athletes needing to feel comfortable with the program—change can happen quickly and event culture can shift. People enjoy taking part in an event that is tied into a movement to solve some of the world's most pressing challenges. It helps them look beyond the race, the performance on stage, or the barrier to change to experience the future our world needs—at least for the days surrounding your event.

Are You Crazy Enough?

Could your event be an incubator for innovative new ideas and businesses serving a future events industry that prioritizes social impact and solutions for the planet?

As you plan your next outdoor event, consider for a moment the impact of more than 70 percent of the plastic bottles from your venue spending the next one thousand years floating in the ocean and ask yourself: Am I designing something with the future in mind?

Maybe we're all waiting for government regulations to catch up to the scale of the problem or perhaps we trust global bottled water companies to innovate their way toward a solution. After all, early indications suggest that single-use water bottles may one day be made with plant-based rather than petroleum-based plastics. That might be a fine solution—*if* they're composted properly in a commercial facility using the latest technology; otherwise, decomposing plant-based plastic releases methane, which has eighty times the warming power of carbon dioxide. So that's not a solution to hold one's breath for.

Will eliminating bottled water from your events solve the world's problems? Unlikely, but you will make a measurable positive impact, be recognized for your voluntary action, and effectively position yourself within an ecosystem of solution seekers and innovators shaping the future.

And if anybody asks you "Are you crazy!?" tell them this: "I have been, but I now see clearly the future of where our event needs to go in the years ahead, and I'm excited to collaborate with you to make it amazing."

5

Go Net Zero

We have to fix climate change with the people we have right now,
and to a large extent with the perspectives we have right now as well.

—Katherine Hayhoe, Climate Scientist

Net-Zero COP

As the host country for the 26th Conference of the Parties (COP26) held in Glasgow, Scotland, in the fall of 2021, the UK was committed to delivering a net-zero emissions event. However, following a significant delay due to COVID-19 and a preoccupation with the G8 Summit, which took place in Cornwall in June of that year, the contract to organize the COP26 event was only awarded in April. That meant COP26 Technical Director Mark Bannister and his team had only six months to pull off one the largest events ever held in the UK, with 38,000 delegates from nearly 200 countries (the highest attendance ever at a COP), with an average of 13,000 delegates on-site each day for two weeks straight—and it had to be net zero.

"The first couple of months were focused on putting the team together and planning up what our approach was going to be," Mark told me during our Zoom conversation. He said, "We developed two very different plans: one for a kind of best-case scenario where some in-person meetings could take place at COP, and then worst-case, with travel restrictions where no one can come to Glasgow."[1]

The team developed a virtual participation option for the first time ever at a COP event. However, as the unpredictable waves of the pandemic escalated and subsided and social distancing requirements were rolled back to five feet, it seemed COP26 was headed toward the best-case scenario, and suddenly the team found themselves managing ballooning delegation sizes and increasing budget pressures.

Events Are Linked to Climate Change

The events industry as a whole has a lot at stake with respect to the impacts of climate change. In addition to its devastating impacts on millions of people, our economy, and the environment, climate change is the biggest event disruptor imaginable. Intensification of extreme weather can cause the cancellation of major events, increase travel risks, make venues inoperable and more expensive, as well as increase your food and insurance costs, and further disrupt already strained supply chains.

Events, themselves, generate significant greenhouse gas emissions, especially when you factor in all the travel required. Therefore, the events industry has a major responsibility to take meaningful action on climate change.

According to Meet Green, the typical conference attendee produces nearly 400 pounds of carbon dioxide (CO_2) emissions per day.[2] Festival and event goers commonly produce over four pounds of waste per day—more than double what they would generate in their regular daily lives. That waste ends up in landfills, which produce more than 10 percent of global greenhouse gas (GHG) emissions. US landfills produce as much GHG as twenty million passenger cars on the road each year.[3]

Climate Chaos at Burning Man Is a Cautionary Tale

One person was found dead and seventy thousand people were left stranded due to a tropical storm during the 2023 Burning Man festival in the Nevada desert.

It was not the only challenge Burning Man faced that year as a coalition of climate and anti-capitalist activists parked a twenty-eight-foot trailer across the road, causing several miles of gridlock until local law enforcement eventually rammed through the blockade.

Both the protest and extreme weather disruption should cause the entire events industry to reflect on the future of major gatherings as we know them.

It Began with Protests

Burning Man is rooted in the ethos of anti-consumerism, self-reliance, and radical self-expression. However, critics have argued that the festival has become a playground for the wealthy elite, Silicon Valley moguls, and billionaires.

The protesters at Burning Man, known as the Seven Circles Alliance, aimed to provoke more aggressive climate action. Their demands included banning private jets, single-use plastics, unnecessary propane burning, and unlimited generator usage during the nine-day event.

According to the Burning Man Project's own estimates, more than 90 percent of the event's carbon footprint comes from travel to and from Black Rock City. Another 5 percent comes from gas- and diesel-burning generators that keep lights and air conditioners on throughout the festival. When you factor these together, Burning Man is responsible for about 100,000 tonnes of carbon dioxide, equivalent to more than what 22,000 gas-powered cars produced in a year.

The climate protest left many burners (Burning Man attendees) feeling confused and agitated. Erika Welch, who attended her first Burning Man this year said, "It was an odd way to protest as the Burner Express Buses dramatically reduce the carbon footprint." Welch was on a shuttle bus from San Francisco to the festival site. "I was also strongly encouraged to buy carbon offset credits for my flight and bus when I bought my Burning Man ticket," she added, which she happily obliged.[4]

Then Came the Rain

The annual nine-day Burning Man festival is held in what is typically an arid and dusty desert town known as Black Rock City. This year the site became a muddy swamp after the clouds opened up and crashed the party with two to three months' worth of rain in just over twenty-four hours. Burning Man attendees were instructed to shelter in place and ration their food, water, and fuel.

Sustainability consultant and academic Shawna McKinley tracks events affected by climate disruptions, and she's seeing a pattern of increasing severity emerging. In addition to Burning Man, McKinley tracked thirty other events that were either canceled, postponed, relocated, or had their agendas notably altered due to the same storm pattern.

A New Playbook Is Needed

Climate change has rewritten the rules, and our existing contingency plans for major events no longer suffice. It's time to throw away the old playbook and reimagine scenarios that account for the intensifying climate events we face. From sudden floods to raging wildfires and extreme heat waves, we must anticipate the unpredictable and adapt accordingly.

Engaging the right stakeholders as part of revised contingency plans is important and should include meteorology experts and local emergency services. Burning Man did both but still underestimated the risks, so more imaginative scenarios are required for adequate preparations.

The Seven Circles Alliance protestors at Burning Man were not just there to highlight the need for more climate action. They were condemning the capitalist economic system and relentless pursuit of profits over well-being, which they argue is perpetuating climate change through greed, overconsumption, and the myth of endless growth.

If Burning Man is a target for these protestors, then all events face the same risk. After all, Burning Man is a leader. Their 2030 road map aims to remove enough CO_2 from the environment to achieve carbon negative as well as become regenerative and ensure "no matter out of place," or zero waste.[5]

Time to Rethink Events

Both the tropical storm and the climate protest are existential threats to Burning Man, as well as all major events. Can the festival continue as it has before? Does it still make sense to burn "the Man" when our world is already burning?

The even bigger question is what is the role of events in our world when their environmental impacts are so big, and the risks of climate disruptions are so consequential?

Adapting to the new risks and contingency measures required for events is only one part of the way forward for events. The entire events industry needs to reimagine its role as a valuable contributor to the most pressing challenges of our time. Events must be part of the solution to climate change, not part of the problem.

Climate Change Is Now

Recent advancements have enabled scientists to directly link—with a high degree of certainty—extreme weather events such as wildfires, droughts, heatwaves, flash floods, and giant hailstorms to climate change caused by combustion of fossil fuels. "Freak" weather events are getting more frequent and more intense, and some of the impacts are already irreversible.[6]

All 195 UN member countries have accepted the findings of the recent reports from the Intergovernmental Panel on Climate Change (IPCC), which highlight the next five years as the most critical in determining to what degree climate change will disrupt our lives. If we take immediate and decisive action, we can limit its severity, but a status quo situation will produce sweeping and irreversible damage to the ecosystems that sustain our economy and quality of life.

There really is only one viable solution to the climate crisis. We need to reach the point where we're producing *net-zero greenhouse gas emissions* from our energy, food, transportation, and infrastructure systems as soon as possible. The scale of this innovation challenge should not be underestimated. It means going from 51 billion tonnes of GHGs, which is what the world typically adds to the atmosphere each year, to net zero by 2050 if we are to avoid the most catastrophic impacts of climate change.[7] Every sector of society is facing pressure to align with this goal. Where is the events industry in this monumental transition?

Industry Response

The events industry doesn't typically think of itself as a single industry. It's often segregated into subsectors such as conferences, sporting events, music festivals, and weddings, not to mention related sectors such as tourism, catering, and transportation. As a result, we're missing the transparent *environmental, social, and governance (ESG) metrics* and data sets that are commonly collected and required across several other sectors. When you look at the energy, mining, and manufacturing industries, for example, it's not hard to find comparable data sets that enable an analysis of the overall industry impacts regionally, nationally, and globally. That doesn't exist for the events industry, but the situation could change rapidly as a result of growing expectations from clients, sponsors, governments, and audiences.

The Net Zero Carbon Events initiative, with support from the United Nations Framework Convention on Climate Change (UNFCCC), was launched at COP26 in 2021 to engage the global events industry in a common ambition toward net zero. That same year, the Net Zero Carbon Events project launched a Net Zero Carbon Events Pledge. More than three hundred organizations in fifty countries have supported the initiative and taken this pledge. The signatories represent event organizers, service providers, venues, destinations, event industry associations, consultants, and media outlets. The Net Zero Carbon Events initiative subsequently released a guidance document laying out an ambitious pathway for the events industry to achieve net zero. This road map calls on the entire events sector worldwide to establish a baseline to compare its carbon footprint against by 2025, to slash its footprint in half by 2030, and reduce the remaining CO_2 to net zero by 2040, with the help of carbon removal processes.[8]

Importance to Your Clients and Sponsors

Climate action is increasingly a priority amongst investors, who also want stable economies, and as a result, ESG investing is gaining momentum. Institutional shareholders are pushing for greater transparency of data from publicly traded companies so they can compare the climate risk exposure their investments are facing today and in the future. Standardization of the measurement and reporting of this data is rapidly converging through initiatives like the Task Force on Climate-Related Financial Disclosure and International Sustainability Standards Board. A number of the OECD member countries, including the US,

UK, Canada, and New Zealand, are already or in the process of enacting new securities legislation, making climate disclosure mandatory across the economy.

California's legislature recently passed the Climate Corporate Data Accountability Act, which will require publicly traded corporations and other large companies to disclose their greenhouse gas emissions and climate-related financial risks. As the world's fifth-largest economy, California's environmental rules impact some of the world's biggest companies, requiring them to account for not only their own pollution, but also the emissions of suppliers and customers using their products. That concept, known as Scope 3, is likely to shape the national standard for reporting in the US.

As an event organizer, you're part of the supply chain for your clients and sponsors. Your activities are part of their *Scope 3 emissions,* so if you want to keep your clients long-term, you should be proactive in determining how you can be a solution provider rather than a hindrance toward the achievement of their carbon-reduction and net-zero goals.

What is Net Zero, Exactly?

Net zero means the amount of carbon emissions released is less than the amount removed from the atmosphere. Achieving a net-zero event requires you to *measure* and *reduce* your direct GHG emissions as well as emissions within your value chain (including supply chains and end use), and then *offsetting* the rest through credible verified programs. Where many people get this wrong is an overreliance on offsets as the starting point; this approach promotes a status quo situation and requires no meaningful change. The other common mistake is to focus solely on direct emissions without addressing supplier and consumer emissions in any way. Understandably, addressing value chain emissions can be challenging, but leaving it out entirely ignores the bulk of the emissions resulting from your event taking place.

The International Standards Organization developed guidelines for what constitutes an effective net-zero target.[9] They include the following:

- **Alignment** with the goals of the Paris Agreement and subsequent UN agreements
- **Urgency** to make immediate contributions to global efforts aimed at keeping global temperatures well below 2°C above pre-industrial levels and ideally 1.5° as soon as possible and by 2050 at the very latest

- **Prioritization** of GHG emissions reduction, with removals used only after all possible emissions reduction actions have been taken
- **Equity and justice** goals are established and actions taken to align with the Sustainable Development Goals and the transition to a net-zero economy while safeguarding the rights of those most vulnerable

Is Net Zero Realistic for Events?

The COP26 team achieved their net-zero goal through a strategy that involved the implementation of various efficiency and sustainability initiatives, significant infrastructure investments by the UK government, innovative partnerships with their suppliers, and offsetting. In the end, Mark Bannister and the COP26 organizing team successfully delivered a net-zero COP26 event—with tens of thousands of delegates and only six months to plan it.

With careful planning, expert advice, strong relationships with your suppliers, an understanding of your data, and year-by-year improvements, you can definitely achieve net zero for your event.

The value chain of the events industry is large and complex, with many and varied stakeholders, including organizers, venues, service providers, as well as exhibiting companies, and, of course, event audiences.

Each event is unique in the way it's delivered and the specific stakeholders it includes. However, all are supported by the systems and relationships that underpin the events industry. This means that, for a specific event to be net zero, the systems and structures that support it need to be net zero. On its own, there is no such thing as a "net-zero event."

The events industry needs to plan and follow its own path to net zero, while at the same time building momentum within the entire value chain so that the system itself also starts to decarbonize. In the current climate of increasing costs, there is an added imperative to "do things differently" across the system and design events that are more efficient.

The Net Zero Carbon Events initiative offers a viable pathway for event organizers to follow to achieve net zero. Figure 5.1 summarizes what this pathway looks like.

> An event is like the leaf on a tree—it can only be healthy if the whole system which supports it is healthy.
>
> — Net Zero Carbon Events

Drawbacks

I asked Mark for his thoughts on the Net Zero Carbon Events initiative and the pathway they developed. After all, he was in the room at COP26 where the initiative was first launched. "There was a good amount of buzz around that," he told me and added, "I'm not sure how successful it's been at engaging the grassroots level of the industry. I think in big international venues, the big associations have come together, and that is a great vehicle to start, but I wouldn't say there has been engagement of the actual supplier base or the agencies of less than five hundred people in terms of actually benefitting or being informed by it."

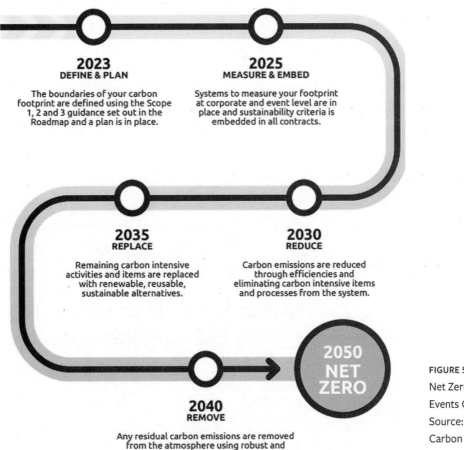

2023
DEFINE & PLAN

The boundaries of your carbon footprint are defined using the Scope 1, 2 and 3 guidance set out in the Roadmap and a plan is in place.

2025
MEASURE & EMBED

Systems to measure your footprint at corporate and event level are in place and sustainability criteria is embedded in all contracts.

2035
REPLACE

Remaining carbon intensive activities and items are replaced with renewable, reusable, sustainable alternatives.

2030
REDUCE

Carbon emissions are reduced through efficiencies and eliminating carbon intensive items and processes from the system.

2050
NET
ZERO

2040
REMOVE

Any residual carbon emissions are removed from the atmosphere using robust and accredited carbon capture or removal processes.

FIGURE 5.1.
Net Zero Pathway for Events Organizers.
Source: Net Zero Carbon Events

As with any voluntary initiative, there is no penalty for not setting a net-zero target, and the incentives are difficult to quantify; therefore, many will choose to ignore it. A recent survey by destination management company Ovation Global DMC revealed that less than 15 percent of current events taking place across the globe focus actively on lowering carbon emissions.[10] There is a lot of work to be done to move the industry from net-zero pledges to taking concrete action.

Furthermore, because the revenue model associated with Net Zero Carbon Events includes tiered sponsorship levels, it may be possible for some organizations with substandard performance to pay their way into the top tiers and get more attention than others who may be demonstrating significantly more advanced leadership.

There is also no verification mechanism being developed, so it will be up to the individual events organizations to measure their own progress. While Net Zero Carbon Events has indicated an intention to develop a standard measurement system, the fact that there isn't one means that current measurement and reporting of net-zero performance differs wildly, so our ability to produce comparable data and arrive at a single set of metrics for the industry as a whole is being lost.

Take the Net Zero Carbon Events Pledge

Despite the many criticisms that have been voiced about the Net Zero Carbon Events project, it has tremendous potential because it takes an industry-wide approach and calls for global collaboration. Combined with a widely used simple tool like the Net-Zero Assessment Tool, it can be a powerful platform to drive action and standardize approaches across event organizations of all shapes and sizes. It's important that the initiative goes beyond its primary audience of large-event venues and organizations—and that it do so sooner, rather than later. While individual action does add up and what you do at your next event truly matters, ultimately these efforts will be insufficient to address the scale of the climate crisis—unless we are committed to engaging the entire value chain to effect change and decarbonize.

Begin by taking the Net Zero Carbon Events Pledge for the Events Industry at netzerocarbonevents.org/the-pledge.[11]

Simple Reporting Tool

I recommend using a simple reporting tool that's already available free online. It's a great tool, especially if you need to be ready for questions from clients, sponsors, and other stakeholders about your GHG inventories, your reduction efforts, and your commitment to net-zero targets. The Net-Zero Assessment Tool (NZAT) is a generic, small and medium-size business-friendly self-assessment tool developed by Bob Willard, author of *The Sustainability Advantage*.[12]

The Net-Zero Assessment Tool uses just five multiple-choice questions to score your commitment to, and progress toward, science-based net-zero targets. It also suggests over two dozen actions that would reduce Scope 1, 2, and 3 GHG emissions.

Best of all, it's an open-source tool, so you can tailor it to better suit your purposes, translate it into other languages, change question weightings, change scoring formulas, use it as a base for an online app, or integrate elements of it into your current tools.

I really like this tool because the data produced is:

- **Simple:** relatively easy with few questions and no quantifications required
- **Comprehensive:** based on questions asked by other credible questionnaires that assess a company's commitment to net-zero targets, such as the Carbon Disclosure Project
- **Verifiable:** clear, specific, and objective
- **Comparable:** appropriate for any organization, in any sector, any size, anywhere
- **Scorable:** scored out of 100 percent and can be used to determine ranking or degree of preferential treatment
- **Educational:** questions also serve as a checklist of criteria with helpful pop-up guidance, explanations, and suggested actions to improve scores

Those taking the pledge commit to the following four actions:
- **Publishing their pathway** to achieve net zero by 2050 at the latest, with an interim target in line with the Paris Agreement's requirement to reduce global GHG emissions by 50 percent by 2030
- **Collaboration with partners**, suppliers, and customers to drive change across their value chains
- **Measuring and tracking** of Scope 1, 2, and 3 greenhouse gas emissions according to industry best practices
- **Reporting on progress** at least every two years

Steps Toward Net Zero Events

Establish or Revisit Your Purpose

Lead with your purpose. Your event likely exists to do more than just sell tickets. Remind the team why your event exists and how integrating climate-related goals into your strategy can help you achieve even greater success.

If taking meaningful action to address climate change does not fit within your event's purpose, seriously ask yourself, why not? Is it possible that you're letting some of the polarization and misinformation around the urgency of this issue distract you from your most substantial long-term risk as an events organizer as well as your greatest opportunity to align with the priorities of your clients and society at large?

Set Reduction Goals and Engage Others

Consider engaging the Science Based Targets Initiative (SBTi) to align with the most credible science-based goals and standards available. SBTi is a collaboration of the World Resources Institute, the Carbon Disclosure Project, the World Wildlife Fund, and the United Nations Global Compact. The initiative defines and promotes best practices in emissions reductions and net-zero targets in line with climate science and the Paris Agreement goals of limiting global warming to well below 2°C above pre-industrial levels. SBTi also provides technical assistance and resources to organizations that set science-based targets as well as independent assessment and validation of targets.

Set ambitious five-to-ten-year goals for reducing emissions at future events and formulate your twenty-plus-year goals to reduce emissions, but don't do it in a vacuum. Engage your team in the process to ensure buy-in and integration of net-zero goals for every area of your event operations and strategy.

Begin by determining the scope of the event, including all activities and sectors that contribute to the overall emissions produced as a result of your event, such as transportation, accommodation, food and beverage, and energy usage. Where does the greatest concentration of energy use exist? Either start there or build up to it, but note that your plan will only be credible if you meaningfully address the largest part of your footprint. No amount of job creation and community goodwill can change that.

Document and discuss any existing environmental initiatives to determine how they can complement a net-zero goal. For example, are you tracking the emissions reductions associated with efforts to divert waste? Each pound of food waste diverted from the landfill prevents up to five pounds of carbon emissions into the atmosphere, according to Project Drawdown. If such programs are done on a limited basis, can they be scaled up or expanded to other areas of operations to make an even bigger contribution toward your net-zero goal?

Who are the key individuals driving these existing initiatives? Can they be engaged further or empowered to drive further results? Assign a respected leader within your organization to champion net zero and provide training for all team members who will be involved. Ensure the concept of net zero is fully understood by everyone in the organization, including contractors.

Align with your finance team to design a budget that prioritizes:

- A venue that's aligned with your goals
- Supplier contracts that incentivize investments into emissions reductions, waste elimination, data collection, and sharing
- Low-emitting equipment rentals
- Renewable energy use or power purchase agreements to buy energy credits from renewable power projects to offset your generated emissions and support the growth of the renewable energy sector
- Offsets for all third-party travel

Coordinate with your communications team, but be careful about communicating publicly too early to avoid getting called out for greenwashing. Engage trusted experts and consultants to verify that your goals and plans are in alignment with credible global standards including Net Zero Carbon Events and the Science Based Targets Initiative.

Engage your suppliers and service providers with the intention of connecting with them on a purpose level rather than a project focus. You don't need to replace all your trusted contractors with net-zero suppliers overnight; you can begin with a conversation to let them know the direction you're going and extend an invitation to them to go on the journey with you. Some may already be on their way while others may not have heard the term *net zero* before. It's an opportunity to educate your supply chain and send a strong signal that there's a market for providing solutions that lower emissions.

Have your competitors already signed the Net Zero Carbon Events Pledge? If so, match their pledge, and if not, lead by example to push your sector forward. Have your clients or sponsors publicly declared a net-zero goal? In Canada, you might want to check if your clients are on Canadian Business for Social Responsibility's Net-Zero Leaderboard.[13]

After you've researched what your clients and competitors are doing to manage their footprint, ask yourself whether your goals are ambitious or competitive enough.[14]

Gather Data and Set a Baseline

Identifying your starting point, or baseline, is a key element for setting carbon reduction targets. The Paris Agreement calls for a 50 percent reduction in emissions by 2030, but it doesn't state a universal baseline. Organizations and industry groups are left to determine their own baselines depending on available data. According to the best practice laid out by the Science Based Targets Initiative, the same base year should be used for your long-term and interim targets, and the base year must be no earlier than 2015.

If you have the resources, I recommend hiring a credible consultant or specialist who can help you establish a baseline calculation and suggest some short- and long-term reduction opportunities as well as a system for ongoing carbon management. But don't fret if you don't have the resources. Measuring the greenhouse gas emissions associated with your event is not rocket science; however, it's also not as straightforward as it should be, given this is something everyone should be doing.

Calculate Total Emissions

There are many free and inexpensive resources you can use to calculate your emissions. See the Tools and Resources chapter for a list of carbon calculators for each activity category such as food, travel, and accommodation. The all-purpose carbon calculator I most often recommend is the free one from the Greenhouse Gas Protocol.[15] Julie's Bicycle Creative Climate Tools are also excellent, free, and simple-to-use online resources to record and understand all aspects of the impacts of your venue, office, tour, production, event, or festival. You can find an up-to-date list of resources on my website, leor.ca.[16]

Test against your estimates using real data on your event's energy consumption, fuel usage, waste production, and associated travel using relevant sources such as utility bills, fuel consumption records, waste management reports from service providers, and travel logs. Sum up the emissions from each of these areas to determine the total emissions for the event and identify a baseline to start from.

Ask the following questions:

- What energy is generated before, after, and throughout the event?
- What types of generators, boilers, and heating and cooling systems are in use and what type of power sources are they drawing from (e.g., gas, coal, petrol, geothermal, solar)?
- What data is available for these items (e.g., digital or equipment meter readings, energy bills)?
- How often is data collected?
- What forms of transportation are used before, after, and throughout the event (e.g., cars, vans, golf carts, transport trucks, shuttles, transit buses, light- and heavy-rail trains, planes, private jets)?
- Is fuel or electric vehicle consumption tracked or monitored? If so, at what level (organizational, departmental, regionally, by supplier)?
- What energy efficiency initiatives are already underway?
- Are they tracked?
- Can you quantify the impact (energy reduction, carbon reduction, cost savings)?

As you engage your suppliers, get them to supply you with data, even if it's imperfect or incomplete. It will be a good starting point to work from.

Decarbonize Where You Can

Explore Edmonton is a nonprofit destination marketing agency managed independently but on behalf of the City of Edmonton, Alberta. It promotes tourism and organizes *K-Days*, Edmonton's largest annual festival. Explore Edmonton also operates two of the city's main event facilities; one of them, the Edmonton Convention Centre, is recognized for having the largest rooftop solar power installation in the country.

In addition to producing this major festival and operating venues, Explore Edmonton also provides a valuable (and free!) service to all conventions, festivals, and events in the city, with the aim of supporting them to become carbon neutral. Explore Edmonton's first step in supporting major events was to develop a waste, water, and emissions reduction plan to address power usage, transportation impacts, and disposal of food, signage, and plastics. They also support the quantification of emissions and facilitate the purchase of carbon offsets as part of their climate resilience mandate to reduce Edmonton's GHG emissions annually to reach their goal of a 30 percent reduction by 2035.[17]

> Events that are taking action to reduce their event emissions most often achieve significantly lower costs.
>
> —Melissa Radu, Explore Edmonton's Director of Social and Environmental Sustainability

Scope 1, 2, and 3 Emissions

Carbon accounting requires figuring out the total tonnes of carbon or CO_2 equivalent (CO_2e) caused by activities that have occurred as a result of your event. The total CO_2 emissions will fall into three main categories: Scope 1, 2, and 3.

Scope 1 emissions are the greenhouse gas emissions produced from *things you directly control*, such as heating or air conditioning, transport vehicles, and onsite gas- or diesel-powered equipment.

For every activity that involves GHG emissions, there will be an emission factor associated with it. For example, the combustion of a gallon of gasoline emits the equivalent of about 8.8 kilograms of CO_2, or a little less than 1 percent of a metric tonne of GHGs. These measurements are well laid out in the free GHG Protocol Tool, which you can use to calculate emissions.

As an example: The COP26 organizers prioritized reduced energy use, renewable power, and low-carbon alternative energy sources such as electric and low-emission vehicles, solar panels, and hydrotreated vegetable oil (made from used cooking oil) in generators instead of diesel.

Diesel Power

Diesel generators are a good example of a Scope 1 emissions source. They also happen to negatively affect your event safety, inclusivity, and bottom line.

Polluting diesel and gas generators are commonly seen at events, especially outdoor ones such as music festivals. Because the generators are so loud and disruptive, they're typically placed far away from the music, even though they power the outdoor speakers, lights, digital screens, and soundboards. So, lots of long wiring is necessary.

This setup is highly inefficient because the farther the power has to travel, the more power loss occurs. Additionally, to operate effectively, manufacturers of diesel generators recommend a load of 60 to 75 percent of its maximum capacity. Yet, many festivals use generators at less than 25 percent capacity *for long periods of time*. This is because lights and speakers don't actually require the volume of power many diesel generators are designed to provide. That produces more emissions and wears the equipment down very quickly.

All that wiring and inefficiency produces more emissions, wears equipment down quickly, and requires expensive electricians and trained personnel on call to monitor and help manage generator maintenance and safety risks on-site. After all, wires are also trip hazards. Site crews often run the wiring through cable guard tracks to reduce the trip hazard, but those protective guards cause difficulty for people with mobility challenges and wheelchairs.

Portable Electric

Mobile electric batteries such as those available from Portable Electric are quiet and safe, and they can be wheeled to wherever power is actually needed. Best of all, the batteries can be recharged using solar panels (or plugged into a common electrical outlet for an even-faster charge) then rolled back out to be used off-grid wherever they're needed.

Mark Rabin, the founder of Portable Electric, primarily worked with festivals and events, but he finds the greatest demand for his batteries is now coming from the film industry, where "quiet on the set" is more than a cliché—it's a necessity.

Rabin told me, "In some cases, we've saved clients up to 90 percent of fuel and maintenance costs by replacing or pairing diesel generators with our portable power stations." He added, "With our remote monitoring software, we give users the ability to monitor the power stations remotely as well as track their CO_2 emissions and reductions."[18]

Scope 2 emissions are associated with *the production of the natural gas or coal that* generates the heat and electricity showing up on your utility bills.

GHGs associated with energy usage largely depend on your location and the source powering your local electricity grid. If coal makes up a big percentage of your local power grid, then you need to get off the grid if you want to make it to net zero.

SBTi has identified 80 percent renewable electricity procurement by 2025 and 100 percent by 2030 as the thresholds consistent with a 1.5°C scenario. Organizations that already source electricity at or above these thresholds should maintain or increase their use of renewable electricity to qualify.

Scope 3 refers to all the emissions *you are indirectly responsible for* across your entire value chain. Some common examples include:
- Travel to and from your event
- Event-related construction
- End-of-life impacts of waste
- Freight transportation of purchased goods and services
- Energy associated with the production of purchased goods
- Mined components used in electronic products
- Food-related emissions from production, transportation, and waste

The organizers of COP26 worked with Tracker+ to develop a bespoke solution for monitoring the carbon footprint of hosting the event; the program allowed suppliers to directly enter their emissions information generated through their activities and product development.[19]

Further Scope 3 measures taken at COP26 included the following:

- Avoiding waste going to landfill by reusing and recycling material
- Encouraging delegates to use sustainable forms of transportation, such as walking, cycling, and public transportation
- Employing local people
- Donating furniture and accessories post-event to individuals and communities in need
- Building sustainability considerations into design and material choices
- Hosting industry-wide workshops to improve standards and capture best practices for future events

Offset the Rest

We'll cover the legitimacy of offsets in chapter 6, but it's important to emphasize at this stage that carbon offsets should not be viewed as a substitute for reducing carbon emissions at the source. The primary goal should be to reduce emissions as much as possible through energy conservation, efficiency, and the use of renewable energy sources. Carbon offsets should only be used as a supplementary measure to address emissions that cannot be avoided or reduced.

COP26 Offset Strategy

After reducing emissions as much as they could, the COP26 team measured the remaining emissions—from such things as crew travel to site visits, distances that equipment was coming from, and the footprint of the equipment itself—using scientific calculations and tools. Then they offset the remaining emissions, known as the *carbon balance*, through an accredited *carbon offset coordinator*.

The offsets used were Gold Standard Certified Emissions Reductions (CERs) located in less developed countries or small island developing states; these offsets were selected for having co-benefits related to the Sustainable Development Goals.

For the organizers of COP26 in Glasgow, air travel was covered within the scope of the Host Country Agreement between the UNFCCC and the UK government, requiring the host country to purchase carbon offsets equivalent to the emissions arising from delegate travel to the conference. Because the majority managed their own travel booking arrangements, the COP26 team did not have detailed delegate flight information. In order to estimate emissions for international travel, a quantification program known as *PAS 2060* was used and validated by a company called Arup. It determined that 136,720 metric tonnes of carbon offsets should be purchased to offset the flights taken by the 38,462 delegates that attended COP26 (including a little buffer).

One detail that drives accountants crazy is the fact that offsets and Scope 3 emissions in general may be *double counted*. If someone else is already accounting for their own emissions and you're including those numbers as part of *your* overall impact, that could lead to miscalculations and duplication of efforts, but let's maintain some perspective.

Emissions are not the same as financial information. Underestimating them is bad, but overestimating demonstrates your commitment to the overall solution, not just the bare minimum. Most important is the trajectory of your emissions. If the numbers aren't perfect, they should at least be as transparent as possible. Double counting will take place. Let's accept that and move forward.

Net Zero VS. Carbon Neutral

In my conversation with Melissa Radu from Explore Edmonton, she emphasized that "offsets should not be the first step to reducing emissions. It should be done after other interventions have been employed to reduce event emissions."[20] Her approach is consistent with the Science Based Targets Initiative, which values eliminating emissions from supply chains and purchasing renewable energy over carbon offsets.[21]

When procuring offsets for events, Melissa explains, "The costs of carbon offsets may differ depending on event size, venue, and how the event is planned." On average, she purchases offsets for flights at about US $22 per person, although she notes that "business travel and economy flights are calculated slightly differently." She buys offsets for participants traveling within the city in vehicles for roughly $2 per person.

In 2022, Explore Edmonton supported 15 carbon-neutral events. All of them took advantage of the service for the first time and therefore set a baseline from which to compare future environmental performance and calculate GHG emissions reduction results.

Nature-Based Solutions

The links between biodiversity and climate change go two ways. While climate change is one of the main drivers of biodiversity loss, the destruction of ecosystems accelerates climate change and increases vulnerability to it by undermining nature's ability to regulate GHG emissions and withstand extreme weather. Thus, the protection of biodiversity and reduction of carbon emissions are increasingly being seen as joint and inextricably linked activities. This is highlighted by the recent addition of biodiversity criteria within the Race to Zero leadership campaign, and the growing momentum behind the Taskforce on Nature-related Financial Disclosure. As plans evolve over time, biodiversity will need to be considered as you make progress toward net zero. This could include ensuring biodiversity impact assessments when building new venues, incorporating biodiversity into buildings via rooftop gardens and biophilic design, ensuring sustainable wood is used or sustainable seafood served.

Carbon offsets can play a critical role in boosting natural ecosystems and human well-being to address major societal issues, including climate change and biodiversity loss. These types of nature-based solutions provide financial incentives to support the protection and restoration of natural ecosystems. Carbon offsets are a way for individuals and organizations to compensate for their carbon emissions by supporting projects that reduce or remove carbon from the atmosphere and sequester carbon in soil, plants, and trees.

While tree planting and forest protection are the most common examples of nature-based solutions, there are many others, including:

- Restoration of coastal wetlands, such as mangroves, salt marshes, and seagrass beds, which act as natural carbon sinks while protecting against storm surges and erosion. Coastal wetlands are under significant threat around the world from development and climate change.

- Regenerative farming practices that increase the amount of carbon stored in the soil, such as reducing tillage, planting cover crops, and using compost and manure as fertilizer. This can help mitigate climate change, enhance soil health, and improve crop yields.
- Protected urban green spaces (e.g., green roofs, parks, gardens, and wildlife corridors) provide numerous benefits, including carbon sequestration, air- and water-quality improvements, and enhanced biodiversity. They can also help to reduce the *urban heat island effect*, a phenomenon in which cities are warmer than surrounding rural areas due to human activities.
- Protected marine ecosystems (e.g., coral reefs, seagrass beds, and kelp forests) can help to mitigate the impacts of climate change, enhance biodiversity, and support sustainable fisheries. Marine conservation can involve a variety of strategies, such as reducing overfishing and restoring degraded habitats.

All these examples can provide exponential positive benefits—especially when combined with strong partnerships that utilize Indigenous knowledge, local employment opportunities, and outdoor education efforts.

Carbon Removal

Rainforest protection generates what's known as *avoidance offsets*, which are activities that prevent emissions from being released into the atmosphere.[22] Tree planting and direct air capture are considered *removal offsets* because they're generated from activities that pull carbon out of the atmosphere.[23]

Some see carbon *offsets* as an interim step on the journey toward carbon *removal*, which usually means capturing existing CO_2 in the atmosphere and permanently storing it somewhere else—in concrete, for example. However, some end-use applications for carbon removal include the development of new fuels or blended fuels, which could reenter the atmosphere over time when combusted.

When I was exploring carbon removal offsets on behalf of the World Petroleum Congress in 2022, I discovered an industry at a nascent stage. There are some terrific organizations, like Canada's Carbon Engineering, (recently sold to oil giant Occidental Petroleum for US$1.1B) that have already mastered the technical challenges associated with direct air capture, but you can't really show up at their door and purchase offsets. You have to do so through third-party aggregators who have secured partnerships with industrial carbon removal technology providers—and you have to procure the credits far in advance. One company I tried to purchase removal offsets from wanted to sell me removal credits three years into the future. That might work for events organizations that plan their events years in advance, but it's not a good way for a one-off event with a short runway to secure credits.

The technology-based and verified carbon removal offsets are cost-prohibitive at this stage. They can cost anywhere from $275 to $400+ per tonnes of CO_2. That would be unrealistic for most events including mega sporting events, which, according to the International Association of Athletics Federation, can generate between 30,000 to 300,000 tonnes of CO_2. That means even at the lowest end possible with today's economies of scale, offsets would cost more than $8 million. It will be some time before carbon removal reaches the scale required to be relied upon as a viable alternative to other voluntary carbon offsets from nature restoration and renewable energy.

There are three main categories of effective offsets: *nature-based solutions*, such as tree planting and habitat restoration; *technology- and engineering-based solutions*, such as direct air capture or flaring gases such as methane; and a *hybrid of the two*.

Report Results

IMEX

Worldwide Exhibition for Incentive Travel, Meetings, and Events has established an impressive goal *"to make the biggest possible impact on a net zero future."* To achieve this, they plan to deliver net-zero events and run a net-zero business by 2030.

The sustainability reports that IMEX produces are a best practice, demonstrating extremely high waste diversion, 100 percent renewable electricity use, and offsets. However, noticeably absent from their main highlights are the total GHG emissions from the event. This might be because they're working on a net-zero road map, which is part of their commitment to the Net Zero Carbon Events industry initiative and expected as part of their next reporting cycle.[24]

IMEX did report a total of 167,609 kWh of venue electricity and 33,756 kWh of booth electricity consumed during the IMEX 2022 conference. The report also claims that because these emissions came from 100 percent renewable sources, an estimated 87 metric tonnes of CO_2 emissions were eliminated—when compared to fossil fuel equivalents. As the report states, this represents reducing roughly the emissions from driving 430 standard gasoline vehicles from the IMEX office in Brighton, UK, to the event venue in Messe, Frankfurt.

IMEX is also piloting the use of the TRACE carbon measurement tool created by a company named isla to serve as a software platform dashboard to store and visualize emissions data, which will be used in future reports.

FIGURE 5.2.
IMEX Frankfurt 2022 Sustainability Highlights.
Source: IMEX Group

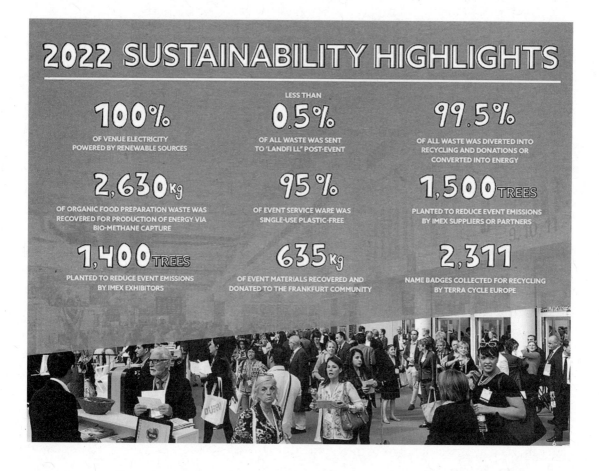

2022 SUSTAINABILITY HIGHLIGHTS

100% OF VENUE ELECTRICITY POWERED BY RENEWABLE SOURCES

LESS THAN **0.5%** OF ALL WASTE WAS SENT TO 'LANDFILL' POST-EVENT

99.5% OF ALL WASTE WAS DIVERTED INTO RECYCLING AND DONATIONS OR CONVERTED INTO ENERGY

2,630kg OF ORGANIC FOOD PREPARATION WASTE WAS RECOVERED FOR PRODUCTION OF ENERGY VIA BIO-METHANE CAPTURE

95% OF EVENT SERVICE WARE WAS SINGLE-USE PLASTIC-FREE

1,500 TREES PLANTED TO REDUCE EVENT EMISSIONS BY IMEX SUPPLIERS OR PARTNERS

1,400 TREES PLANTED TO REDUCE EVENT EMISSIONS BY IMEX EXHIBITORS

635kg OF EVENT MATERIALS RECOVERED AND DONATED TO THE FRANKFURT COMMUNITY

2,311 NAME BADGES COLLECTED FOR RECYCLING BY TERRA CYCLE EUROPE

Collaboration Required

The events industry is made up of a complex network of stakeholders and a deep supply chain, all of whom will need to work together to reduce their emissions for the industry to achieve net zero. Collaboration is required for real change to happen. It will not be sufficient for a single organization or group of organizations to take steps to decarbonize in isolation. A rethink in how events are planned, designed, and delivered across the whole system must be incentivized, inspired, and required.

As a global industry that generates substantial employment and economic impact, the events sector must recognize the part it can and must play in reducing carbon emissions and mitigating the most catastrophic impacts of climate change.

6

Be Proactive to
Avoid Greenwashing

We all have dreams. But in order to make dreams come into reality,
it takes an awful lot of determination, dedication, self-discipline and effort.

— Jesse Owens

Green Goals VS. Greenwash

It was the most exciting World Cup in decades with legendary footballer Lionel
Messi leading Argentina to a historic victory. It was also billed as the *greenest*
World Cup ever. The 2022 FIFA World Cup in Qatar promised the soccer tournament would be the first "fully carbon-neutral" World Cup, and its organizers
set out to inspire a new sustainability standard for future mega-events. But
less than a year later, the Swiss Fairness Commission, Switzerland's advertising
regulator, upheld complaints brought forward by five European nations, accus-
ing FIFA World Cup 2022 of greenwashing.[1]

In 2020, the tournament organizers published a greenhouse gas accounting
report carried out by Swiss carbon finance consultancy South Pole. The findings
informed the FIFA tournament's emissions reduction plan and offsets strategy."

The sustainability strategy they developed was organized around five pil-
lars: environmental, social, governance, economic, and human. It encompassed
twenty material issues, twenty-two objectives, and almost eighty projects to
address emissions reduction and offsetting, sustainable building construction,
workers' rights, waste reduction, and water conservation.[2]

The 2022 World Cup in Qatar committed to measure, mitigate, and offset all Scope 1, 2, and 3 emissions associated with the 2022 FIFA World Cup. According to the pre-tournament GHG accounting report, those emissions were estimated at approximately 3.5 million tonnes, but the final number may be revised in the final calculation included in the post-tournament report, which was late and still unreleased at the time of writing this book.

Controversial Journey to the Cup

Skepticism about the event's carbon-neutral claims was abundant.[3] "This promise of carbon neutrality is absolutely not credible," said Gilles Dufrasne, lead author of a Carbon Market Watch report published in May 2022 examining Qatar's environmental claims and concluding, "This is a blatant example of greenwashing."[4]

In November 2022, Carbon Market Watch along with five other NGOs filed complaints against FIFA in five European countries. The relevant authorities in those countries transferred the complaints to Switzerland, where FIFA is headquartered.

The evidence that the Swiss Fairness Commission examined was based primarily on the Carbon Market Watch report, which claimed the World Cup's emissions levels were grossly underestimated. The report hinted at a number of flaws in FIFA's assessment, including FIFA's failure to account for the climate impact of the maintenance and operation of the stadiums built specifically for the World Cup in the many years following the event, as well as to the uncertain efficacy of some of the climate mitigation measures announced, such as the creation of a large-scale tree and turf nursery in the middle of the desert.

In its decision, the Swiss Fairness Commission remarked that stricter standards apply when it comes to environmental claims in commercial communications. The Commission rejected FIFA's claim that the statements were "efforts in transparency and accountability" and not a form of commercial communication. The Commission determined that the disputed statements qualified as "advertisements" and emphasized that claims of carbon neutrality create specific expectations for the average recipient that the World Cup would take place "with the same result, in terms of carbon emissions, as if the tournament had not taken place at all."[5]

FIFA had to prove that the methods used to calculate emissions from the tournament were generally accepted, covered all sources of emissions, and were fully offset. FIFA did not satisfy these requirements and therefore was advised to drop the claim that the 2022 Qatar World Cup was carbon or climate neutral.

The greenwashing accusations were layered onto the already vociferous condemnations of human rights abuses associated with the construction of seven stadiums leading up to the World Cup. In February 2021, the UK's *Guardian* newspaper published an explosive accusation about 6,500 migrant worker deaths associated with the Qatar World Cup.[6,7] These accusations were damaging and maintained a dark shadow on the World Cup henceforth.

The *Guardian*'s investigation focused on non-Qatari residents who had died in the country over a ten-year period using death records produced by the embassies of five countries with large numbers of nationals in Qatar (India, Bangladesh, Nepal, Sri Lanka, and Pakistan). The British newspaper confirmed 6,751 deaths. But those numbers may have little to no connection to World Cup stadium construction and even included death by natural causes.

It's valid to ask whether the Qatar World Cup was an example of greenwashing, but to fully answer the question requires a deep dive into what greenwashing looks like before we conclude how the World Cup holds up against scrutiny.

What Is Greenwashing?

There are many definitions of greenwashing, but generally they involve the intersection of poor environmental performance and positive communication about that performance or the disseminating of exaggerated, misleading disinformation regarding environmental practices.[8,9]

Greenwashing is a major risk for event organizers. The reputational damage from greenwashing and perceived greenwashing can be significant. Your audience, staff members, clients, and sponsors are all looking for you to provide credible data on your environmental progress.[10] If your purpose, messaging, and image turn out to be disingenuous, the loss of trust could result in a shrinking audience, talent pool, sponsorship, and client list.

Overstating environmental performance also opens new risks of lawsuits and fines. There is a growing body of class-action lawsuits against organizations overstating their environmental claims.[11] The European Union is building greenwashing into its Unfair Commercial Practices Directive; the Competition Bureau in Canada has fined companies and is currently investigating others for greenwashing; and individual countries are taking similar actions and imposing severe penalties.[12, 13]

More broadly, greenwashing is a major obstacle to sustainability progress. It covers up the continuation of practices that desperately need to be innovated. It makes it easier for event goers, governments, and the event organizers themselves to become complacent in the false belief that enough action is taking place to address environmental problems, when in reality an environmental emergency is being largely ignored.

Why Greenwashing Occurs

Greenwashing occurs because it usually works, and it can contribute to short-term profitability. Despite the public being increasingly sensitive to greenwashing, there's still a wide gap in education and awareness to correctly identify what greenwashing looks like. A global study of ten thousand people between the ages of sixteen and twenty-five, found that 57 percent of respondents believed that greenwashed claims were a reliable source of information.[14]

Studies also consistently show a growing number of people value the environment more than ever before and are willing to pay more to demonstrate their values. Naturally, marketers want to tap into this growing and lucrative market.

Greenwashing can be intentional or unintentional—and there's a wide range from slight exaggeration to full untruth. Event organizers may lack the expertise to know what is genuinely environmentally beneficial, or that expertise may be siloed in a committee or with an individual without penetrating the core strategy and operations of the event.

Marketing and communications teams may be too eager to communicate a short-term good news story without an understanding of how the story fits into a broader narrative such as labor law reform. There may also be a cultural dimension to the way communication takes place as some countries place a greater emphasis on "saving face," avoiding embarrassment, being the first, best, or largest. Terms and knowledge are constantly evolving, and event professionals may not realize what terms like *net zero*, *carbon neutral*, *sustainable*, or *compostable* actually mean in the context of their event.[15]

Greenwashing can also be hard to spot. Event goers don't typically have the time or expertise to investigate claims. Tracing a product's supply chain, for example, is difficult even for the experts.[16] Misrepresentation is relatively easy to get away with because the world of communications and disinformation can be chaotic. Condensed communications through social media can remove the required nuance, and misinformation can spread quickly.[17]

Fear of Greenwashing Can Drive Action

Major events *can* be strong drivers for low-carbon infrastructure investments. Just prior to COP26, the UK government realized that hosting the world for a massive climate change conference carried some reputation risks if the energy system powering the bulk of the event was based on fossil fuel infrastructure. After all, the British tabloids are notoriously vicious, and even a misplaced recycling bin can be turned into a greenwashing scandal. So, what chance would a climate conference powered by inefficient generators have? The government engaged Scottish Power and made a massive multi-million-dollar investment to expand grid connections and distribution substations so the event venues could access renewable power as their main source of energy. The investments would almost certainly not have been made were there not fear of greenwashing accusations.

The 6-Headed Hydra of Greenwashing

Planet Tracker has done a good job of outlining the most common types of greenwashing, which they picture as a six-headed snake:

Greenhushing refers to underreporting or hiding sustainability credentials in order to evade scrutiny. South Pole, a social enterprise that implements emission reduction projects around the world, surveyed 1,200 organizations across 12 countries and found that 23 percent of them chose not to publicize their science-based milestones beyond what was mandated, despite having net-zero targets in place.[18] Keeping organizational targets away from

FIGURE 6.1. The 6-Headed Hydra of Greenwashing. Source: Planet Tracker

the public not only limits scrutiny and accountability, it also limits input and collaboration—at a time when collaboration is a key driver to achieving net-zero goals.

Greenrinsing occurs when targets are revised before they're achieved. It makes an organization appear closer to its goal than they actually are relative to their original target. The energy giant BP recently received negative press coverage for revising their climate targets from 35 to 40 percent emissions reduction by 2030 to 20 to 30 percent while simultaneously reporting record profits.

Greenshifting is when it's implied the consumer is at fault, insinuating that individual consumer choices will be what reforms the unfolding ecological crisis of mega-events. This approach blunts the reality that mega-events like the World Cup are vehicles for driving global capital into tourism, infrastructure spending, and engineering services, with significant and long-lasting effects on cities, ecosystems, and local cultures. It's unfair to shift responsibility to consumers or fans when the event's footprint and influence is so significant.

Greenlighting occurs when a particularly green feature, however small, is selectively disclosed or spotlighted in order to draw attention away from a lack of action or environmentally damaging activities elsewhere in the operations. Governments are famous for doing this. For example, they might announce that all government contracts over a certain dollar value are subject to Scope 1 and 2 carbon emissions disclosure, but they fail to mention that the small number of large contracts covered by that stipulation are already disclosing that information while thousands of other contracts are not bound by such a clause.

Greencrowding is when a laggard organization blends in with a cluster of other organizations or groups to avoid discovery. This often shows up as participation on an industry association committee tasked with recommending sustainability policies while the organization lobbies against stronger environmental rules. The progress of such groups tends to move at the speed of the participant dragging their feet most, but that participant is protected by their association with the reputable players in the same group.

Green labeling occurs when exaggerated claims or voluntary certifications are used to imply something is *green, sustainable, environmentally friendly,* or *carbon neutral* but a close examination reveals those claims to be inconsistent, misleading, or lacking proof. That's what the World Cup in Qatar was accused of. The Keurig Dr. Pepper story is another example. The Canadian Competition Bureau fined the company because they labeled their K-Cup pods "recyclable" despite not being so in every major jurisdiction where they were sold. There were some instructions on the packaging to explain this, but that was determined to be too small and unclear.

Steps to Avoid Greenwashing

Lead with Purpose

Tie metrics of success for the initiative back to your purpose. Lead all internal and external communications by articulating how the action taken enables you to live out your purpose and how the metrics demonstrate impact, not just output.

The Olympic and Paralympic Games have a stated purpose to *"contribute to building a peaceful and better world by educating youth through sport practiced without discrimination of any kind,"* but some might be dubious of the statement as "purpose-washing" because the awarding of the Games to host countries like Russia has been so controversial and inconsistent with that purpose.[19]

Be Specific in Your Communications

Base your messaging on facts about your event using knowledge about what resonates with your audience.

For example, instead of saying, "Our travel footprint was X," you might choose to communicate, "Our travel footprint was X tonnes of CO_2, representing X percent of people who traveled by plane and X percent of those traveling by car. We are aiming to reduce our footprint by X, which would be equivalent to taking X number of trucks with internal combustion engines off the road for an entire year, and if you do XYZ, this will help us get there."

Align with Industry-level Campaigns

Focus on collective impact regarding what "we" can do: meaning the combined impact "we" can have, which is much more powerful and compelling than the prospect of tiny isolated efforts.

Engage your audience by leveraging assets and networks associated with industry campaigns such as Net Zero Carbon Events, Global Citizen, Music

Declares Emergency, or the UN Framework Convention on Climate Change (UNFCCC)'s Climate Neutral Now campaign. Interestingly, FIFA was the first international sports organization to join the UNFCCC campaign.

Consider engaging with performers or speakers to find out who shares your concerns and has the willingness to speak about environmental messages in a short video to be shown before your event or on stage during the main show to inspire your audience into action.

"Focus More on Upstream Versus Downstream Efforts"

That's the excellent advice offered by Natalie Lowe, award-winning co-founder of the Sustainable Events Forum about where to focus efforts, so they address the core issues stakeholders care about most.

Natalie noted, "Downstream efforts to reduce an event's environmental footprint, such as recycling, composting, offsets, and reuse of materials, address the negative impacts created by the event. These are good efforts, but unless they are paired with upstream solutions, they don't make much of a dent in the overwhelming backlog of emissions that our modern meetings produce."[20]

Upstream solutions might include switching to lower-impact and vegan sources of protein such as chickpeas and lentils, as well as choosing venues with energy-efficiency and water-smart programs associated with LEED best practices. Natalie reminds us that "the bottom line with upstream solutions is that you're avoiding the problem rather than solving for it later."

The organizers of the FIFA World Cup in Qatar were able to recycle or compost approximately 80 percent of the waste produced at all eight stadiums because they focused on avoiding single-use plastics and sourcing recyclable and compostable alternatives during their procurement process.

Make It Bold

As a sustainability advisor, I'm often asked about the key to setting ambitious sustainability plans in motion. In my experience, it's best to package the entire long-term business transition strategy together rather than try to address it one initiative at a time and seek approvals from senior leaders every time. Timing is everything, but once your full long-term plan is in place, the rest of the organization will figure out how to reposition around it and implement it.

Leverage the process of establishing stretch goals as an opportunity to engage your community of stakeholders, including staff, suppliers, and sponsors. Aim to set science-aligned emissions targets and phase out the combustion of fossil fuels as part of your long-term plan.

Break it down into phases and begin with a pilot to identify unforeseen challenges and work out the details before scaling up. However, if scaling becomes contingent on audience participation rates, then you might be missing the tipping point effect, which occurs when your audience views an initiative as legitimate due to scale and impact.

Plastic Bottle Ban

I had this process in mind when my team and I eliminated bottled water from the Calgary Folk Music Festival. Previous initiatives to reduce plastic waste and encourage audience members to bring their own reusable bottles had had no measurable impact. Banning single-use plastic bottles got people's attention. The positive impact was immediate and significant, and the bold action generated international media attention.

Certify Your Performance

The FIFA World Cup in Qatar was the first of its kind to get ISO 20121 certified.

International Standards Organization (ISO) 20121 is a sustainable management systems standard for events, which was born out of the process developed for the 2012 Olympics in London. ISO 20121 offers guidance and best practice to manage social, economic, and environmental impacts at major events. It addresses all stages of an event's supply chain and includes monitoring and measuring guidelines. The best part of the standard is the PLAN—DO—CHECK—ACT methodology, which can lead to a robust approach to sustainability management.

There are several benefits to ISO 20121; however, it's not the right fit for all events. It's quite a time-intensive and costly process, ranging from a few thousand to tens of thousands of dollars depending on the size and scope of the event. There are fees associated with the accredited certification body that conducts an audit and issues the certificate, which could involve travel expenses in addition to hourly rates. Hiring consultants to develop a gap analysis and help prepare for the audit is also commonly budgeted as part of the process of ISO 20121 certification, even though it's not mandatory.

Finally, ISO 20121 is not a net-zero certification. It doesn't provide any guidance or targets for decarbonization. There is a free net-zero guidance document available from ISO that can serve as a valuable resource in your planning, and you are welcome to download a copy of the ISO 20121 standard for US$125 and self-declare conformity to ISO 20121 without involving a third-party auditor. It may not provide the same level of credibility or recognition, but coupled with a transparent reporting process may be an effective option for you.

Another lower-cost environmental certification option is Green Mark, which was developed specifically for the events industry to cover energy, water, waste, procurement, transport, and communication. It also provides support and guidance to help event organizations improve their environmental performance.

Measure the Impact

Transparency in your impact measurement builds trust and credibility with your stakeholders and can help you avoid potential criticism or backlash. It also enables you to evaluate your performance and learn from your successes and setbacks. You can adjust your strategies and actions accordingly to achieve your social impact and environmental goals.

To demonstrate transparency, you should share all the information about your impact claims, including any limitations or shortcomings. You should also use reliable methods and tools to fill any data gaps, verify your results, audit your emissions reductions, use a credible third-party auditor whenever possible, and report your progress annually.

Be sure to spend more time and resources on achieving your sustainability goals than communicating *about* your sustainability goals.

Link Social and Environmental Outcomes

The first-ever World Cup in the Middle East aspired to instill confidence in the region as a safe and reliable place to build infrastructure aligned with a low-carbon future.

The credibility of FIFA World Cup Qatar's environmental claims was at least in part questioned due to the country's human rights record. The *Guardian* led an investigation in 2013, when Qatar was first awarded the World Cup, and described situations of "forced labor, a form of modern slavery," which led to several dozen deaths during that summer. It documented the daily lives of Nepalese construction workers in the city of Lusail whose travel documents had been confiscated, who were not paid their wages, and who were housed in insanitary conditions.

Qatar's Supreme Committee for Delivery and Legacy tried to address the problems with the development of significant labor law reforms as well as opportunities to establish and grow local and regional businesses and skills. New contractually binding national Workers' Welfare Standards were established to ensure proper working and living conditions. The program covered thirty thousand construction workers, and the two hundred thousand workers engaged with the wider tournament services, including hospitality, transportation, and security. The Standards were enforced through a four-tier audit and inspection system consisting of audits conducted by contractors, the Supreme Committee, ad hoc inspections by the Qatar Ministry of Labor, and a leading consultancy called Impactt, which specializes in ethical trade and human rights.

A dedicated hotline was made available in eleven languages for the anonymous reporting of grievances. Of the 2,441 cases opened through the hotline, 80 percent were resolved.

The Supreme Committee also established a major fund to reimburse workers who were charged illegal recruitment fees for the opportunity to work on the stadium construction projects. As part of this initiative, a whopping US$24 million was paid out to 49,000 workers regardless of whether they had evidence or not of paying recruitment fees.

For the first time in a FIFA World Cup, the Qatar committee had a team of almost one hundred human rights volunteers monitoring all stadiums and the FIFA Fan Festival. Human rights volunteers went through specialized training delivered by experts in the field. During the tournament, they engaged with fans to learn about their experiences and report any incidents affecting attendees' human rights for follow-up by tournament organizers. For the delivery of the human rights volunteer project, organizers partnered with the Centre for Sport and Human Rights, a global organization promoting human rights in sports.[21]

Make It Credible

Through effective communication about your sustainability commitments, efforts, and impacts as well as a strong call to action, you can help your audience to demonstrate their purpose and values while deepening their trust and loyalty toward your event.

Audiences can be powerful agents of change, and event organizers can ask their audiences to create change with them. Organizers of live music events can also work together with other local events; through networks and trade associations, organizers can call for greater policy support and systemic change backed by the combined social, cultural, and economic muscle of their collective audiences.

To ensure your communications are credible and trustworthy, avoid vague or misleading terms, such as *green* or *eco-friendly*, and back up your claims with solid, independent, and verifiable evidence that shows your impact and progress.

> When trust is high, the dividend you receive is like a performance multiplier...high trust materially improves communication, collaboration, execution, innovation, strategy, engagement, partnering, and relationships with all stakeholders.
>
> — Stephen Covey

Specify which aspects of your event are demonstrating sustainability leadership and which areas are still a work in progress. You should also be clear about whether your actions are voluntary or mandatory, and how you address your responsibilities along the entire value chain of the event, including supply chains and audience impacts.

It's OK to say you're still working toward meaningfully addressing your Scope 3 impacts or that you are in a learning phase with respect to advancing justice, equity, diversity, and inclusion issues. That would put you in the same category as 99 percent of everyone else working on these same challenges.

Confusing Fatality Numbers

Qatar leveraged the World Cup as an opportunity to modernize its labor laws, and significant improvements were made. The measures taken have improved the working and living conditions for hundreds of thousands of workers. However, there's still a long way to go, and the inconsistent communications around this fact led to mistrust and confusion.

After a period of intense negotiations, the State of Qatar and the International Labour Organization (ILO) agreed on and launched a program to support major labor reforms. The ILO report entitled *One Is Too Many* found that at least fifty workers had lost their lives in 2020 and just over five hundred were severely injured in connection with World Cup related construction. This is a far cry from the three reported fatalities and thirty-seven non-work-related deaths officially acknowledged in the FIFA World Cup Sustainability Progress Report.[22, 23]

The most confusing communication arose during a televised interview where World Cup chief Hassan Al-Thawadi was asked about the migrant worker fatalities. He repeated the claim that three had died in incidents directly connected with construction of stadiums and thirty-seven deaths were attributed to other reasons. But after being pressed by television host Piers Morgan about the number of deaths among migrant workers in the wider efforts to get Qatar ready for the World Cup, Al-Thawadi said, "The estimate is between four hundred and five hundred."

The main problem comes back to the different definitions and lack of harmonized approach being used by various institutions in the country with varying levels of quality data collection. This is a matter the ILO is also working with Qatar's Government to improve.

Demonstrating some vulnerability by acknowledging where you are in your journey through timely reporting is key to establishing trust among key stakeholders and communicating a willingness to improve.

Don't Rely on Offsets Alone

There's simply not enough land on Earth or available technology to offset everyone's carbon emissions, therefore you cannot rely on offsets alone. You must do all you can to reduce the emissions you can control in your operations and the emissions you can influence through your supply chains.

There will be emissions that are simply out of your control and influence (air travel to some degree, for example), and you can invest in offset projects as a meaningful part of your overall strategy to remove carbon dioxide from the atmosphere and reduce your footprint as close to net zero as possible.

The World Cup Qatar 2022 had a sustainability strategy that included eliminating single-use plastic, diverting waste from the landfill, utilizing electric vehicles and solar power, and minimizing emissions throughout. However, they were significantly challenged by the need to build stadiums from scratch and operate them with packed crowds *in the desert*.[24]

The FIFA World Cup also attracted crowds from all around the world, which generated significant travel-related GHG emissions. The carbon footprint from travel alone accounted for 52 percent of the Qatar World Cup emissions.

According to the sustainability progress report published in 2022, Scope 1 and 2 impacts represented only 2 percent of the total emissions. Most of the Scope 3 emissions came from three sources: international travel, accommodation, and construction and operation of stadiums. Nevertheless, the organizers of the 2022 World Cup committed to offset all unavoidable emissions, which involved millions of dollars of investments in offset projects.

Many have questioned the legitimacy of carbon offsets in general, but the methods and calculations used to get the Qatar World Cup to net zero saw a level of scrutiny not previously seen.

It's Complicated

Those that believe all carbon offsets are meaningless and highly suspect are often influenced by the negative media attention offsets receive. This is understandable, especially considering the explosive 2023 article in the *Guardian* that reported more than 90 percent of the rainforest offset credits verified by Verra, the world's leading carbon standard for the rapidly growing $2 billion voluntary offsets market, were "phantom credits" that don't represent genuine carbon reductions.[25]

Verra responded to the controversy by disputing the claims made in the *Guardian* article, which were based on a research study that Verra said reached incorrect conclusions because it relied on synthetic controls that didn't accurately represent the pre-project conditions in the area, as the studies' authors themselves acknowledged. The same study also didn't account for the urgent risks from deforestation in the UN-backed Reducing Emissions from Deforestation and Forest Degradation (REDD) project.

Deforestation credits do require a certain level of faith in a system that calculates carbon avoidance rather than direct carbon removal from the atmosphere. To put it in perspective, these credits direct capital investments into vulnerable communities for the purpose of sustainable development and protection of local forests. This may involve hiring local scientists and forest managers as well as rangers to discourage illegal farming and poaching. These types of programs aim to protect local forests, reduce corruption, and stimulate local economic activity, while respecting Indigenous rights. It's definitely no easy task.

"We still stand by all of our current methodologies as the best in class," said Julie Baroody, Verra's senior director of forest carbon innovation, who is responsible for the rainforest offsets program.

Verra is a US-based nonprofit organization that functions like a stock exchange's IPO department. It creates listing rules that need to be adhered to by companies or project developers who may be public organizations or private companies. Verra certifies tens of millions of offset credits each year and earns $0.10 on each one to pay for staffing costs, lawyers, climate scientists, and management of the exchange listing. Their job is to continuously improve standards and listing rules, and they have already made major updates to their methodology since the *Guardian* article was released.

Another negative story involved the Kachung tree plantation carbon offsetting project in Uganda, which was established as a carbon credit by Norwegian company Green Resources.[26, 27] A report by the Oakland Institute concluded that the project required the eviction of multiple villages to get enough land to build the plantation. Although the project was validated under the Climate, Community and Biodiversity (CCB) Standards program in 2011 as having a sound design and evaluation plan, it was never verified, as is required within five years of the project's validation. Since the project was never verified, its validation expired in 2016 and was never certified. Obviously, due diligence is required to ensure the offsets you purchase are verified by a credible organization and certified to be in alignment with legal and ethical standards.

All the negative media regarding carbon offsets has largely been constructive in that it's led to the development of governance, calculation, and methodology improvements, which is quickly professionalizing the industry and driving capital to the most efficient and effective projects in the world that keep carbon out of the atmosphere.

At times it feels like the early days of shopping for "organic" foods. There was a lot of loose use of the term until the standards consolidated and forced the nonconforming products off the shelves. Until that happens, it's up to you to ensure that your offset purchase meets at least some kind of recognized third-party standard that assures the offset was developed and sold legitimately.

More than US$36 billion was invested in carbon credit projects over the past decade, and $18 billion of that was invested in the last three years alone. That recent growth means there are many more intermediaries, accounting firms, engineering firms, and insurance companies who have done the work to simplify the message and add trust to carbon offsets markets. There is significant value to look for these trust-adding services, especially for first-time offset buyers.

There are many expectations for perfection in carbon offset markets. In addition to demonstrating clear evidence of climate action, offsets are expected to reduce poverty, create local employment, strengthen Indigenous rights, and support women. No pressure.

Verra

In 2005, carbon markets investment advisory firm Climate Wedge and its partner Cheyne Capital designed the Voluntary Carbon Standard, intended as a quality standard for transacting and developing "non-Kyoto" Protocol carbon credits. The Kyoto Protocol's Clean Development Mechanism (CDM) for carbon offsets under the UN Framework Convention on Climate Change was focused on emerging economies only, so voluntary credits from mature markets were not eligible due to geographic or timing constraints of the Kyoto rulebook (e.g., carbon offset projects in the US, Hong Kong, and Turkey that were not eligible for the CDM).

In March 2006, Climate Wedge and Cheyne Capital transferred the Voluntary Carbon Standard (VCS) version 1.0 to The Climate Group, International Emissions Trading Association and World Economic Forum, and provided the initial sponsor capital for these nonprofit organizations to convene a team of global carbon market experts to further draft the VCS requirements. The team later formed the VCS Steering Committee, which worked to draft the second and subsequent versions of the VCS Standard.

As of October 2022, Verra has certified 1,848 projects globally.

Offsets Are Not Going Away

While there are complexities in the carbon offset market and there can be reputational consequences for offsetting without also taking other actions to decarbonize, offsets are a viable option to address unavoidable emissions associated with events, such as air travel, freight, and embodied carbon. However, they should not be a replacement for long-term decarbonization solutions.

The Science Based Targets Initiative refers to carbon offsets as *business value mitigation* and views them as an important mechanism to address emissions that fall beyond an organization's direct control.

When done right, offsets are an effective way to enable capital investment to reach high-quality climate action activities on the ground and build up a more inclusive, low-carbon economy. The UK, the EU, and the US are all in the process of addressing greenwashing as it relates to carbon credits through growing regulatory scrutiny of what companies can say, including claims of carbon neutrality.

Gold Standard

The Gold Standard or Gold Standard for the Global Goals is a standard and logo certification mark program for nongovernmental emission reductions projects in the Clean Development Mechanism, the Voluntary Carbon Market and other climate and development interventions. It's published and administered by the Gold Standard Foundation, a nonprofit foundation headquartered in Geneva, Switzerland. It was designed with the intent to ensure that carbon credits are real and verifiable and that projects make measurable contributions to sustainable development. The objective of the Gold Standard is to add branding, with a quality label, to carbon credits generated by projects, which can then be bought and traded by countries that have a binding legal commitment according to the Kyoto Protocol, by businesses or other organizations, for carbon offsetting purposes.

As of October 2022, The Gold Standard has certified 2,600 projects across 98 countries.

Which Offsets to Buy

You should begin by deciding which kind of offsets you want to purchase. There are renewable energy credits, clean cooking schemes, nature restoration, local, and even Indigenous community-focused offsets.

There are two major types of carbon markets to buy and sell offsets. *Compliance markets* are regulated by government agencies and used by companies and governments legally mandated to offset their emissions.[28] The type you're more likely to encounter, though, are known as *voluntary markets*, which are used by those not legally required or regulated to purchase offsets.[29] In most cases, the carbon credits from the voluntary market cannot be used in the compliance market unless explicitly accepted.

While the compliance markets are governed by programs like the Clean Development Mechanism created under the Kyoto Protocol and the California Cap-and-Trade Program, the voluntary market is governed by a handful of registries that evaluate potential carbon offset projects and either approve them or deny them.[30, 31, 32]

Unfortunately, the market for offsets has been slow to react to the growing demand for voluntary credits, and therefore the shortage of supply has led to the growth of lower-quality offset products in some geographic regions.

The voluntary carbon offsets market, if relied on too heavily, allows a lot of wiggle room to achieve "net zero" without actually lowering operational and supply chain emissions. Research done by the Columbia Center on Sustainable Investment analyzed thirty-five organizations with publicly disclosed net-zero commitments and discovered that 66 percent of them overly relied on carbon offsets in their net-zero strategies.[33]

Where to Source Offsets

The World Wildlife Fund (WWF) published a comparison of the most common offset standards (you can also find this in the Tools and Resources chapter of this book as well as on my website, leor.ca).[34]

Natalie Lowe of the Sustainable Events Forum recommends looking for certifications approved by the Global Sustainable Tourism Council.[35]

As already mentioned, Melissa Radu and her team at Explore Edmonton provide a valuable service to all conventions, festivals, and other events taking place in the city of Edmonton, Alberta—absolutely free of charge—with the aim of helping events become carbon neutral. Melissa procures offset credits on behalf of event organizers through Ostrom Climate, which are verified by Verra.[36,37]

World Cup Offsets

The FIFA World Cup Qatar 2022 sourced their carbon offsets from an independent organization called the Global Carbon Council and prioritized offsets from countries in the Middle East region or in Asian and African countries that contributed to the workforce that made the World Cup a reality. The tournament organizers aimed to create a diversified portfolio of different types of offsets from different parts of the world, including renewable energy projects, habitat preservation, gas leakage reductions, and energy-efficient cookstoves, which were all certified as Gold or Verified Carbon Standard from Verra.[38]

Cookstove credits are associated with projects that replace inefficient stoves that burn firewood, charcoal, agriculture residues, or dung. These projects can produce significant emissions reductions while improving the health and quality of life for some of the poorest of the poor. A credible third-party verifier is required to visit households in the project areas to confirm efficient cookstoves are in use.

Other examples of offset projects supported by FIFA World Cup Qatar included an energy-efficiency project in Oman, which utilized an ecological wetland solution and replaced a high-pressure pump for a produced water disposal system. This project resulted in 85,000 total CO_2 offsets certified by the Global Carbon Council.

Another project in Indonesia preserved 64,000 hectares of tropical peat swamp forest, which is home to the endangered Bornean orangutan. The area was slated by the Provincial government to be converted into palm oil estates. The investment resulted in 28,000 total CO_2 offsets certified by Voluntary Carbon Standard.

FIFA commissioned a third-party study that determined the Global Sustainability Assessment System was the standard best suited for the World Cup in the Middle East region.

Additionality

Gilles Dufrasne of a Carbon Market Watch was critical of the offsets employed by the FIFA World Cup Qatar, telling *Le Monde* newspaper that one of the renewable energy projects used to generate carbon credits was a wind farm in Turkey, which he claimed was, "an economically viable project that would have seen the light of day with or without Qatar's help."[39] Dufrasne's criticism of the project in Turkey is a reference to *additionality*.

For a carbon offset to be considered *additional*, the reduction in greenhouse gas emissions being credited to the offset would not have occurred without the creation and sale of the offset. In other words, the carbon offset project is additional to what would have happened anyway, in the absence of the offset project.

This concept is important because it ensures the carbon offset represents a real and verifiable reduction in emissions that would not have occurred otherwise. It also helps to prevent the "double counting" of emissions reductions, where the same emissions reduction is claimed by multiple parties.

In practice, determining the additionality of a carbon offset project can be challenging; it requires a rigorous assessment of the baseline scenario or what would have happened without the offset project. Typically, this work is carried out by the project developer and then verified by a credible third-party, factoring considerations such as current government policies, market trends, and the status of existing technology and infrastructure.

Third-party Verifications

Carbon credit verification is a rigorous process to ensure the legitimacy of offset credits. Verification typically starts with the project developers who implement carbon reduction activities and generate the credits. They need to provide evidence of the carbon reduction, such as monitoring data, project reports, and other relevant documentation. They can get the protocols and methodologies and even the project validated.

Then the data is submitted to a third-party verifier such as Verra and Gold Standard who ensure that the project meets all the requirements of the chosen carbon credit standard. The verifier will also check for any errors or inconsistencies in the data and verify the accuracy of the project report. If the verifier is satisfied that the project meets all the requirements, it issues carbon credits, which can be traded on the carbon market.

Attributes of Effective Offset Verification

Accredited: Verifiers should be accredited under the ISO 14065 series or another applicable standard, and they should apply ISO 14064-3 or another applicable standard to provide verification of ex-post credits.

Additional: Offsets should be additional, meaning they represent an emission reduction or carbon removal that would not have taken place if not for the offset activity.

Accountable: Offsets should be tracked using a publicly accessible registry to ensure they're only sold to one buyer.

Certified: Carbon offsets should be certified against a recognized standard.

Co-beneficial: Besides being environmentally beneficial, offset projects must not negatively affect the local population, and ideally should offer social benefit to them.

Consistent: Offset providers should convert greenhouse gases like methane into CO_2 terms according to their actual warming impact.

Independent: The same organization should never verify a project that they compiled or consulted on.

Minimal Forward-selling: The time gap between the purchase of offset and the execution of the action to remove carbon or reduce emissions should be minimized, and there should be some sort of insurance in place.

Permanence: This refers to how long a greenhouse gas stays out of the atmosphere. Ideally, it should be kept out of the atmosphere forever. Where there is a risk of reversal, e.g., where reforested or afforested plots are destroyed and carbon is released, it must be acknowledged and accounted for in the offset plan.

Transparent: The standard should describe the methodology to be used for the verification that pertains to the process and/or system controls and the data. It should be available for scrutiny.

The above attributes are a modified version of the guidelines from Net Zero Carbon Events and the Net Zero Methodology for Hotels.

Leave a Legacy Not a White Elephant
Since FIFA and the International Olympic Committee ramped up their environmental claims back in the 1990s, their events have only become bigger, and their impacts have only become more severe.[40] One recent study found that

between 1964 and 2018, the Olympics and World Cup grew sixty-fold in terms of the number of sports, athletes, journalists, spectators, marketing, and costs involved.[41] The ever-expanding size of these events seems to push the promise of net-zero emissions further and further out of reach.

Mandating the elimination of fresh stadium construction could help limit emissions, but that would essentially mean creating a short list of potential hosts with existing infrastructure and shutting out most of the developing world. Ironically, those countries with existing infrastructure to support mega sporting events are the ones historically most responsible for climate change.

One of the stadiums built for the World Cup in Qatar, known as 974, was designed to be disassembled and donated to other countries hosting major tournaments in the future. It's the first-ever fully *demountable* World Cup stadium. Most of the other 2022 World Cup stadiums were designed to have their upper tiers demounted and donated.

It's terrific that part of the World Cup legacy will be the stadiums donated to other countries hosting future tournaments. The approach should be made a requirement for all future mega-event bids as long as the sustainability impacts are not more than those associated to permanent facilities. FIFA, the Olympics, and other global mega-events can be better designed as pop-up-like experiences rather than requiring millions of dollars of sports infrastructure investments that will likely be obsolete in a few short years.

Was It Greenwashing?

Is the World Cup Qatar 2022 guilty of greenwashing? The answer may be based on your response to whether low-impact mega sporting events are even possible. If events of this scale are seen as just environmental, social, and economic disasters leveraged for prestige and advertisements, then no amount of effort will suffice. If, however, you believe the journey toward purposeful, accessible, net-zero, and zero-waste events are possible at any scale, then the 2022 World Cup could be seen as a major step in the right direction with lots of difficult lessons learned.

It's possible, when the final World Cup report is eventually made public, that Qatar's new eight-hundred-megawatt solar power plant may be identified as an offset against some of the tournament's associated emissions. However, that claim would be greenwashing since the project could not be considered additional or verified by any credible organization.

FIFA World Cup Qatar 2022 faced the kind of intense scrutiny that events are certain to come across more often in the future. Proactively getting ahead of the scrutiny while the whole world is paying close attention requires demonstrating transparent, game-changing climate action and positive social breakthroughs at a Lionel Messi kind of level.

7

Change the Venue without Changing the Venue

Some people look for a beautiful place.
Others make a place beautiful.

— Hazrat Inayat Khan

We Forgot About the After-Party!

We were high-fiving each other after a successful and exhausting finish to the Calgary Folk Music Festival weekend; we were happy to be on track to divert more than 70 percent of all the waste generated. In subsequent years, that target became 90 percent (and we met it!). We left the island victorious and arrived at the after-party ready to unwind and celebrate. We were horrified to find it in progress with overflowing garbage bins of paper plates, red solo beer cups, and empty pizza boxes. We had such a sophisticated plan in place for the main festival venue, where we engaged hundreds of people to execute our waste strategy, but we forgot to talk to the secondary venue hosting our after-party. It definitely sent the wrong message to staff, volunteers, sponsors, and artists about our level of commitment to a zero-waste festival.

After travel, your venues are usually the most significant contributors to your event's overall footprint, especially if major construction is involved or large built elements are required such as trade show exhibitions, pavilions, or set designs.

For corporate events, the most significant carbon impact tends to come from the food served. Freight and logistics—the transportation of equipment and goods to an event—is also an important contributor, especially for exhibitions. Depending on the type of venue and the size of the event, venue energy will be important to account for.

Demand Is Growing

In 2020, just before COVID-19 led to countless event cancellations, a report, known as the Meeting Room of the Future Barometer, found that sustainability was named as the most important issue for the future by venue operators. Two years later, despite the pandemic remaining front-page news and the effects touching everyone around the world, the updated *Meeting Room of the Future Barometer 2022* found that sustainability was still the number one issue for venues, and 87 percent of responding venues said they had recently developed environmental or sustainability policy statements.[1]

This focus on sustainability is the result of increased requests venues are receiving from clients to show their *environmental*, *social*, and *governance* (ESG) performance. In fact, 46 percent of venues worldwide reported that their clients were increasingly asking about their ESG or sustainability initiatives.[2] Although only 13 percent of responding venues were asked specifically about their carbon footprint, it was noted that this is a fast-rising area of interest for clients.

Are you receiving increased requests from your clients to either state or provide your social responsibility and environmental credentials?

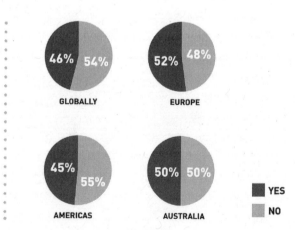

FIGURE 7.1. Roughly half of venues worldwide are increasingly asked about their sustainability initiatives Source: International Association of Conference Centers

Net-Zero Venues

An analysis of fifty leading venues by the World Travel and Tourism Council (WTTC) found that seventeen hotel chains (34 percent) had set a carbon reduction target; 76 percent of venues had established interim targets; and 24 percent of venues included both interim and long-term targets in their sustainability plans. Furthermore, almost 60 percent of these commitments were aligned with science-based targets.[3] Four of the analyzed accommodation providers are part of the Race to Zero campaign—a global initiative of the UN Framework Convention on Climate Change (UNFCCC) to rally support from businesses, cities, and investors to halve global emissions by 2030.[4]

Carbon offsetting is being utilized by 82 percent of the surveyed venues, and 50 percent of the evaluated accommodation providers report Scope 3 emissions partially. Because Scope 3 includes emissions from each franchised hotel, it's an important part of the overall footprint, so collecting data from franchisees is critical for any large chain setting emissions reduction targets.[5]

Venues Are Moving on Plastics

In a recent survey conducted by Development Counselors International (DCI) on behalf of the International Association of Conference Centers (IACC), 82 percent of the venues were actively reducing single-use plastics.[6] Venues in Europe and Australia have a significant lead in reducing single-use products, including guest room amenities, plastic drink bottles, plastic food utensils, hot drinks cups, and straws in both guest rooms and meeting rooms.[7]

Donate More Food

However, according to that same DCI and IACC study, venues in the Americas have a slight edge on programs to reduce food waste, healthy menus, and unused food donations.[8] Of the venues surveyed, 94 percent are providing menus that focus on healthy food, and 91 percent are striving to manage food waste. The most notable improvements have been the donation of unused food from group events to local community organizations. More than half, 54 percent, now say they have this option available, compared to less than a quarter two years prior.

Food at Venues

Food and beverage is an interesting area to explore because it's a significant part of events—some might argue it's the most significant part—and the responsibility for procurement is split between the venue and event organizer. The latter is responsible for determining the volume and type of food and beverages; however, most venues have preferred caterers or long-term contracts with a specific catering company and beverage supplier. Therefore, it's the venue that sets the parameters for what's possible based on their choice of preferred suppliers.

Influencing the menu options and environmental practices—including packaging—offered by those preferred caterers may be difficult, but change management always is. Ideally, the environmental practices of the caterer should be in line with your purpose, and objectives are written into the venue agreement and banquet event order to as great an extent as possible.

If there are no sustainability-minded caterers on that preapproved list, do your best to influence a change in who's allowed on that list—to help not just your event reach its goals but also every other event that will use that venue.

Collaborate with your chosen venue to establish common goals and share lessons learned and resources. If contract renewals with food and beverage suppliers are coming up, see if you can influence the process to ensure social and environmental goals are written into contracts or request for proposals (RFPs).

If the scale of your event does not afford you influence with the venue, you may need to select one that is more aligned with your purpose. You could also consider approaching the venue as part of an industry effort or consortium of event organizers and sponsors.

If the existing food and beverage provider is unwilling or incapable of working toward your intended outcomes, explore the opportunity to pilot your caterer of choice for *a portion* of the event or as a subcontractor to the existing supplier. This would be a great way to introduce a social enterprise like Ethnicity Catering, which I mentioned in chapter 2—they provide Canadian work experience and training to immigrants in transition to Canada while relying on their traditional cuisine to offer unique and delicious menus to all types of clients.[9, 10]

Congratulations! You were successful in getting a vegan or sustainability-focused caterer onto the venue's preapproved vendors list. It's now up to you to find an appropriate way to acknowledge that newly added supplier to help generate future demand. This could be done in the labeling at serving points, in the post-event report, or even during a separate lunch and learn event, particularly if an industry association effort was required to influence the change. Doing these things may help to generate further demand for the caterer, which ensures they are kept on rather than being removed from the preferred vendors list following your event.

Go All in on Vegan

According to a 2021 study by the University of Illinois, the production of meat accounts for a whopping 60 percent of all greenhouse gases from food production.[11] It also indicated that global food production is responsible for a third of all planet-heating gases emitted by human activity, with the use of animals for meat causing twice the pollution of producing plant-based foods. Vegetarian meals alone can reduce the upstream emissions of production and manufacturing by an estimated 90 percent per serving. Therefore, serving plant-based foods in place of meat can cause a significant decrease in the greenhouse gas footprint of your next event.

> We're eating the way people will eat in the future. We're just doing it early.
>
> — James Cameron, Filmmaker, after revealing that all catering provided to cast and crew on *Avatar: The Way of the Water* was plant-based in an effort to stay true to the film production's dedication to preserving the environment.

There was some pushback when Explore Edmonton implemented a 100 percent plant-based menu at the Edmonton Convention Centre in 2019.[12] Organizers met the initial pushback with health and environmental data to support the decision, and the Explore Edmonton team discovered a lot of support once they clearly articulated the rationale. It also helped that the food was prepared by an award-winning chef, and the menu offered lots of delicious protein options.

Perhaps going fully plant-based at your event sounds impossible. We often predict that people will be displeased about vegetarian-only options. But if it can work in Alberta, where cowboy hats are not uncommon and bumper stickers regularly proclaim "I love Alberta beef," then it can work anywhere.

> Alternative proteins are to meat production as renewables are to energy: the future.
>
> — Caroline Bushnell, Senior VP corporate engagement, The Good Food Institute

No matter how you slice it, vegan and plant-based protein foods boast much lower emissions than the "sustainable beef" approach, which relies heavily on offsetting emissions rather than reducing them. A life cycle assessment from the University of Michigan showed that a Beyond Burger, for example, which is now sold at A&W, Denny's, Carl's Jr., and elsewhere, produces 90 percent fewer GHGs compared to a beef burger.[13]

Food Donations and Misconceptions

The Edmonton Convention Centre partnered with another food rescue program, Second Helping, to donate leftover food to the local food bank. In the first year of the program's inception, more than five thousand pounds of leftover food from events were donated to Edmontonians experiencing food insecurity.

> Green events happen in green venues.
> — Amanda Simons,
> Program Manager at Greenview

Some venues commonly tell event organizers that all leftover food is taken to a staff room for employees to enjoy. I recommend pushing back on that unless the venue has an explicit policy in place about hiring marginalized demographics.

I've also been told multiple times by several venues they can't assume the liability associated with donating food because it might cause an allergic reaction or illness. However, this is an uninformed position that ignores the Samaritan laws passed across North America which are specifically designed to make it easier to donate "apparently wholesome food" and exclude donor liability except in cases of gross negligence or intentional misconduct. In the US, this law is known as the Bill Emerson Good Samaritan Food Donation Act, passed in 1996.

How to Find the Right Venue

Here are some key questions to ask a venue and/or a destinations organization, such as a tourism board or economic development authority:

Does the venue have its own net-zero or decarbonization goal in place?

What electrical power source are they drawing from?

- If it's the local power grid, what percentage of the energy comes from coal (highest emissions profile), natural gas (marginally better), nuclear power (waste disposal concerns), and renewables such as solar, wind, hydro, or geothermal (lowest emissions footprint)?

- If they have solar panels, are they in good working order, and what percentage of total power do they supply?

What kind of certifications do they have?
- Leadership in Energy and Environmental Design (LEED)?[14]
- U.S. Green Building Code?
- UNESCO Sustainable Travel Pledge?
- Sustainable Event Standards?
- Global Sustainability Assessment System (GSAS)?

Is there any support available to decarbonize the event and address other social and environmental impacts?
- Is there a local tourism or economic development bureau committee like Explore Edmonton that can help offset emissions and secure complimentary public transit passes for attendees?

What local infrastructure can support the event's sustainability performance?
- Electric vehicle charging stations?
- Compost facilities?
- Waste-to-power technology?
- Local food suppliers?
- Partnerships with local Indigenous groups or environmental organizations?

What metrics and methodologies are they using (if any) to measure and report on sustainability impacts?
- Do they have data (that you can trust) on energy use, waste diversion, biodiversity, and social impact from previous events?

Who is on their preferred list of caterers?
- Are they open to expanding the list?
- Do they have a food donation policy?

Are they willing to work with you to demonstrably improve year after year?

Are they education focused and willing to help your participants become better informed?

Do they have a good working relationship with the municipality, and are they a preferred venue carrying out city priorities?

Are they accessible to those with mobility challenges?

> An inspiring space has the power to ignite creativity, ignite energy, and spur innovation.
>
> — Jeff Shinabarger

Accessibility

Your venue selection says a lot about your purpose and event culture with respect to how accessible it is via public transportation or biking and walking. It speaks volumes about inclusivity when mobility challenges are considered. Looking to see how the venue is ranked on Maayan Ziv's AccessNow app and asking whether they have an accessibility certification, such as the one offered by the Rick Hansen Foundation, are simple ways to focus the conversation and send a strong signal to the market about your priorities.

Even a modest curb step at the entrance of your venue can be a hindrance and send a message about how welcoming your event is or isn't. The Toronto-based Stop Gap Foundation helps venues with a simple custom ramp to enable accessibility for under $500. They ship these ramps all over North America.

Narrow spaces and stairs without the option of an elevator are more significant limitations that will prevent the participation of certain demographics at your event. Even if there is an elevator, if your event is on a rooftop or penthouse, note that some participants in wheelchairs may struggle to reach the top elevator buttons.

The Great Outdoors

Outdoor venues and destinations can also be made more accessible. For example, Greece is making nearly three hundred beaches wheelchair-friendly by installing the Greek-designed SeaTrac system for wheelchairs, which offers unassisted sea access to people with disabilities and mobility issues. This innovative technological assistant promotes autonomy, quality, and wellness in everyday life. It will be complemented by other essential facility upgrades to parking lots, bathrooms and change rooms, ramps, corridors, and refreshment bars.

Interestingly, Greece is also home to the world's first zero-waste island. The small island of Tilos achieved a national park designation and is powered completely by renewable energy. The destination transformed from sending nearly 90 percent of its waste to the landfill to eventually closing its landfill and diverting 100 percent of its waste through a Center for Creative Upcycling, where items can be repaired, reused, and converted into raw art supplies or building materials.

Waste Infrastructure

Your locale has a lot to do with your ability to divert waste from your event. Some cities and countries are far behind with respect to recycling and compost infrastructure. Transporting waste to another city for processing may be required in some circumstances.

Ideally, your location and/or venue of choice has infrastructure in place to make it easy for people to separate waste into different streams and direct it to the appropriate facility for processing. If compost bins are not available in your venue, you may need to rent some equipment. This may be especially important in the kitchen areas. Ensuring chefs have access to compost bins and recycling bins is key. They may need to receive simple training on how to avoid contamination. Training is also required for the cleaning and janitorial crew to help ensure they dispose of waste in separated waste streams as part of their regular cleanup. Non-invasive spot checks in the kitchen and with the cleanup crew are recommended.

Consolidating all the event waste at a loading dock or other centralized location should be done to enable weighing of the different streams; ideally, waste in the wrong stream should be removed. Loading docks are typically already outfitted with scales able to handle this. I recommend doing this—even when you have a service provider offering to send you the post-event cargo weights. If you have more than one service provider, some may be more dependable than others, and they may all be using different equipment and assumptions to calculate the weight, so totals can be inconsistent and full of gaps.

Separately calculating *your own event's* footprint using event staff, volunteers, or a sustainable events specialist may be important if you are to obtain accurate data. The venue may not actually have this data if they are aggregating your waste along with waste picked up from multiple other events before the hauling trip to the landfill or compost facility.

Climate Change Is Changing Venues

In June 2013, Calgary and surrounding areas were hit by a catastrophic flood that killed five people and displaced more than one hundred thousand others. Total damage estimates exceeded $4 billion.

Vancouver Convention Centre

The GLOBE Forum takes place every two years at the Vancouver Convention Centre (VCC) in British Columbia.[15] The VCC holds the distinction of being the world's first double LEED Platinum-certified convention center.

The VCC has implemented several nature-based solutions to reduce its environmental impact, including a green roof, which covers six acres of the facility's roof and includes over four hundred thousand native plants and grasses. This serves as a natural filter for rainwater, reducing the amount of runoff that enters the surrounding waterways. It also helps to insulate the building, reducing energy consumption for heating and cooling. The green roof provides a unique setting for events, with views of the city skyline and the nearby harbor.

The VCC's black-water treatment plant cleans and recycles water for irrigation for the living roof and washrooms. The facility uses a sea-water heat pump system, which draws water from the harbor and uses it to regulate the temperature inside the building. This system reduces energy consumption and carbon emissions associated with traditional heating and cooling. They even have an artificial reef built into their foundation, which has improved water quality and biodiversity in that section of Vancouver Harbor.

However, despite having a fairly robust composting, recycling, and waste reduction program, the VCC only diverts a little more than half its waste from the landfill. This is very low for such a world-class venue with so many sustainability-related amenities. Their example highlights the challenge and causes one to ponder the average diversion rate for venues without such sophisticated sustainability programs in place.

The Calgary Stampede grounds were completely underwater—less than two weeks before the scheduled opening. However, organizers vowed the event would go on, come "hell or high water," which became their slogan that year.[16]

Calgary's main indoor arena, the Scotiabank Saddledome, situated in Stampede Park, was among the many facilities damaged; flood waters filled the first ten rows of the lower seating bowl.[17]

The disaster was followed by a bitter showdown involving Calgary city council and the wealthy and influential owners of the local NHL sports team, Calgary Flames, over a new arena. The Saddledome sports stadium, originally built in 1983 ahead of the 1988 Winter Olympics, was an iconic backdrop for underdog-turned-cinematic hero stories about the Jamaican bobsled team and unlikely ski-jump champion Eddie the Eagle.

Many in the community felt the stadium still had many years left and that the city didn't need a new arena, especially at the hotly debated price tag of US$413 million, even though the cost would have been split between City Hall and the Flames owners.

Newly elected Mayor Jyoti Gondek had to be the one to inform the public that the owners decided to walk away from the project due to some relatively minor additional costs added to the project. She was immediately blamed for the outcome. Those extra costs included $3 million for solar panels and climate mitigation measures.

At the time of writing, a new arena deal had been reached "in principle" worth more than $860 million, split between the city and Flames owners, but this time with the provincial government on board as a partner too. While many details are not yet available to the public, there seems to be more than $165 million allocated to transportation, infrastructure, and district and $40 million for "other" costs.

Governments, sports team owners, and anxious sports fans alike should get used to the fact that climate mitigation is essential for any major infrastructure project. Owners and operators of both indoor and outdoor venues need to rethink and redesign for greater resilience in the face of extreme weather events becoming more frequent and intense due to climate change.

Embodied Carbon

In addition to designing for climate resilience, developers of major new infrastructure should leverage the opportunity to account for embodied carbon in their build decisions.

Embodied carbon refers to the total GHG emissions associated with the entire life cycle of a building, from raw material extraction and manufacturing to transportation, construction, and eventual decommissioning and disposal—everything except the actual operation of the venue.

According to statistics released by the World Building Council, the building sector is responsible for roughly 40 percent of annual global GHG emissions, of which 28 percent is attributed to building operations (also known as operational carbon) and 11 percent to materials and construction processes (considered embodied carbon). As operational efficiencies continue to improve, embodied carbon is likely to overcome operational carbon as a bigger risk than operational carbon.

Tips to Address Embodied Carbon
Conduct a Life Cycle Assessment

Conducting a thorough life cycle assessment is the critical first step to understand the full accounting of emissions associated with each stage of the venue construction process as well as to identify areas for improvement.

Engage Your Stakeholders

Engage and train the engineering and design teams as well as suppliers and contractors working on the project with regard to your purpose and priorities around efficient and sustainable designs that minimize future emissions. Early buy-in and design decisions can have a profound impact on embodied carbon.

Effectively communicate your commitment to reducing embodied carbon to all of your stakeholders, including media, to build support for your sustainability efforts. Be mindful of increased scrutiny regarding your sustainability communications to avoid accusations of greenwashing later.

Stay engaged with the construction industry long term to effect change across systems through active involvement in industry-wide initiatives and working groups to change technical specifications and influence the future of the built environment.

Work Closely with Suppliers

It is essential to select and collaborate with the right suppliers who disclose their emissions and implement carbon reduction strategies. Transparent supply chains enable informed choices about the materials you use.

These choices of construction materials and fixtures have a considerable impact on embodied carbon. Using low-carbon materials, such as recycled and sustainable options, can significantly reduce your carbon footprint.

Reduce the distance products and materials travel to lower transportation-related emissions. Prioritize sourcing materials locally whenever possible.

Manufacture 2030 is a unique platform and support service that simplifies the process to engage your suppliers with regard to **measuring**, **managing**, and **reducing** emissions. It provides some level of certainty that your carbon commitments will be met, while creating opportunities for your suppliers to enhance their operational and resource efficiency, procure more sustainably, and drive down costs.

Go Carbon Negative

What's needed is a massive deployment of carbon-negative products that remove more CO_2 from the atmosphere than it takes to produce them. Scaling these innovations requires you to demand their use and pay for them to be deployed.

Carbon utilization in cement and concrete production is a promising innovation that holds the potential to significantly reduce the carbon footprint of venue construction. By capturing and utilizing carbon dioxide emissions in the manufacturing process, these technologies not only address a critical environmental challenge but also enhance the performance of construction materials. Two notable examples of such solutions are Carbon Cure and Carbon Upcycling Technologies. Carbon Cure injects CO_2 into the concrete mix, where it chemically transforms into a mineral, resulting in both reduced emissions and increased concrete strength. Carbon Upcycling Technologies, on the other hand, captures CO_2 emissions and converts them into advanced nanoparticles that can enhance the properties of various materials, including concrete. These innovations not only contribute to more resilient and sustainable venues, but also showcase the transformative potential of sequestering carbon in the built environment and keeping it out of the atmosphere.

Think Circular

Encourage the reuse and recycling of materials including those from previous infrastructure the new build is intended to replace. This reduces the need for new production, may lead to cost savings, and lowers your overall embodied carbon. Integrate your zero-waste or circularity strategy into the design process, rather than as an afterthought.

For example, the FIFA World Cup in Qatar designed stadiums to collect water vapor from the cooling systems for use in irrigation of the surrounding areas. This helped the World Cup stadiums use 40 percent less water compared to minimum requirements set by the International Plumbing Code.[18]

Leverage Global Best Practices

Major infrastructure projects are long-term investments. Leveraging recognized international frameworks and best practices as a basis for complying with future carbon-related regulations can help ensure the longevity and resiliency of the venue. It can also help secure favorable insurance rates during future renewal cycles and protect the value of the asset.

Environmental Product Declarations (EPDs) are quickly emerging as a best practice to provide comprehensive and objective information about construction materials and sustainable decision-making, assigning points in adherence with green building rating tools.

Building Transparency provides open access data and necessary tools to enable action across the building industry in addressing embodied carbon's role in climate change. It helps to develop scenarios using steel, cement, and flooring and maintains the Embodied Carbon in Construction Calculator (EC3)—a free database of construction EPDs—and a matching building impact calculator for use in design and material procurement.

Trade Shows

The landscape for trade shows is undergoing a remarkable transformation, with a growing shift away from extravagant wasteful displays and pavilions toward more intentional and sustainable meeting spaces. This shift reflects the broader industry trend toward sustainability and responsible event management.

According to a report by UFI, the Global Association of the Exhibition Industry, the demand for more sustainable and efficient booth designs is rising, driven by exhibitors' desire to reduce costs and minimize their environmental impact.[19] Moreover, a growing percentage of exhibitors and visitors said they would not attend a trade show that didn't have a reasonable approach to sustainability.

Sustainable event practices, including the use of reusable materials, LED lighting, and modular booth structures, are becoming the norm as they not only align with environmental values, but also offer practical benefits such as reduced setup time and shipping costs. This evolution signifies a promising future for trade shows, where meaningful interactions and purposeful engagements take precedence over flashy extravagance.

Find out if your venue already has guidance and requirements for limiting the footprint of trade shows and whether the contractors used to design the pavilions have any environmental credentials. If not, develop your own criteria and share them with the venue so they might incorporate them for future expositions.

COP Sustainability Guidance for Exhibitors and Suppliers

Exhibitor guidance for COP26 in 2021 focused on the impact of their materials and procurement choices and discouraged the use of disposable items, such as paper handouts and promotional merchandise. Applicants for exhibitor space at the Green Zone were asked to explain how they would embed the COP26 Sustainability Governing Principles into their exhibits, and their applications were assessed on this basis.

Supplier guidance focused on the impacts of the wider supply chain and the subconsultants chosen to help deliver the contract, business travel impacts, and behaviors on-site, such as catering choices and waste management.

COP26 provided direct engagement with delegations on embedding sustainable decision-making into their pavilion designs. Where possible, they were asked to self-monitor the impacts of their materials via Tracker+ to get the most comprehensive overview of the impacts of the delegation pavilions captured for any COP to date. Orientation Events worked with the organizers of COP26 to provide one-on-one support to delegations on designing the most sustainable pavilion possible, and they also captured information on the materials used.

Tips to Reduce Your Trade Show Footprint

Choose Wood

Choose wood frames for the booths or consider reused or recyclable options instead of PVC plastic or steel frames. Wood has a significantly lower footprint and is much easier to recycle and reuse.

Promote Modular

Promote modular display pieces to avoid premade custom designs whenever possible. You can offer a "kit-style" trade show booth that snaps together in a wide variety of configurations and is easily disassembled and reused for office panels.

Reduce Energy Use

Reduce energy use by eliminating extra lights and video monitors.

Reuse, Recycle, Repurpose, and Rent

Rent trade show hardware whenever possible and avoid buying or custom-designing hardware and visuals without planning how to reuse them after the event.

Think long-term about multiple uses for your set. One TEDxYYC event I worked on, for example, partnered with a creative production company called RocketHouse to produce a five-minute live-action trailer version of Mind-Fire, a parkour-inspired theater production that tells a mental health story. A railroad-inspired steel structure was commissioned as part of a TEDxYYC artist-in-residence program, and after being featured on stage during a full day of provocative TEDxTalks, the legacy set piece was reused multiple times, traveling to venues in several cities as part of the MindFire theater show.

Make Waste Capture Easy

Provide a convenient waste-capture process for all the cardboard and plastic wrapping waste generated during set up and tear down.

Eliminate Paper and Plastic

Avoid paper handouts. Most of it winds up in the trash bin, anyway. Choose paperless options such as QR codes, email collection, stations for reading on tablets, or hand out preconfigured USB thumb drives.

Lower Food and Beverage Footprint

If you plan to have food and beverages at your booth, source locally and choose fair trade coffee and vegetarian or vegan options, which have a lower footprint; it doesn't go bad as quickly and is easier to compost. Donate leftover food and beverages to local food rescue programs. Ask your venue to support this choice.

Choose compostable or reusable (washable) cups, glasses, and plates. Avoid individually packaged condiments, stir sticks, and other coffee accessories, as these produce a lot of waste.

Don't Use Single-Use Signs

Use large rented monitors instead of vinyl banners and booth panels that are custom produced specifically for the show and never used again.

Avoid Single-Use Carpets

Many carpets and area rugs used for trade show booths and stages are cast away immediately following the event. Consider sourcing future flooring needs from Interface Flooring. They design modular carpet tiles that are carbon neutral across their full product life cycle as part of a third-party verified program.

Interface also designs its products to be fully recyclable and uses old fishing nets in place of nylon. Through the Interface Net-Works program, the company pays local community members in the Philippines and Indonesia to collect discarded nylon fishing nets, which Interface then recycles into carpet tiles. This initiative reduces marine pollution by removing discarded fishing nets from the ocean, which can harm marine life and damage ecosystems. It also provides a positive social impact for community members who gain a sustainable livelihood for their conservation work.

Interface also has a reclamation program so the used tiles from your event or trade show can be repurposed by charities, local businesses, and other deserving organizations and groups.

Ban SWAG

Level the playing field for all vendors and eliminate all branded disposable giveaways, especially those made from single-use plastic. If banning swag giveaways altogether is not an option, consider locally sourced, recyclable, eco-conscious items such as reusable water bottles, food ware, or local Indigenous arts.

SWAG Is a Drag

For many events, a significant source of single-use plastic and waste is the coveted Stuff We Always Give Away (SWAG). These are wasteful and ubiquitous.

I'd like to tell you that SWAG is on its way out, but it's still so common at large consumer shows and several other exhibitions. Race events often provide grab bags full of SWAG and free samples from sponsors, and conferences offer opportunities to provide SWAG items as part of the sponsorships. Companies also typically make large purchases of branded items for employees with the intention of using excess items as giveaways.

"SWAG is a sign of bad marketing," said David Betke of GreenShows when I asked for his perspective on the matter. "Poor marketing," he explained, "is unsustainable for the planet or anyone's budget."[20] *Shotgun marketing* and *attention marketing* create a lot of physical and budget waste, while a more effective approach demonstrates a brand's purpose. Selecting marketing materials that increase waste and have a negative environmental footprint is a significant brand risk.

GreenShows has a section on their website where they review sustainable marketing products based on five key metrics: *Freight, Materials, Packaging, Lifecycle,* and *Living Up to Supplier's Claims.*

GreenShows offer trees as an alternative to plastic SWAG. They plant the trees physically. Each tree gets a code. Then they provide those codes as giveaways, incentives, and gifts. The recipient can then virtually plant and dedicate the tree with a photo or logo, their website URL, and tweet in GreenShows' virtual forest.

Explore Edmonton advises event organizers to lose the tote bag giveaways and consider partnering with Fill-It-Forward to promote people bringing their own reusable bottles and cups; their advice has led to several successful campaigns.[21]

GreenShows also offers opportunities for trade shows to reduce printing and go paperless. By utilizing QR codes, attendees can see which printed materials are available at a trade show booth, and receive it digitally without having to track down an attendant and hear a sales pitch. This eliminates the need for pamphlets, brochures, and business cards since the same technology also collects contact information for those downloading the material. The app offers exhibitors a finely segmented list of leads showing precisely who was interested in what.

After-Party

Influencing the culture of your event toward a meaningful purpose requires careful planning and continuous improvements in all its aspects. The moment your audience arrives and the last impression you leave them with are particularly memorable, so be sure to integrate a user experience mindset and use those memorable moments to reinforce your call to action and how it will bring your event's purpose to life.

The Calgary Folk Fest after-party story I began this chapter with was an example of an afterthought moment. The environmental footprint of that event was overshadowed by all the progress made at the main event site, but unfortunately, the inconsistencies stand out even more when there's lots of progress elsewhere. When such inconsistencies are illuminated, it's important to stay humble and acknowledge the need for improvement. Debrief with the venue after the event and ask them to address the issue in the future. If, like the Folk Fest, your event takes place annually, invite key venue contacts to participate in your annual planning cycle and schedule a kickoff meeting. Note that once you've acknowledged an area for improvement, resources must be directed toward addressing the challenge.

A challenge like this can be a great point of collaboration with your venue. It may also be a source of tension. It's imperative that your venue shares your purpose and is directly involved in your journey toward greater sustainability and inclusion. Remember that you're the customer, and it's your responsibility to articulate your purpose and needs. If a contract renewal process is upcoming, these elements—along with specific goals and outcomes—can be incorporated into the new contract.

8

Make Mobility More Sustainable

'Cause I'm leavin' on a jet plane. Don't know when I'll be back again.
Oh babe, I hate to go.

— John Denver

When Bicycles Arrived at a Cowboy Festival

The Calgary Stampede and Cyclepalooza may seem like an unlikely pair. One is a mainstream celebration of rural and agricultural ways of life, while the other is a small fledgling festival loved by urban cycling enthusiasts. However, a partnership between the two helped legitimize the fringe event *and* unlock a demographic for the Stampede that was previously inaccessible and determined to *avoid* the annual ten-day rodeo and music festival.

The Calgary Stampede is an event some people love to hate because it's perceived to be rowdy, disruptive, wasteful, and out of touch with its cosmopolitan surroundings. When a colleague learned I was managing the Stampede's compost program, he memorably said, "I half expected them to roll it up, stick it in a barrel, light it on fire, and shoot it out of a cannon."

The Calgary Stampede is a one-hundred-plus-year-old event delivered with the help of more than 2,500 community volunteers. With such an event, change can take time. Their decentralized model involved numerous satellite events across the city, but for some reason, bike infrastructure was not prioritized until demand reached a pivotal peak—and then a program blazed into being.

Cyclepalooza was a complete contrast to Stampede. Widely seen as a diverse and inclusive community-based bicycle-themed festival promoting arts and culture. Not coincidentally, it overlapped the Calgary Stampede, and like the Stampede, Cyclepalooza also incorporated a decentralized model with satellite events around the city and lasted for ten days. It thrived as a sort of *anti*-Stampede and was welcomed as an alternative to ten days of twangy country music, stiff cowboy boots, and bravado. One year, the organizers aspired to promote their fledgling festival through participation in the Stampede parade, but their bikes were not welcome.

The following year, a left-leaning elected Member of the Legislative Assembly (MLA) and biking enthusiast, Dr. David Swan, decided he didn't want to wave to the three-hundred-thousand-person Stampede crowd from a gas-guzzling vintage automobile or on the back of a horse, which was customary for the kickoff parade. Swann wanted to cycle instead. The biking community was incensed when the news broke that Dr. Swann decided not to participate in the parade because his request was denied. The media coverage of the story was unkind to the Stampede.

Discouraging the use of bicycles in the parade was a misguided decision that failed to see the biking community as an influential demographic shaping the future of the city's infrastructure. When it comes to long-term infrastructure planning, most major cosmopolitan centers are now designing around more inclusive mobility options with a lower carbon footprint.

Elephant in the Room

Events certifying as "carbon neutral" that don't account for their full value chain (including audience travel) are choosing to ignore industry best practices. They're also opening themselves up to accusations of greenwashing.

Flying is the most environmentally damaging way to travel. Aviation is currently responsible for 3 percent of global CO_2 emissions. However, as other industries decarbonize in line with some projections, and air travel continues to grow, flying could account for up to 24 percent of global emissions by 2050 unless there's a significant technological shift.[1]

It's not just the CO_2 pumped out from jet engines that has an impact. Other substances, including water in the form of contrails, as well as soot and nitrous oxides, all trap additional heat in our atmosphere. Transportation emissions significantly contribute to air pollution, and long-term exposure can cause chronic conditions such as cardiovascular and respiratory diseases as well as lung cancer.

Research on the US and Canadian exhibition industry uncovered that up to 85 percent of carbon emissions were generated by attendee travel. Data collected from the events industry in France over a two-year period came to a similar conclusion—even for national events where travel distances are shorter than for international events.[2] This contributed to the decision by the government of France to ban domestic short-haul flights where train alternatives exist.[3]

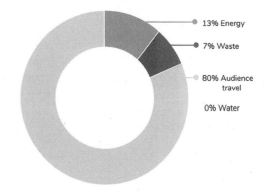

FIGURE 8.1. Average UK Festival Carbon Footprint Breakdown with Audience Travel. Source: ecolibrium

Net-Zero Travel

The travel sector has developed a road map to net zero through the World Travel and Tourism Council, which encompasses aviation, accommodation, cruise, and tour operations. The aviation sector has also published its own net-zero road map through the International Air Transport Association, which is heavily based on the rapid expansion of sustainable aviation fuels (SAFs) and new technologies, such as hydrogen fuel cells and hydrogen propulsion engines. Airbus for example, has revealed a hydrogen-powered zero-emission engine that can be used as a power source for aircraft propulsion.

Several large reputable airlines (including British Airways and Air Canada) have announced net-zero targets. United Airlines was the first to commit to reducing its GHG emissions—by 100 percent by 2050 without relying on offsets. Their plan includes a combination of constant fleet renewal, operational improvements, investments in SAF, and direct air capture technology for carbon removal contributed to this achievement.

The bold assertions have attracted a wave of anti-greenwashing litigation seeking to hold major players in the aviation industry accountable for sensational claims of being sustainable, low-carbon, or contributing to net zero. Consumers can use legal mechanisms such as commercial practice or consumer protection regulations, as was done in a recent greenwashing complaint to the European Commission filed by consumer groups in nineteen countries against seventeen airlines.[4]

So far, six climate change-related cases have been brought against major airlines: four in Europe, one in the US, and one in Brazil. They stemmed from complaints received by UK and US advertising standards boards as well as the European Commission, which have already successfully ordered Ryanair, Lufthansa, and Etihad to pull their ad campaigns.[5]

In each of these three cases, authorities found that terminology like "protecting the future," "sustainable aviation," or "low-emissions airline" amounted to willful misleading of consumers and breached advertising regulations.

Sustainable Aviation Fuels

The aviation industry is placing some big bets on the future of sustainable aviation fuels to reduce CO_2 emissions by up to 80 percent over conventional jet fuels. SAF-enabled airplanes can be fueled by oil from plants and nuts, forestry and agricultural waste, and gases from steel mills.

Because of limited production and distribution capacity, the cost of SAF is high. However, since 2011, the year they were certified for commercial aviation, more than 225,000 commercial flights have been powered by SAFs and six billion liters of SAFs are in current forward purchase agreements by airlines.[6]

The main challenge surrounding SAFs is that producing them on a global scale is currently unsustainable. For example, it would require about half of the UK's agricultural land to keep that country's airlines flying on SAF at today's levels of travel—which will only increase in the future.[7] That same agricultural land is also earmarked for food production and renewable energy growth, so competition for available land is set to heat up.

Innovation Breakthroughs Required

Hydrogen is a clean-burning fuel that's seen as a longer-term solution to sustainable aviation, but producing sufficient green hydrogen fuel is a major challenge. Globally, the aviation demand for hydrogen by 2050 could be as much as 70 million tonnes per year—coincidentally about the same as the world's recent annual production of hydrogen, but most of that was grey hydrogen used for petrochemicals and ammonia.

"Grey hydrogen" is a term used to describe hydrogen produced from natural gas (primarily methane) and high-temperature steam. It's called "grey" because it releases greenhouse gas emissions into the atmosphere.

"Blue hydrogen" is the same as grey hydrogen except that it's coupled with carbon capture and storage technology, so the CO_2 is not emitted into the atmosphere. It's most commonly stored in underground formations.

Green hydrogen is produced using renewable energy sources, such as wind, solar, and hydropower, to split water into hydrogen and oxygen (a process known as electrolysis). This is the most ideal form of hydrogen because it has a much lower CO_2 footprint, but there simply isn't enough renewable power available to produce enough green hydrogen to fly us all.

According to the International Renewable Energy Agency (IRENA), the world will need another 19 exajoules of green hydrogen in the energy system in 2050.[8] That's an enormous amount of energy, equivalent to the energy consumption of many continents.

While annual growth rates for wind and solar are increasing, it's nowhere near fast enough for the world to align with Paris Agreement goals. The share of available renewables must increase six times faster to meet agreed climate goals, according to a 2019 IRENA report. Several terawatts of renewable energy will be needed to produce a sufficient supply of green hydrogen, but that seems secondary to the demand from the rapidly growing electricity sector, which needs to decarbonize while simultaneously powering ever-larger shares of the heating and transport sectors.[9]

The Jet Zero Council was formed by the UK Government in 2021 to help meet the government's "net zero by 2050" commitment. The council, a partnership between industry and government, brings together senior leaders in aviation, aerospace, and academia to drive the development of new technologies and innovative ways to cut aviation emissions. The council is working to industrialize and commercialize clean aviation and aerospace technologies and develop a coordinated approach to the policy and regulatory framework needed to deliver net-zero aviation by 2050.[10]

The Jet Zero Council aims to deliver a zero-emission transatlantic flight within a generation—a groundbreaking milestone as worthy of commemoration as the Wright Brothers' first flight.

Challenges to Making Mobility More Sustainable

Awareness and Motivation: There's a lack of awareness and demand for sustainable transport options among event attendees. Many may not be aware of the environmental impacts of their travel choices, or they may lack the incentives to choose more sustainable modes of transport. For example, a survey by ecolibrium found that 50 percent of UK festivalgoers were aware of their travel carbon footprint, but only 20 percent were willing to pay more for greener options.

However, as the impacts of climate change and air pollution become increasingly evident and urgent, more people are becoming conscious of their travel choices, and demand for sustainable transport options is growing among event attendees and stakeholders. We're going to have to figure out ways to incentivize and simplify sustainable travel for audiences.

Infrastructure: There may be a lack of infrastructure and policy support for sustainable transport solutions in and around your venue. Many event destinations may not have adequate services to accommodate different modes of sustainable transport, such as bike lanes, electric vehicle (EV) charging stations, mass transit, rail, coaches, or car-sharing platforms. However, if you do have access to any of these options, utilize them as much as possible.

Political Will: Many countries do not have policies or regulations to support the development and adoption of sustainable transport solutions, such as subsidies, taxes, standards, or targets. You have an opportunity to inspire change by demonstrating to event participants what the future could look like if these solutions were prioritized.

Complexity: Events may have different travel characteristics depending on their size, location, duration, audience, and purpose. Take advantage of those characteristics when you can. For example, a large international conference will have more air travel emissions than a small local festival, but it may also have more opportunities to influence attendee behavior through ticketing or communication strategies.

Tips to Advancing Sustainable Mobility

Make Your Purpose Worth It

Transportation and mobility are commonly seen as essential for putting on live events. Even at the height of the global pandemic—for a conference about climate change—there was still a strong desire on the part of international delegates to participate in person at COP26, even though virtual participation was completely enabled.

"They had to be in the room," Mark Bannister, one of the COP26 organizers, told me. "Yes, they could stay at home and participate, but those delegations felt they would be at a disadvantage if they weren't there at the event." He added, "And I can see that. Having seen the amounts of discussion and the little huddles happening outside the room, none of that could have really been facilitated virtually." [11]

Then Mark said, "I kind of get why the travel and the carbon related to that was felt to be a worthy sacrifice. Because, hopefully, the benefit of being there in person would have outweighed the carbon cost of getting there. And I personally feel it did."

Effectively, what Mark is saying is that if the purpose behind the event is meaningful and the potential impact is significant, then the associated emissions may be worth it.

Ask yourself the question: Is my event worth it?

Focus on the event's main purpose, make sure it's something the world really needs, and keep it specific enough so that you know whether you've achieved it or not when it ends.

Encourage Low-Carbon Audience Travel

Promote walking, running clubs, cycling, carpooling programs, car sharing, shuttle buses, trains, coaches, and public transit to and from the event venue. Support for those transportation modes could come in the form of user-friendly maps, timing estimates for these options, shuttle bus services, or free public transit passes. You can leverage social media to promote sustainable options and incentivize participation with prize draws, early entry, VIP passes, or priority parking.

Provide concise information about the environmental impacts of travel. Use solutions-focused framing so that decisions (such as taking public transit) are consciously communicated as active and positive choices made by a like-minded group of audience members, rather than selfless sacrifices or inconveniences made by individuals acting alone.

Focus on user involvement; leverage carpooling and shuttle buses as community-building activations for your audience members to experience. Use professional photography to capture images of actual participants taking advantage of these options and amplify human stories that "show the change" and model positive behavior, rather than relying only on facts and figures to tell the story.

Activate Your Audience

In 2016, legendary Canadian marathoner Martin Parnell and filmmaker Kate McKenzie traveled to Afghanistan to participate in the second Marathon of Afghanistan and document the brave women and girls who risked their lives to train and participate. When they returned to Canada to tell this story of courage and hope through a book and award-winning documentary, both entitled *The Secret Marathon*, they uncovered many reports of people in their local community who also felt unsafe to go for a run or participate in the outdoors, especially at night.

Kate and Martin were inspired by what they saw in Afghanistan and what they heard in Canada to establish an annual walk and run event, known as the Secret 3K, which is held worldwide on International Women's Day to promote the idea that everyone should be free to run.

When *The Secret Marathon* film premiered in different markets, the local Secret 3K organizers and running clubs mobilized to coordinate meetups and runs to attend the screenings during film festivals and stand-alone events. It was a great way to engage their audience, strengthen community, and promote active, sustainable commuting.

Package Travel and Entry Together

Link travel opportunities to ticket purchase options at the outset of the user experience to produce the best results for encouraging more sustainable mobility, which may include advantageous pricing for travel by train or coach.

Engaging people about travel to the event during the point of purchase helps them to make decisions and plans in advance; more delayed communications about sustainable travel might require users to log back in (after losing the link, forgetting their password, etc.) to make changes. Most people simply won't do that. The simpler the process, the better.

Ask your staff and volunteers to register for the event online using a complimentary code and solicit their feedback to improve the user experience as it relates to planning for sustainable mobility during the registration process.

You can set defaults to opt **out** of shuttle buses rather than opt **in**. This creates an assumption that everyone is in unless they tell you otherwise.

In 2022, a music, art, and spiritualism festival called the Greenbelt Festival in the UK offered free shuttle buses from the train station directly to people's campsites. As a result, public transport users doubled that year to 9 percent.[12]

Links to public transit and car-sharing platforms can be included in the event registration section along with clear travel information that might include a map of the site, nearest bus stops, train stations, EV charging stations, and safe cycle routes.

Provide secure cycle storage at the event, and ensure people are aware of it in advance. Consider having a bike mechanic service on-site. Offer incentives for people traveling by bike, such as a free program or reserved camping. Offer guided rides led by a local cycling organization or encourage people to self-organize cycle groups using an online discussion forum.

Charge extra for car and camper van passes. If ticket sales are robust enough, increase parking charges to encourage people to share or leave their car at home. Make it clear that driving impacts the environment and (if possible) that the additional parking fees will be reinvested into increasing sustainable mobility initiatives.

A Tyndall Centre for Climate Change report proposed that reducing car parking by 20 percent could lower festival audience travel emissions (excluding flights) by 10 percent. They recommend that festivals set targets to incrementally reduce car parking use over a few years.[13]

Subsidize Commutes

OpenAir St. Gallen attracts nearly thirty thousand people and is one of the oldest and biggest open-air music festivals in Switzerland.[14] It takes place in the Sittertobel nature reserve, just fifteen minutes from the local train station, which forms a natural border of the festival site. "What is unique about OpenAir St. Gallen is that the campsite is integrated into the festival site," explained Désirée Messmer, who manages staff and volunteers and is responsible for the event's sustainability.

The organizers of OpenAir St. Gallen recognized one of the reasons festival-goers preferred to arrive by car rather than public transport was because the latter is often more expensive. As a result, the festival subsidizes travel by public transport to make it more affordable. It works with Swiss Federal Railways to offer festivalgoers a 50 percent discount on train tickets to the festival.

City buses as well as shuttle buses between the parking area, the main train station, and the festival site have been included in the festival ticket, and the festival tries to make traveling by car less attractive by limiting the parking spaces available and making them expensive to secure.

The festival has invested in new mobility-related programs each year, and they were able to increase the number of visitors arriving by public transport, bike, or on foot from 47 percent in 2010 to 83 percent in 2019.

Fly Efficiently

It's best to offer sustainable options to your audience, but some will still fly, regardless. Plan your event with their travel experience in mind and explore partnership opportunities to offset the cost of public transit, trains, or coaches. Encourage audience members to select a direct flight with an airline that's demonstrably committed to reducing its impact on the planet.

By any means necessary, strongly discourage using private planes to attend your event. "A private jet is the most polluting form of transport you can take," according to a report by Transport & Environment, a European clean transport campaign organization. "The average private jet emits two tonnes of carbon an hour," which is fourteen times more polluting, per passenger, than commercial planes and fifty times more polluting than trains.[15]

You. Smart. Thing.

A digital travel assistance service in the UK called You. Smart. Thing. offers multi-modal routing, which can be customized to enable event organizers to send content-enhanced wayfinding and curated door-to-door travel plans that nudge visitors toward low-carbon travel options such as cycle hubs, charge points, shuttle bus service, or a rideshare to drop-off and pickup points. The platform can be used for travel demand management, to handle disruptions, improve accessibility, promote active travel, measure transit-based CO_2 emissions, and for highly targeted marketing to incentivize behavior change and enhance the visitor experience.

You. Smart. Thing. claims on average, events utilizing their service experienced a 30 percent decrease in visitor CO_2e by influencing modal choice.

Address Supplier Footprint

Encourage procurement managers and bookers to consider minimizing transport wherever possible; combining loads or ordering numbers of units that are transport efficient are two ways of doing this.

Moving goods by road typically consumes about 50 percent of all global diesel. Light commercial vehicles and heavy goods vehicles (HGV) make up 15 percent and 5 percent, respectively, of travel miles in the UK. Empty-load HGV mileage (the miles a truck that has delivered goods has to travel empty to base) is estimated at 30 percent of the total.

In the Vision: 2025 Green Industry survey results from 2022, about half of the 119 festivals and events that responded reported they had comprehensive travel services in place (such as shuttle buses, dedicated coaches, and secure cycle parking). Four out of five events are communicating with audiences about travel choices, but only 50 percent are doing so with their crews, and less than 40 percent with their artists, speakers, or suppliers.[16]

It seems inevitable that road freight using diesel fuel will eventually transition to new technologies including electric trucks, hydrogen fuel cells, liquified natural gas, and advanced biofuels, but all these solutions are currently very challenging to deploy at scale. We can therefore expect that contractor transport will be diesel-powered for some time and produce significant greenhouse gas emissions as part of your supply chain. As a result, your focus should be on reducing the number of contractor vehicle miles.

Engage Artists and Speakers

Consider booking artists who are already on tour in your area to save them from making a direct flight to your venue. For this reason, the Greenbelt Festival adopted a policy of inviting performers with tour dates around the time of their event.

Investing in a local talent pipeline can also have positive environmental impacts over the long term. For example, the Folk Fest has managed a dynamic singer-songwriter program over multiple decades; this has produced several local emerging artists that were featured at the annual festival. They did not need to be flown in for the event, and, best of all, they remained loyal returning performers even after achieving notoriety, as was the case with one of my favorites, Reuben and the Dark.

Another amazing band—Coldplay—recently released a sustainability report illustrating the impact they had while touring, with a focus on reducing their environmental impact. The report highlights the need to start by measuring the current state to determine a benchmark. Coldplay aimed to reduce their footprint by 50 percent against their benchmark. Coldplay sent a "sustainability rider" to venues ahead of time and worked with Showpower to design and deploy a first-of-its-kind smart grid battery power system for the 12-show European tour. The Coldplay concert in Coimbra, Portugal, marked the world's first major stadium show powered by 100 percent battery power.

Some performers travel long distances on tour buses. These are ecological emergencies on wheels, especially if diesel-powered and left idling for long periods of time. I've seen musicians dump full loads of raw sewage from their tour buses right in the middle of a pristine event site on their way out. Provide the tour an opportunity to sustainably dispose of their raw sewage and wastewater as well as recycling and compost. Be sure to communicate with handlers in advance that you have a plan for managing their waste. Encourage positive environmental behavior by outlining expectations in the booking contracts and seek media coverage for your most savvy eco-conscious talent. Then celebrate their efforts as part of your audience communications.

Go Electric

A number of countries, including the US, Canada, and the UK, are in the process of phasing out sales of new cars and vans that run on gasoline and diesel. This is expected to significantly ramp up the adoption of electric vehicles.

The transition from fossil fuels to biofuels, hydrogen, and renewable power is a monumental shift, and it's likely to take longer than we need it to. We can't take anything for granted because all the emissions reductions we produce at events now buy us more time to make the major shifts we'll need in our infrastructure, food, energy, and mobility systems later.

A transition to EVs alone won't be sufficient. The decarbonization pathway can't be all about replacing fossil-fueled vehicles with electric ones; it also offers an important opportunity to change behavior and the way people view mobility in general. What we need is not just a policy and a technologically led transition but a motivational breakthrough.

The increase in EVs leads to greater demand for charging stations at events.

Consider establishing partnerships to enable the installation of several EV charging stations, ideally under a canopy of solar panels to provide shadow and shelter against inhospitable weather.

One of the legacies left behind by the 2022 World Cup in Qatar is the electricity infrastructure built for the tournament. More than 25 percent of public transit buses were converted to electric, and one hundred new EV charging stations were installed.

A fleet of 311 eco-friendly hybrid and electric vehicles and 10 electric buses were provided by sponsors Hyundai and Kia for transporting teams, officials, and VIPs at the FIFA World Cup Qatar 2022.

Although the country is a significant producer, exporter, and consumer of fossil fuels, Qatar's new 800-megawatt solar power plant was a key feature of the World Cup's sizable construction efforts. This facility has the capacity to meet 10 percent of the country's peak power consumption, which is not insignificant in a desert country where all-day air conditioning is a part of life.

Upgrading the vehicle fleets and power equipment used for your event from fossil-fuel-powered to electric may seem like a disruptive, unbudgeted expense, but when you're playing catchup a few years from now, you may not have the luxury of time for incremental improvements, and you definitely won't be seen as a leader once it's common or mandatory. These changes make a significant difference to your overall emissions footprint, and the data you can collect from these vehicles will also be material for your tracking and reporting.

Some areas to consider going electric include:
- Vehicle rentals
- Transport trucks
- Shuttle buses
- Luxury vehicles for VIP airport pickups
- Golf carts and buggies
- Forklifts
- Parade vehicles and floats

Get started early. Explore partnerships with EV makers and resellers and engage your event venue to start the process of installing electric vehicle charging stations.

Measure Travel

The Net Zero Events Roadmap recommends that event organizers begin immediately to measure and report the travel emissions related to attendees and develop a net-zero pathway.[17]

If you don't have a dedicated sustainability officer, appoint a Green Champion or team who will be responsible for gathering and calculating travel data. Ask them to collect information from your whole team, including flight and gas station receipts.

Choose local suppliers and contractors when possible and collect information on *their* vehicle types and mileage, and the empty-load mileage associated with your event—especially from your key contractors. You can add a request for this in your service agreements.

Collect travel data from your artists and speakers when they arrive on-site or directly from their travel agent. Make this a part of contracts. For artists doing multiple dates on the same tour, apportion flight impacts accordingly.

Some of the travel data to collect will include:

- How people traveled, e.g., car, coach, plane, type of public transport, walking, or cycling
- How far they traveled, including return journeys
- How many they traveled with. If they used a private vehicle, e.g., a car, or camper van, how many passengers were there?

How to collect audience travel data:

- You may have zip code data from your ticket agent, which can be used to calculate the total and average mileage traveled by your audience.
- Use a survey to verify how your audience traveled—either at the event or as a follow-up online.
- You can ask your crew of volunteers to count how many people arrive by foot, bicycle, train, or car.
- If you charge for car parking or provide dedicated buses, travel data will be available in the ticketing information.

Despite what your instincts may tell you, the data you collect and report doesn't have to be perfect. If you don't know the exact mileage of your audience travel, for example, you can use an average based on the demographics of your attendee locations or from a survey that represents a good sample size. The consistency of measurement is important and the trajectory of whether that number is going up or down matters most.

Invest in Bicycle Infrastructure

Cycling is on the rise as young people are driving less. In a comprehensive 2018 study of driving trends, only 29 percent of seventeen-to-twenty-year-olds and 63 percent of twenty-one-to-twenty-nine-year-olds held driver's licences, down from 48 percent and 75 percent respectively for these age groups in the 1990s.[18]

Like many cities around the world, Calgary has an active biking community that mobilized very effectively around the political advocacy for more and safer municipal biking infrastructure. That city infrastructure, including an impressive network of separated bike lanes, can take cyclists right to the front gates of Stampede Park faster and safer than ever before, but once they arrived at the urban venue covering roughly ten square city blocks, there was no obvious place to lock up their bikes. This noticeable lack of infrastructure resulted in hundreds of bikes chained to trees, lampposts, and other strange places. They often blocked pedestrian pathways and made it especially difficult for those with mobility challenges, wheelchairs, or strollers. The bikes were often kicked, vandalized, or stolen. The frustrations over this issue, combined with the parade controversy mentioned earlier, caused a major public relations problem, frequently highlighted over social media.

Because of our existing relationship and the successful waste management program we developed for the Calgary Stampede, my environmental services company was in a strong position to pitch a new Bike Valet program.

The plan was to staff the Bike Valet with friendly attendants who would check people's bicycles in and out, like a coat check system. Even though most would be locked up, we ensured the bike cage was staffed to give people greater confidence that their bikes wouldn't be stolen or vandalized.

In 2015, we launched the new program with a musical celebration and pancake breakfast on the first day of Stampede in partnership with Cyclepalooza—the

> Bicycle, bicycle, better than a car.
> Spokes on my wheels and shiny handlebars.
> With the wind in my hair and pedals under my feet.
> Bicycle, bicycle, fly over concrete.
> — Frances England

small fringe festival celebrating cycling culture in the city. The main organizer, Gerardo Marquez, promoted the launch to the cycling community as a satellite event, calling it Stampedepalooza. The City was also involved and leveraged the opportunity to promote Calgary's brand-new cycle tracks—an impressive network of separated and protected biking lanes throughout the city core, newly opened that very week, after years of squabbling at City Hall.

A stationary bike powered a bubble-making machine at the launch event—a visual spectacle for the media who arrived to cover this unusual partnership. None of us could have predicted how popular the Stampede Bike Valet would be.

> I thought of that while riding my bicycle.
> — Albert Einstein on the theory of relativity

A surprising number of cyclists showed up. Some used the service because they didn't have their own locks, and some families chose to leave child bike trailers and baby carriages at the Bike Valet so they could better maneuver through the crush of the crowds.

The program was oversubscribed, so we expanded it later from the one small pilot at a single entrance to bike parking at three different locations. My team innovated the idea further, providing opt-in opportunities for cyclists to have their chains greased or get other simple tune-ups while they spent the day in the park.

One of my team members began photographing particularly stylish cyclists and young families (with permission, of course) and posting the pics to social media under the hashtag #BikeChicYYC. (YYC, the Calgary airport code, is often used as shorthand for the city.) It became a meme.

We checked in approximately five hundred bikes in that first year, and the program grew to serve more than one thousand cyclists over time. Cyclepalooza saw record numbers at their festival after appearing on the news alongside the Calgary Stampede, and the next year, cyclists became a common fixture during the Stampede parade.

Take Responsibility

The GHG emissions associated with travel are your greatest reputational risk. However, given the perceived low level of influence event organizers have over attendee travel emissions, they're often excluded from events' Scope 3 emissions calculations. That is a grave mistake.

As an event organizer, you must take responsibility for this difficult challenge that is central to the future of this industry. Although there are no easy answers, there are tremendous opportunities to influence supplier practices and audience travel choices. There's a lot of room for creative enhancements to the visitor experience and possibilities for collaboration with speakers, performers, travel bookers, venues, tourism boards, local transit authorities, and airlines.

9

Leverage Procurement to Build a Circular Economy

Sustainable procurement ensures that buyers obtain the best value
for money when purchasing the most sustainable goods and services
from the most sustainable suppliers, in support of the buyer's
organizational purpose and strategic goals.

— Bob Willard, *The Sustainability Advantage:
Seven Business Case Benefits of a Triple Bottom Line*

Who Killed the Plates?

When festivalgoers purchase their delicious food from a vendor at the Calgary
Folk Music Festival, their meal is typically served on a compostable plate or food
shell. Until recently, however, the plates at the family-friendly Folk Fest were
reusable plastic. What changed?

Folk Fest organizers began to question the life-cycle impacts associated with
transporting the plates for washing and reuse throughout the festival. I assured
them that reused material is superior to single-use items 100 percent of the
time. Anyone focused (as was in this case) on the footprint of a golf cart run
to a nearby hotel and the wastewater associated with washing is ignoring the
emissions, water use, and biodiversity impacts associated with grazing land,
extracting materials, manufacturing, and transporting new products to market
regardless of whether they are plastic or compostable.

In fact, 70 percent of greenhouse gas emissions and 90 percent of biodiversity loss and water stress are tied to material extraction handling and

long-haul transport of manufactured goods, according to the 2023 Circularity Gap Report.[1]

Having a circular product supply should always be encouraged over the linear supply-and-disposal model used at most major events and festivals. The reusable plates program at the Calgary Folk Music Festival was a great example of a circular *supply*, a business model central to a circular economy.

The five circular business models are: *circular supply*, *sharing*, *resource recovery*, *product life extension*, and *product-as-a-service*.

Rise of the Circular Economy

The temporary nature of events has caused the industry to evolve such that infrastructure is specifically designed for short-term use. The production and disposal of items significantly contribute to an event's carbon footprint. To move toward net zero, the industry must adopt a more *circular* approach to producing events by using reusable items and sustainable materials in a thoughtful approach to significantly reduce waste.

This approach is counter to the "take-make-use-waste" economic model that rewards companies for extracting as much raw material as possible to produce and sell as many products to customers as possible. This model also rewards suppliers of disposable items because single use often translates into continuous sales.

Because this linear system has achieved maturity in our society, it's almost always cheaper to source goods and services using this approach. This is true not only for food and beverage orders but for everything you need for your event: electronics, power equipment, building materials, fleets, tents, linens, centerpieces, and speaker gifts.

The approach has led to deficiencies at both the extraction end, where the mining or sourcing of raw materials has created tremendous ecological and social harm, as well as the waste end, where we've amassed mountains of garbage that can't be broken down naturally or processed efficiently.

In a circular economy, the outputs of one

> In our current economy, we take materials from the Earth, make products from them, and eventually throw them away as waste—the process is linear. In a circular economy, by contrast, we stop waste being produced in the first place.
>
> — Ellen MacArthur

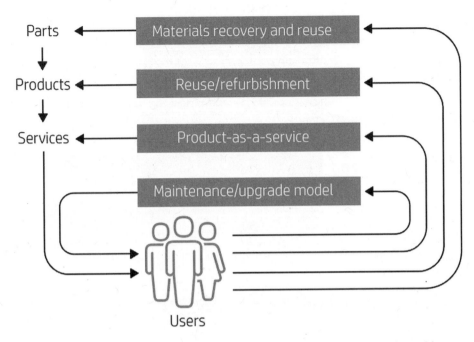

FIGURE 9.1. Circular Economy Ecosystem. Source: HP Sustainable IT Purchasing Guide

production process become the inputs of another, and the process is repeated this way as long as possible. Such a system significantly reduces the need to extract more resources and discard them after only one use—into waterways and oceans, landfills, and the broken recycling system discussed earlier in the book.

As you consider your purpose, I encourage you to engage your suppliers to find a new balance between upfront costs and long-term value. When you choose the cheaper option, you're voting with your dollars against the circular economy.

Circular Procurement

Circular procurement requires securing agreements with your suppliers to ensure you purchase products for your event that align with one of the five circular business models so they will/can be reused or further processed after their initial use.

It may seem counterintuitive to use another lens to screen suppliers when inflation has driven prices higher and supply chain disruptions are more common than ever. Even finding suppliers with enough capacity to deliver on time can be challenging. However, procurement is almost certainly your greatest expenditure. So, it's the single most powerful tool you have to influence a positive impact. Institutional purchasing of goods and services represents more than $10 trillion of spending in the US each year according to the Sustainable Purchasing Leadership Council.[2]

There may be roadblocks to a more sophisticated procurement process, so start now and learn as you go. Collect, learn from, and analyze procurement data to test and plan a new approach that helps deliver the impact you're striving for.

Circularity at COP26

The COP26 that took place in Glasgow in 2021 set some great circularity benchmarks for international conferences by renting what they could and either returning or donating material post-event. Approximately 96 percent of all products were reused and reusable. Mark Bannister and his COP26 team sourced as many certified sustainable materials as possible, and the recycled content of all products were determined to be approximately 25 percent.

They also focused on increasing their efficiency and avoided significant volumes of GHG emissions by consolidating their transport services. Rather than rely on each supplier to provide their own transportation of goods, COP26 organizers contracted one company to manage all collections from suppliers so there were no half-empty trucks arriving on-site. Similarly, furniture rental returns and donations of set design pieces were optimized to limit the number of trips required. Best of all, the transport trucks being used were fueled with biofuel rather than biodiesel or gasoline.

Procurement Is the Trojan Horse

All too often, short-term cost savings drive purchasing decisions, while the massive opportunity that purchasing offers to drive change into core business operations goes unaddressed.

Author Bob Willard calls procurement a "Trojan horse" for legitimizing sustainability considerations when making important business decisions. Sustainable procurement assigns heavy weighting to the sustainability attributes of both the products and the suppliers themselves. Sustainable procurement makes sustainability matter enough that it incentivizes suppliers to want to outperform their competitors with more positive impacts on people and planet. When buyers realize that they get the best value by taking sustainability factors into consideration when making procurement decisions, they will start to take sustainability-related factors into consideration when they make *any* important business decisions. Sustainable procurement is the Trojan horse that enables this transition by both buyers/event planners and suppliers to more sustainable mindsets and business models.

Perhaps diversity, local content, human rights, or environmental footprint is addressed in a code of conduct or broad contractual commitment to *do your reasonable best*, but every study I've seen about supply chain practices confirms the vast majority of requests for proposals (RFPs) in the market do not award or even consider any form of social or environmental benefits in procurement decisions. Behavior change requires formal mutual consent, strategic planning, training, constant reinforcement, and monitoring—and consequences when targets are missed. A desired outcome vaguely worded in a code of conduct that isn't regularly revisited is not going to do the trick.

People often assume sustainable procurement refers to securing "local" suppliers because sourcing locally can be a viable way to eliminate many environmental impacts associated with long-haul transportation while injecting revenue into the community most impacted by the event, but that may not necessarily be the best solution available to you. Larger suppliers have the capacity to invest in solutions that integrate a cross-section of important concerns at scale such as product design, waste reuse, and access to data to track impacts, including emissions.

Sustainable procurement is a tool that can be used to address many types of issues. If you're concerned about climate change, materials usage, biodiversity, child labor, human rights, diversity and inclusion, and/or Indigenous reconciliation, you can leverage your procurement processes to address these concerns in a very practical way. For example, you can:

- Require product-level certifications such as Fair Trade, Energy Star, and Forest Stewardship Council (FSC)

- Introduce requirements that suppliers establish science-based targets
- Require living wages from all your suppliers and their subcontractors
- Allocate a percentage of your overall spending to certified Indigenous-owned businesses and equity-seeking populations

In essence, procurement is a market force, and the signals you send to that market can create awareness and profound change.

What the Research Tells Us

A 2020 research study by York University's Schulich School of Business in Toronto looked at fifty RFPs from a broad range of national, regional, and local public sector institutions. It found that, despite many having clear commitments to achieving net-zero emissions, only 12 percent of the RFPs had any weighting[3] attached to sustainability considerations, and it was largely insignificant compared to what was actually scored. You can guess that, in the end, it came down to the lowest-cost provider and perceived "*most dependable*," which is code for "we've worked with them before, and we get on well."

Unconscious bias shows up here, too, because less well-known suppliers who might represent a cultural community and employ underemployed or undereducated local workers may not be viewed as "most dependable" when compared to a well-known global brand that outsources to low-wage labor and regularly undercuts competitors to secure contracts.

The lack of sustainability integration into supply chains is a significant missed opportunity given the urgent need for action, the limited resources available, and the potential associated with procurement—your largest, most consequential area of spending.

No Net Zero Without Supply Chains

International climate negotiations like the ones taking place at COP were supposed to harness global consensus around climate solutions. However, they are not delivering on the urgent need to reduce emissions in all areas of society. While most governments and big banks are on board, small and medium-sized companies and suppliers are largely disengaged from the process. This is a major problem because these organizations represent the majority of activity in our economy and, therefore, any real reduction of emissions requires their participation.

Establishing sustainable business-to-business relationships with these smaller companies is one of the most effective levers to address climate change today. These companies are going to be incentivized into action if their customers demand it, and there's a reasonable expectation of a return on investment.

As an event organizer, you're the customer. If you're not questioning your suppliers about purpose, net zero, circularity, diversity, and inclusion and integrating that language into your bid documents and service agreements (along with data and performance expectations), then you're basically communicating it's not that important to you.

Working with suppliers to identify meaningful emissions reductions that are relevant for their business is a large part of where the change must take place and where your stakeholders likely expect you to take more responsibility.

Gone are the days when we could say that recycling was done and donations were made. Those are minimum expectations. The easy stuff is commonplace. We're entering a more sophisticated era. We have to accept our responsibility to address the more difficult systemic challenges such as the broken recycling system, an economy that rewards the lowest cost over the greatest long-term value, and the fact that no laws exist to enforce such things.

Net-Zero Procurement

Net-zero procurement focuses buyers on obtaining the *best value* when purchasing the *most climate-friendly goods and services* from suppliers who are *committed to science-based net-zero targets*. It's a focused subset of *sustainable* procurement and can be used to quick-start sustainable procurement by focusing on climate-related aspects of suppliers' sustainability performance (rather than the supplier's *overall* sustainability performance) on a number of complex and intersectional matters such as soil and ocean impacts, waste, transportation, and energy use.

Structuring an RFP and service agreement around net-zero procurement means heavily weighting the suppliers' performance on embedding climate change considerations into their strategy, operations, and public communication about their GHG reductions. Doing this intentionally during the tender process gives *preferential treatment* to suppliers who are the most committed to net-zero targets, who offer low-carbon goods and services, and who are transitioning toward decarbonized business models.

Scope 3 Is Where the Action Is

While a significant portion of your event's impact falls outside your direct control, it does squarely land within your sphere of influence. The time to significantly scale up supply chain action is now.

What we're witnessing is a gradual shift in focus from direct operational impacts to Scope 3 impacts. Scope 3 management is critical if you want to stay ahead of new regulations, expand value creation, and better manage your risks. The tricky part is that meaningfully addressing Scope 3 impacts means that everyone you work with *and everyone they work with* also needs to address it.

According to a 2021 McKinsey and Company report, purchased goods and services typically make up 70 percent of any organization's Scope 3 emissions.[4] Some of the organizations I worked with through CBSR's Sustainable Procurement Fellowship see up to 90 percent of their emissions as Scope 3.

Furthermore, the Carbon Disclosure Project (CDP) estimates that supply chain emissions are more than eleven times higher than operational emissions,

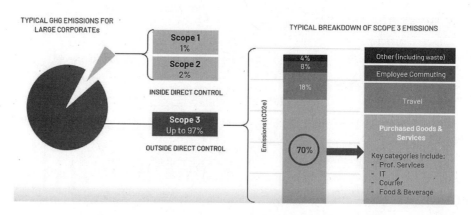

FIGURE 9.2. Largest Share of Emissions Is Outside Your Direct Control.
Source: Carbon Intelligence

and yet only 38 percent of organizations reported engaging their suppliers to reduce their carbon footprint.[5]

Social Procurement

Every purchase has a social, economic, cultural, and environmental impact. Social procurement is about using your existing purchasing budget and process to capture those impacts and help shape inclusive, vibrant, and healthy communities.

Local

When I speak to people about redirecting their procurement dollars, they assume I am encouraging them to buy local, and they often complain about the higher prices and fewer options available in local communities. There is little doubt that sourcing close to the event venue is a powerful way to localize the benefits and maintain positive relationships. This is especially true where your event brings in a lot of tourists (which may have both positive and negative effects on the community).

However, "local" is not the only lens I recommend applying to strategic decisions. Procurement targets should reflect your overall purpose and most material impacts. You should be asking, Who are my priority stakeholders, partners, and future audience members? Then leverage your procurement as a strategic tool to establish relationships and shared prosperity with those groups.

However, it's not uncommon for event planning to go on autopilot—to the point where they're sourcing the same high-end meat served in the same chafing set with the same bouquet of flowers used at several previous events. The result can be a generic and uninteresting esthetic no different from similar events. Sourcing locally and from cultural communities adds a unique flare, a tip of the hat, and inclusivity to your event, not to mention an economic bump to the local community.

Social Procurement at COP26

COP26 was an early adopter of the UK Government's commitment to embedding social values and measures to combat climate change into major contracts. Organizers incorporated a 10 percent weighting, which arguably is not enough but had the desired effect of sending a strong signal to the market about the circular, reduced emissions, and supplier diversity preferences most important to them.

The COP26 team identified opportunities to deliver social value through engagement with local charities and small and mid-size enterprises and to provide charitable donations derived from the event build and disassembly. A large number of items used for COP26 were donated to local charities, projects, and low-income families. These were facilitated by EventCycle that helps event planners reduce leftover materials by repurposing and redistributing them to charities and community groups that are in need, creating a positive social impact in the process.

Donations included:
- 18,000 yd² (15,000 m²) of carpets
- 1,400 yd² (1,200 m²) of textiles
- 5,000 lb (2,300 kg) of sandbags
- 2,700 scenic set pieces
- 63 gallons (240 L) of paint
- 6 tonnes of wood

Social Procurement at Live Nation

Live Nation recently committed to *"dedicating more of our annual $2B spend on global sourcing to Black and minority-owned vendors by 2025."* This is a welcome move, but it would have been even more effective with some clarification of a percentage. Nevertheless, they have sparked the discussion, and that's important in the drive toward circularity and net zero.

Social Impact of Reusable Plates

The reusable plates discontinued at the Calgary Folk Music Festival have an unlimited lifespan, which reduced waste and resource use. The program had some other unexpected results too. It harnessed the circularity principle of the sharing economy and created economic opportunities in addition to reduced resource consumption. As a way of promoting the event year-round and providing a valuable community service, the Calgary Folk Music Festival rented the plates out to trusted community partners on the condition they be returned clean and intact.

During the main festival, food vendors paid $1.50 (CAD $2) to the organizers for each reusable plate, and that cost was passed on to festivalgoers, who were encouraged to take their soiled plates to one of the return areas (which included waste stations to scrape leftover food into). Anyone who returned a plate received a *toonie*, a two-dollar coin.

Without fail, you could count on several enterprising kids to approach festivalgoers and offer to save them the trouble of returning the plates. Some of those kids probably finished the weekend with enough toonies to buy a Star Wars animatronic droid.

Don't Let Vendors Drive Your Sustainability Programs

Approximately fifteen thousand reusable plates were in circulation during any given Folk Fest weekend. These were branded with the funding sponsor's name, the Calgary Folk Music Festival name, and the signature prairie cow logo that has adorned Folk Fest swag for more than three decades.

Some festival staff didn't like the logistics of handling money except entrance fees and concessions, and others worried that the free plates offered to performers backstage end up being returned to the front of the house and come out of pocket for the festival. Many went missing over the years—costing the festival more than a toonie each. There are probably several Folk Fest fans out there who have amassed matching festival plate sets in their cupboards at home.

However, it was the food vendors who ultimately killed the plate return program at the Calgary Folk Music Festival. They didn't like having to charge $2 on top of their already expensive meals, and they didn't want to buy the plates at the beginning of the festival. Vendors wanted their food packaged in clamshell containers, and since the festival was already pushing them to source compostable cutlery, adding compostable clamshells to their order felt like a natural extension.

The cost of abandoning the much-loved reusable festival plates was high. In addition to the sponsor benefits, valuable service to partner organizations, and the entrepreneurship lessons to kids at the Calgary Folk Fest, the plate-return program was an effective audience education tool. It created micro-moments of engagement, learning, and feedback at the plate-return stations. The home-style feeling associated with each festival meal helped to shape a culture of responsibility, environmental awareness, and community.

All the logistical challenges involved with a plate program are solvable. If enough sponsorship were secured to buy more plates, store them during the off-season, and make up for the cost of missing plates, it might even compensate for the money exchange associated with the program (sorry, kids). There's a need for incentives to ensure the success of a plate return program, but it might be better as an earned credit system associated with a broader environmental program—perhaps audience members could earn points to cash in for festival souvenirs like water bottles, t-shirts, and music.

Steps for an Effective Sustainable Procurement Program

Align with Purpose

Procurement goals need to be connected to your purpose and integrated within your overall strategy, systems, structures, and processes. This translates to *specific*, *measurable*, *realistic*, and *timely* (SMART) procurement goals that are tied to strategic sustainability outcomes.

When engaging suppliers regarding your purpose, begin with a focus on the impact you want to have, then explore how to best achieve that impact in collaboration with your suppliers—with the most effective return on your and their investment. Your suppliers should realize business benefits from helping you achieve your goals.

Align with Partners that Share Your Purpose

The most common objection I hear when encouraging more supplier engagement is something along the lines of this: "We represent such a small percentage of their business that we're not influential enough to change their behavior."

Approaching suppliers as part of an industry or inter-industry consortium is one way to address this, and it is a very powerful tactic. But remember that change will not happen overnight. It may require you to continue working with a large global supplier while investing time and resources into a smaller supplier and mentoring them to scale up to meet your long-term needs.

It's up to you to clearly articulate your purpose and find the right partners that share the same or similar purpose. You are the conductor of your orchestra, and all those that are part of your value chain represent your event to some degree.

COP26 Sustainability Governing Principles

As an example, suppliers for COP26 were selected based on the strength of their stated ability to help achieve the following Sustainability Governing Principles:

- Actively manage the potential impact on the environment of their activity
- Provide an accessible and inclusive setting
- Encourage healthy living
- Ensure a safe and secure atmosphere
- Encourage more sustainable behavior
- Promote the use of responsible resources throughout the supply chain
- Leave a positive legacy

"We asked prospective suppliers to demonstrate how they could support our commitments and aspirations and commit to more sustainable ways of working themselves," said Mark Bannister about the COP26 event. He added, "This formed part of the evaluation of their tenders." [6]

Integrate It

The Sustainable Procurement Toolkit is a wonderfully simple and free open-source tool you can use to quickly integrate sustainability considerations into any procurement process. It was developed by Bob Willard and is available on his website at sustainabilityadvantage.com/sp/toolkit.

Contract Management

It's very important that sustainable procurement outcomes and expectations are embedded into banquet event orders, supplier contracts, and management processes. It can't simply be written into a supplier code of conduct and expected to be followed because codes of conduct have no mechanism for accountability. Sustainability performance metrics must be incorporated into the agreements to provide clarity on how progress is going to be assessed.

Requests for Proposals

The most underutilized solution for addressing sustainability priorities and attracting sustainable suppliers is the transformation of your procurement process to focus on reducing emissions, enabling circularity, and incorporating social impacts, including preferences for certified Indigenous, Black, and women-owned businesses and social enterprises. It sounds quite simple to revise your RFP to communicate your environmental or social impact preferences, but it's rarely done. Most RFPs do not mention emission reductions or sustainability requirements of any kind.

Integration

Expectations for COP26 suppliers were aligned with the COP26 Sustainability Governing Principles (given just above) and communicated at the tender stage. Suppliers were evaluated not just on value for money but on their approach to circularity and decarbonization, and demonstrating beneficial outcomes for the local environment, economy, and society.

By communicating emissions-reduction and sustainability ambitions upfront, they ensured that everyone involved was truly committed to the Governing Principles of sustainable development. This also encouraged suppliers to consider how they could improve the sustainability outcomes of their goods and services in the contract and propose innovative ways of working.

Make the Weighting Count

One of the most practical and effective things you can do to reduce your footprint and enhance the positive impact of your event is to allocate a significant-enough weighting in the supplier selection criteria toward those aligned with your desired sustainability outcomes. A minimum of 20 percent is best practice if you want to have a demonstrable effect.

You may need to work collaboratively with the person or team responsible for purchasing in order to change the allocation. And it may be that the venue you choose is the most critical decision in this area. Discuss your expectations as early as possible with them and consider making willingness to participate in this strategy a condition for venue selection.

Prioritize Using HIPO

When you're getting started, be careful about trying to do too much and pushing your suppliers too far too fast. Take on just a few initiatives at a time but focus on the most material and strategic opportunities by creating your *highest impact procurement opportunities* (HIPO) list. This is a targeted list of products, services, or projects that are deemed to have a high sustainability risk for the organization, or they are categories that are deemed to have highly positive or easy-to-achieve sustainability impacts.[7]

Recognize that 5 percent of your procurement is likely where 65 percent of your impacts, risks, and opportunities lie. Don't seek to create a checkbox exercise in contract clauses. Instead, seek to align your suppliers around your purpose and integrate more sustainability criteria into negotiations with new suppliers. Maintain clauses in your contracts that allow you to exit with 60 days' notice for nonperformance, sustainability included, so you're not stuck in bad contracts.

Manage Risks

In November 2022, the Canada Border Services seized two large shipments of clothing linked to forced labor in China.[8] In 2021, the German Parliament passed the Supply Chain Due Diligence Act, which renders large companies based in Germany responsible for social and environmental issues arising from their global supply chain networks. Those who violate the law in Germany face a fine of up to 2 percent of their annual revenue. Similar Canadian and American legislation is currently being considered. This includes prohibitions on child labor and forced labor and attention to occupational health and safety throughout the entire supply chain.

Be sure you never find yourself weeks or days out from your event and suddenly have to pivot because the government has seized your shipment of essential items because you didn't do the necessary due diligence to avoid exposure to forced labor. Too often, due diligence looks like a broad, meaningless statement in a code of conduct to *"do your reasonable best,"* but if you don't pursue suppliers with social and environmental goals as their primary driver, you are stuck with the reasonable best of a mediocre bunch.

Create Social Value

Some communities have a practice of developing Community Benefit Agreements (CBAs), particularly when new building infrastructure is involved. These legal agreements and contractual requirements can be powerful tools to ensure that local community members and disadvantaged people benefit from subcontracts issued by your prime contractors. They may involve negotiations between event organizers, local governments, and community representatives to outline specific commitments that address the unique needs and concerns of the affected neighborhoods.

One notable example was the CBA developed in collaboration with the Vancouver Organizing Committee for the 2010 Olympic and Paralympic Winter Games, the City of Vancouver, the Province of British Columbia, and the Government of Canada to drive investments into affordable housing, public transportation improvements, and sustainable urban development.

Such agreements can also be used to mitigate potential negative impacts while creating hiring, training, and procurement opportunities, cultural and environmental preservation initiatives, and other programs prioritized by and implemented in partnership with the local community.

Buy Social Canada has several excellent resources available to design and implement successful CBAs.[9]

Explore whether there's a fit for you and your event to take the 15 Percent Pledge (or one of the other pledge initiatives being fostered around the world). This is a US-based supportive ecosystem of buyers and sellers, mostly in the retail sector, who have committed to directing 15 percent of their sourcing toward Black-owned businesses.

The Canadian Council for Aboriginal Business is contributing to the push toward the CAD$100 billion Indigenous economy in Canada through an initiative called #SupplyChange. They are actively working to raise private and public sector procurement from Indigenous businesses to at least 5 percent of their total spend via an Aboriginal Procurement Marketplace. If the private sector in Canada were to increase procurement from Indigenous businesses to 5 percent, it would translate into US$17 billion. That would be a significant boost for the self-determination of Indigenous Peoples and communities, and it doesn't involve spending any additional funds outside of existing budgets.

Supplier Diversity

Given that procurement represents an event's largest spend, you might assume that diversity, local content, human rights, or environmental footprint are commonly factored into such decisions, but you would be incorrect. In reality, these issues almost never factor in, and it's a huge risk.

Can you better leverage your purchasing power to expand economic opportunities to Black, Indigenous, people of color (BIPOC), and women-owned services and goods providers? Even small changes can have a big impact on this often overlooked but essential part of event planning.

> It is time. It is time to increase the presence, visibility, and role of the emerging modern Indigenous economy.
>
> — Carol Anne Hilton, Author and Founder of Indigenomics Institute

There are over 60,000 Indigenous-owned businesses in Canada and roughly 26,000 in the US. Nearly all are small or medium-sized enterprises, which were some of the hardest hit by the COVID-19 pandemic.

Indigenous business owners face reduced access to traditional lenders such as banks, in part because those living on reservations (in the US) and reserves (in Canada) don't have ownership over their properties. The federal governments in both countries hold these lands in trust, which means they were set aside for the use and benefit of specific Indigenous tribes, but the government retained ownership. It also means Indigenous business owners typically can't leverage their homes as collateral to secure loans and are dependent on retained earnings, private savings, or specialized development corporations.[10]

Despite these and other challenges, Indigenous businesses contributed an estimated $36 billion to the US economy in 2020 and about the same amount in Canada. That number could quickly surge if these businesses were prioritized in more procurement policies.[11]

Social and sustainable procurement policies can send a strong signal to the market that this is an emerging priority. It provides a competitive advantage to the most sustainable, socially responsible, and best-managed organizations in the events industry, and provides a vested interest in the success of your event among your target audience, partners, and stakeholders.

Incorporate Total Cost of Ownership

It's commonly understood that most of a product's sustainability impacts are determined during the design stage. Continually improving design and encouraging organizations and their supply chains to do the same will drive the circular economy. For example, many organizations purchase technology without considering product lifespan and the end of the (first) life of those products. The potential for reuse is a critical design element that can be specified in bid documents. Value can be derived for your organization by including these costs in purchasing decisions and the concept of *total cost of ownership* (TCO).

Total cost of ownership involves considering *all* the costs associated with a product over its lifetime—from initial purchase through delivery and installation, use, maintenance, and disposal.[12] Many of these secondary costs are associated with social and environmental impacts, such as energy use, worker exposure, and landfill/incineration. Therefore, reducing a procurement's TCO is often a win for an organization's bottom line *and* a win for the sustainability impact you can have.[13]

Engage Suppliers

Long before you decide which suppliers to keep and which to exclude, start by using simple voluntary disclosure tools to collect data from your suppliers and set a basic baseline. Some of them may not be there yet, but may get there if they see the market moving in that direction. Others may surprise you by demonstrating they're already offering some sustainable options; you just never asked them about it.

The COP26 team also worked closely with their suppliers to reuse or rent items, minimizing bespoke builds and ensuring that materials would be repurposed after the event to give them a future life. "We wanted to show suppliers that there is a different way of doing things," said Mark, "and I know a couple of those key suppliers have carried on that way."

How to Find Sustainable Suppliers

To attract top suppliers who are loyal, innovative, and purpose-driven themselves, you need to communicate your purpose and goals to the market. As I mentioned, your RFP is a great place to do that.

Engage all your existing suppliers and invite them to join you on a purpose-driven journey with shared goals. Let them know you require tangible sustainability results that can be clearly communicated to your stakeholders.

There are software solutions you can invest in that enable you to screen for suppliers with a credible sustainability track record. EcoVadis is one example. You could also screen for suppliers certified by the International Standards Organization 14001, which would have assessed their performance and impacts against environmental commitments made. All these options are better suited to large international organizations such as the FIFA World Cup; they are cost prohibitive for most suppliers who fall into the small and medium-sized business category.

> The fastest way to green your business is to purchase from one that has already greened theirs.
>
> — adapted from Ray Anderson, former CEO of Interface Flooring

I've teamed up with Meegan Jones—author of *Sustainable Event Management: A Practical Guide,* and together we've built out an online database featuring suppliers with sustainability-related specialties. You can access the database at: suppliers.greeneventbook.com.[14]

The Vendry is another great event industry resource offering listings of venues and vendors local to your city in many parts of the world. You can filter the information to act as a resource for Black-owned businesses in your community.[15]

Buy Social Canada also has a directory on its website of social enterprise companies.[16]

Certified Social Enterprises

When you research event suppliers or agencies, look for organizations that qualify as a Minority Business Enterprise. The certification is given to a business that is at least 51 percent owned, operated, capitalized, and controlled by a woman or citizen of an ethnic minority. Similarly, Women Owned is an international initiative in support of female entrepreneurs and those who do business

> We can no longer define success as just greater profits. That's obviously important (no margin, no mission) but true success leads to a stronger and healthier community and environment as well.
>
> — Jay Coen Gilbert, Cofounder, B Labs

with them. The Women Owned logo certifies a business as being at least 51 percent owned, operated, and controlled by a woman or women.

Certifications can sometimes feel like paying someone to assess that you are who you say you are and then charging you an annual fee to reaffirm it. However, the most effective certification bodies also act as an ecosystem of like-minded business and community leaders with an aim to have a positive impact. In the case of B Corp certification for social enterprises, it is more like a movement.

B Corporation, run by a global nonprofit called B Lab, certifies the social and environmental performance of companies that undergo a self-assessment and verification process. To obtain and to maintain certification, companies must receive a minimum score of 80 on their assessment and integrate B Corp commitments to stakeholders into their governing documents. Companies must recertify every three years to retain their B Corp status as well as pay a yearly fee based on annual sales.

Having helped a number of companies obtain their B Corp certifications, including my own, I can attest that the process is rigorous and time-consuming. No fly-by-night organization would bother going through such a laborious process. There are currently 5,300 or so certified B Corps in 83 countries.

COP26 Supplier Engagement Program

Mark and his COP26 team worked collaboratively with suppliers throughout the planning and delivery of the event to reinforce the Sustainability Governing Principles and encourage suppliers to step up to the challenge. They also hosted training sessions for suppliers, encouraged them to appoint sustainability champions, and provided tips for using alternatives to plastic packaging in order to comply with the ban on anything wrapped in plastic brought to the site.

Mark told me that, despite the compressed timeline his team worked under, COP26 was strict with their sustainability demands: "We set out a two-page document." It laid out: "Here is how we expect you to work, here's how we expect you to source materials, and here's how we expect these materials to arrive on site."[17] In addition to the centralized transporting process mentioned earlier, suppliers could not provide any materials wrapped in plastic. All materials had to be banded together using cables that could be reused during strike or some other method that produced zero waste.

Awareness Required

We need a lot more event organizers demanding sustainability performance from their vendors. However, few small businesses and suppliers even know about circularity, net zero, and social impact, let alone how to advance these opportunities through procurement. To do your part in transforming the status quo, get more intimately involved in your procurement processes. If you have an individual or group that is responsible for procurement, engage them and solicit their support in the development of measurable targets. And don't forget to recognize your suppliers as well as procurement team members through storytelling via social media and applying for awards such as A Greener Future.

Disclose Performance

It's important to communicate your results and impacts against your key performance indicators in order to maintain the buy-in you worked hard to secure from your internal procurement team and external suppliers.

However, obtaining reliable data from suppliers can be a major challenge. Verification and auditing of that data can be difficult and expensive.

Some of this stuff is complicated. For example, calculating embodied carbon is more of an art than a science at this stage. But don't let imperfect or incomplete data stop you from moving forward. Ask your suppliers for the best available information and start doing and learning as you go.

Mark Bannister from the COP26 project told me, "We actually tied the measurement and data collection from suppliers into their final payment schedules." As his team informed them, "Until we get your measurement data, you are not getting your final invoice." Mark added, "We put that in the contract at the beginning, sort of fearing we might need to use that a bit more than we did, but there was a lot less resistance than we expected to get that buy-in that we wanted from our suppliers."[18]

Be honest with your audience about where you can improve. It will make your disclosure that much more credible. Transparency is the basis for supply chain collaboration. Without transparency, suppliers and their customers are not speaking the same language and are not on the same page about where they are today—or where they're going together in the future.

Build Long-Term Supplier Relationships

Procurement of venue, catering, electronics, furniture, speaker gifts, cleaning services, etc. are all opportunities to address the issues outlined in this book from diversity and inclusion to net-zero emissions, circularity, and more.

I recommend entering those relationships with the same spirit you enter any long-term partnership. Trusted suppliers who can help you achieve your purpose should not be pushed to undercut other competitors. They should be paid fairly to deliver long-term value and reinvest in their own longevity and in their relationship with your event.

Tell me and I'll forget.
Show me and I may remember.
Involve me and I'll understand.
— Chinese Proverb

Establishing supplier agreements based on shared values and common objectives beyond making money will make your supplier relationships more resilient to market shocks like a future pandemic or catastrophic climate event.

Perhaps you believe your service agreements are already purpose-built, but if it's not in writing, if there's no verification process, and if there's no tracking or reporting of sustainability or social impact metrics, then your supply contracts are unlikely to produce any meaningful sustainability-related outcomes. Suppliers might even be greenwashing their results, which can present a risk to your event and reputation.

One of the main reasons suppliers are not delivering sustainability outcomes to you is that it's cheaper not to. Unless you've expressly communicated your willingness to pay more for long-term value over short-term deliverables, you're likely getting inferior products and uncreative services from mediocre suppliers.

Building relationships with suppliers and aligning on sustainability goals drives innovation and helps create a ripple effect through the supply chain. It also means a compounded positive impact on your organizational objectives—social, environmental, financial, etc.

Suppliers can inform you of capabilities that are available today and what will be possible tomorrow as you collaborate to develop a more sustainable future. Procurement is a strong tool that drives innovation in the technology industry. Working with your suppliers to understand how your goals might align will result in a more circular economy.

10

Embrace Hybrid Events

Most people doubt
online meetings can work
but they somehow overlook
that most in-person meetings
don't work either.

— Scott Berkun

"What the heck did I just do?"
That's what Elizabeth Shirt asked herself after accepting the prestigious role as managing director of GLOBE Series, Canada's largest, longest-running, and most successful sustainability event series, just as the bottom fell out of the entire events industry in 2020.

Elizabeth left her role as Executive Director of Policy and Strategy for Emissions Reduction Alberta and moved to Vancouver for her new gig with GLOBE just two weeks before the World Health Organization officially declared COVID-19 a global pandemic.

Air travel was grounded, gatherings were labeled *super-spreader events*, and painful cancellations followed for thousands of conferences, weddings, sporting events, and much more around the world. This had devastating consequences not only for the events industry and those that support it, but also for people's livelihoods, especially those already in precarious situations.

It couldn't have been a more challenging time to start as the head of an events business.

Rise of Virtual Events

While virtual events were steadily on the rise prior to the pandemic, COVID-19 propelled them to a whole new stratosphere in 2020. Some virtual event platforms experienced a growth rate of 1,000 percent, with Zoom emerging as the dominant platform of choice. Zoom began 2020 with a market cap of $19 billion and saw it grow to more than $125 billion by year's end.[1]

Prior to COVID-19, many event organizers recognized that there were audiences unable to attend in person, but providing virtual participation was simply cost prohibitive. COVID-19 forced the events industry to overcome its inertia. The forced move online was embraced by many eventgoers and organizers.

The move fundamentally changed how people think about events, including how and if to travel to them, as well as how to engage diverse audiences not previously accessible to event organizers. It's clear that increased use of digital solutions and opportunities for hybrid events are now embedded in the future of the industry, and they provide a significant opportunity to make event content accessible to wider audiences, many of whom could not have previously accessed the content or event in person.

Broaden Your Reach and Increase Engagement

"Virtual events can attract people that for economic, geographic, or accessibility reasons, would be less likely to attend an in-person event," said David Betke, president and founder of GreenShows and Do Better Marketing. "A local event can quickly become an event with global reach and participation."[2]

Global reach translates to greater brand exposure, higher return per marketing dollar, and more innovation due to the increased opportunity to hear different perspectives and encourage the cross-pollination of ideas.

Speaker questions at in-person events tend to be dominated by extroverts, while introverts seem likelier to contribute through typed chat during virtual events. Greater participation can spark further discussions, new insights, and solutions that might have been missed otherwise. Because chats can be saved and videos easily recorded, they can form the basis for a final report and serve as downloadable resources for an even broader reach.

Unfortunately, harassment can still occur online. GreenShows, which offers a virtual platform for conferences and tradeshows, offers a "Report Abuse" button on the platform and has a zero-tolerance policy for hate, bullying, or abuse, as do many other virtual platforms. GreenShows also offers closed captions for the hearing impaired and the option to change interface backgrounds to make the experience more accessible for the visually impaired. Enabling closed captioning capabilities and plug-ins for the hearing impaired can be a very simple setting change in Zoom and other online meeting platforms, but they're rarely used because organizers have not adequately tested them with affected stakeholders.

Although we're more connected than ever before, it's important to remember that not everyone has access to high-speed internet. In fact, 42 million Americans don't have such access, so it's also important to provide download options or a chance to watch the virtual event after its conclusion.[3]

How Accessible Is Your Website?

The first impression that people with disabilities will have of your event is through your website. This is where they will go to access your virtual event as well as research whether your in-person event makes any accommodations for them. If your website does not take disabilities into account, that will be the perception of your event as well.

The World Health Organization estimates that about 285 million people have visual impairments worldwide; 39 million of them are blind, and 246 million have low vision. Individuals diagnosed with low vision are able to see colors but struggle with vision that is obscured or fuzzy. Adapting to this audience online is a good first step toward prioritizing inclusion for your event.

Some simple steps include allowing for manual font size adjustment. People with visual impairments will likely use magnifying software to view your website, so it's important to provide the ability to adjust text size in browser settings. However, many people with low vision (especially older people who may be experiencing age-related vision loss) do not use magnifying software, and they may not be familiar with their browser's text size adjustment options, so use large fonts, regardless.

Keyboard shortcuts can make navigation for visually impaired users far easier. A mouse is not useful for navigating because it requires hand-eye coordination. This is especially true for users who are blind and use screen readers to surf the web. For people with low vision, keyboard commands make it possible to navigate a site without having to strenuously focus and follow a mouse cursor across the screen.

Use explicit and descriptive labels for links and buttons and avoid using vague link labels such as "click here." People who use screen-readers often use a keyboard shortcut to list all the links on a page to navigate more efficiently.[4] If this list of links has no surrounding text, it creates a contextless state. As such, it's imperative to create descriptive and explicit link labels that make sense out of context. Screen readers go line by line, so get your point across in as few words as possible through your text and alt text—read aloud by screen readers to describe images for visually impaired users. These are logical best practices that benefit all users.

Descriptive link labels can make your site easier to quickly scan through for sighted users too, and, as an added bonus, they help boost the search engine optimization for your website.

Color Blindness

Don't rely on colors to communicate important information on your website and be sure to provide sufficient contrast using colors and textures. According to the Howard Hughes Medical Institute, about 3.7 percent of Americans, or 12 million, are diagnosed as color-blind.[5]

When it comes to alerts, warnings, and actionable page elements such as text links and buttons, your web developer should clarify that these are meaningful to the user by incorporating more than a simple color change. Almost universally, people understand that underlined blue text is a link. However, many websites underline blue text that doesn't link to anything. Color-blind users should be able to trust that when the color treatment is taken away, the underline will let them know it's a link.

Virtual Events as a Climate Solution

Virtual events provide a powerful tool for reducing our collective emissions by eliminating travel, lodging, food, and venue emissions so you can focus purely on what matters most: connections and content.

Most people don't know it, but digital events have a footprint, too. Quantification of the footprint of virtual events and the digital elements of in-person events is an evolving field. The carbon footprint of virtual events includes the life-cycle emissions from attendee computers, network data transfer energy use, server energy use, and other needs such as lighting and monitors, which would not be needed if the event had not taken place.[6]

In one example, for a virtual conference in May 2022, 64 percent of emissions were from network data transfer, 19 percent from preconference planning meetings, and 11 percent from computer use during the conference.[7] Surprisingly, other analyses have shown that the carbon emissions of a virtual event can be more or less the same as the on-site elements of a live event, not including the emissions associated with transportation, which, as noted in previous chapters, is often the biggest footprint associated with events.

Through carbon offsetting, David Betke's company offsets its virtual event emissions by 1 kilogram per hour per person of video consumed. They advise customers to turn off their cameras during slideshows because leaving them on generates approximately 1 kilogram per hour per person of GHG emissions. This seems to be the most accepted metric for GHG emissions from virtual meetings.

Virtual Costs Less

Virtual events reduce costs, can shorten the sales cycle, offer greater reach, increase engagement from "introverts," supply better analytics, and lower GHG emissions.

The cost to produce a virtual event is usually a fraction of producing an in-person event. The venue costs are lower or even nonexistent, food costs can be eliminated, and virtual events require less staff on the ground. There are no freight, travel, or lodging expenses for exhibitors or attendees. The result is that virtual events can free up the budget to hire more and higher-profile speakers to create better content and more monetization opportunities in the future. For example, the cost savings for food alone could pay for that keynote you never thought you could afford.

Lowered Opportunity Costs

A good virtual event platform can segment leads, shorten the sales cycle, and significantly reduce opportunity costs.

Typically, an exhibitor is out of the office for up to a week for a three-day trade show. Yes, they may be producing leads, but they are also playing catchup when they return to their office, which leads to productivity loss. If exhibitors do not have a good event strategy, including lead capture, qualification, and segmentation, they create unnecessary work for their sales and marketing teams. When they return to the office, they're likely handing off data about who attended their booth, but rarely does this result in segmented or qualified leads. This lack of pertinent data can lead to longer sales cycles or time to revenue and a lower return on investment.

Superior Analytics

The granulated data you can gather from a virtual event far exceeds that of any in-person event from the perspective of engagement, leads, and per-person GHG consumption. An excellent virtual platform generates complete profiles of attendees, including which virtual booths they visited, what they expressed interest in, and who they interacted with at each booth (and for how long). It can segment leads by interest, geography, and position. It can tell you if they participated in networking, commented, asked questions, or reacted to content.

We can also determine the duration of individual camera activation and the length of time they viewed each session. This information allows us to define attendees' GHG emissions far more accurately than you could with an in-person event. Other key performance indicators can be formulated and measured throughout the customer journey.

Innovation Breakthroughs

After taking a few deep breaths, Elizabeth Shirt recognized that bringing people together during a time of social isolation to find solutions to some of the world's most pressing sustainability challenges was more important than ever, and she leaned into her new role with GLOBE.

Elizabeth's first major test as managing director was the delivery of GLOBE Capital—a completely virtual three-day sustainability conference with a focus on scaling investments and solutions across sectors. It was stressful because registration numbers were lower than expected just two weeks out from the event. However, the last-minute crowd definitely showed up, and it was oversubscribed in the end.

The event combined presentations and panel discussions with workshops and virtual networking opportunities for participants. One of the key innovations that stemmed from the GLOBE Capital experience was the development of a virtual matchmaking process, where delegates could identify individuals they'd like to connect with for a fifteen-minute virtual speed-dating-like experience. Participation in the matchmaking program earned points for those that participated, which added a gamification aspect to the event.

Gamify Your Event

Including a leaderboard for participants to earn points toward can stimulate more of your audience's senses and leave a positive lasting impression. For some attendees, their internal gratification of winning is enough, but most will want some tangible rewards such as e-gift cards, sought-after products from your sponsors, or arts and crafts from Indigenous and other local partners.

However, the steps you incentivize your audience to take should not be frivolous distractions. Cheap gimmicks and blatant sales-related demonstrations from sponsors will turn people off. The best event gamification ideas put user experience first. Points for early registration, social media shares, participation in a digital scavenger hunt, educational trivia, attending a networking session or virtual trade show, or contributing content in a discussion board are some possibilities. Whatever you offer, it should align with your purpose, create deeper connections, engage audiences in the content, and enhance the overall user experience.

Disadvantages

The most difficult part of creating virtual events is convincing audiences that your highly engaging and professionally produced virtual event is not just another Zoom call. Some are hesitant about paying for a virtual event when there is so much good-quality free content available. This really raises the bar for the quality required to wow audiences online.

Attendance and Engagement

Free events that are open to the public tend to have a lower attendance from registrants—on average 35 percent attendance rate—while closed, exclusive, and paid events tend to attract around 75 percent.[8] Many closed events offer an incentive to attend, such as a gift, which seems to help increase the number as well.

The digital marketing conference known as SocialWest pivoted to a virtual event and rebranded as Social @ Home during the height of the pandemic in 2020. Each registered participant received a gift package by mail that included sponsor gifts, a funky pair of custom socks, a bingo card for a game called *Cross-Dressed Bingo*, and sealed items they were told to not open until the *big reveal*. This thoughtful welcome package and intriguing items resulted in an extremely low no-show rate.

Attendee engagement can be challenging for online events, especially if it's a very passive experience for your audience. However, through the successful use of incentives, well-facilitated breakout groups, and interactive whiteboard tools like Miro, it's absolutely possible to achieve more than 90 percent engagement rates—even for events spanning several hours.[9]

Multiverse

In 2020, the annual Burning Man festival was canceled due to the COVID-19 pandemic. Organizers decided to create a virtual version of the festival called *Multiverse*, which allowed participants to explore interactive virtual worlds, meet other attendees, and interact during live events and performances over the course of eight days.

The Virtual Burning Man Multiverse had more than one hundred thousand registered attendees from around the world. They reported high engagement rates, including:

- Over 10,000 concurrent attendees at the peak of the event
- Over 1,500 hours of live-streamed content, which included performances, talks, and interactive experiences
- Over 500 virtual camps and art installations—all created by Burning Man participants and volunteers

The Burning Man project attributed the success of Multiverse to several factors, including the creative and interactive nature of the event, the use of technology to connect and engage with attendees, and the community-driven ethos of Burning Man. Additionally, Burning Man masterfully leveraged social media and digital marketing to promote the event and engage with attendees before, during, and after the event.

You're on Mute

The level of speaker and attendee technological proficiency can present challenges, especially if guests are using a new meeting platform or whiteboard tool. It's important to address the varying degrees of technical abilities through pre-event speaker training and how-to videos for attendees.

Post-COVID

While opinions vary depending on the country, people are still wanting to attend virtual events post-COVID-19. European countries and Australia tend to favor in-person events the most.[10] In the UK, only 39 percent of respondents will do both video conferencing and in-person meetings, while 56 percent prefer to meet in-person only. Of American respondents, 52 percent report they will attend both types of events; in Japan, the number is even higher, at 65 percent. Worldwide, however, the percentage of people who plan to attend only virtual events after the pandemic is typically below 10 percent. Yet, according to research from Skift Meetings, 71 percent of event planners said they will continue to employ a digital strategy.[11]

After a hard pivot to virtual programming, GLOBE Series has emerged from the pandemic stronger. In addition to producing their signature events, GLOBE Forum and GLOBExCHANGE (formerly GLOBE Capital) now offer virtual, hybrid, and in-person conference support to many other event clients worldwide.

The virtual matchmaking platform that was created for GLOBE Capital (which has since been enhanced) not only has been integrated into all of GLOBE's in-person events, but it has become a revenue-generating service they offer to other event clients, including WPC Energy, to facilitate meaningful connections that aren't just left to chance encounters, while still leaving plenty of time in the agenda for serendipitous meetings, too.

Side Door

Canadian musician Dan Mangan and his business partner, music promoter Laura Simpson, appeared on the popular television show *Dragons' Den*, which is very similar to the start-up business pitch program *Shark Tank* on US television.[12] They pitched their house concert project, Side Door, and attracted $370,000 in financing from one of the show's Dragons, Arlene Dickinson.[13]

Mangan and Simpson noticed that artists were struggling, partly because of the lack of suitable venues. "We were both experiencing difficulty finding shows that were meaningful and profitable for the artist," Simpson said. The Side Door platform was designed to bridge the gap between people who have space for artists to perform and artists who need a venue. Both the artist and host were then paid automatically through the platform. They've done more than two thousand shows since launching the company.

It was launched in 2019, one year before the COVID-19 pandemic forced venues to put events on hold. In response, Side Door launched ticketed live-streamed shows. Unlike many live-streamed free performances during the pandemic, Side Door set up private ticketed streaming events to generate revenue for artists.

During the height of the pandemic, Dan Mangan performed online each Saturday for fans across the world, donating his proceeds to local causes such as the Vancouver Food Bank and Shelter Movers. The result was large online gatherings of people from all walks of life who interacted via video, dancing, singing along, and cracking jokes on the chat thread.

Hybrid Events

Hybrid events enable panelists and audiences to virtually join in-person events. They became more common as we moved out of the pandemic toward a more endemic COVID-19 reality, and 67 percent of the events professionals surveyed by Skift Meetings stated that hybrid is the future of events.[14]

When done effectively, hybrid events do more than just broadcast face-to-face content. They are a distinct online experience, with their own unique content.

Elizabeth Shirt says that "including virtual speakers is definitely more of an exception than the norm." She told me, "Pure hybrid events are like organizing two parallel events at the same time, and there is a high probability that neither the live nor virtual audience will feel prioritized in the process."[15]

Although they're a lot of work, as Elizabeth noted, you can take advantage of the nature of hybrid events taking place in multiple locations simultaneously. For example, in 2021, the International Association of Conference Centers replaced their one large Americas Connect conference with several localized *pods*.

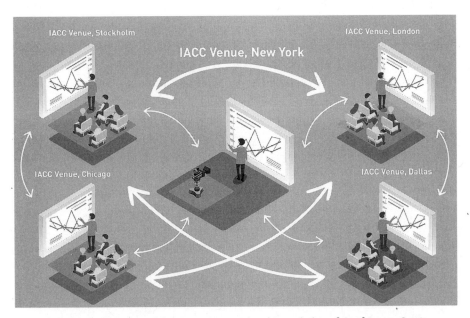

FIGURE 10.1. IACC Pod Model. Source: International Association of Conference Centers.

These operated in person but were all connected virtually to deliver the experience of a full-sized conference.[16]

Hybrid events require many more screens—not just in homes but at the venues themselves, which does increase electricity use. But hybrid events do incorporate more digital signage in place of printed single-use banners and coroplast signs (those ubiquitous corrugated plastic signs) for agendas, directions, and such.

TED Active

The best hybrid event I ever attended was the TED Active event for TEDx organizers from around the world who congregated in Whistler—a first-class ski resort in British Columbia. There was lots of interactive content, TED presentations, and a vibrant community of participants. Throughout the two-day event, we curled up on beanbag chairs and hammocks to watch amazing speakers take the main TED stage, broadcasting live on big screens from the convention center in nearby Vancouver. Some speakers visited us in Whistler afterward to debrief about their talks. It was a unique and enjoyable experience.

In-Person Is Back

The innovative technology solutions that arose through necessity due to the pandemic have not negated the value of face-to-face interactions and events. The rapid growth of virtual events during the pandemic demonstrated that content can be successfully delivered online and to more people. The virtual events space is still anticipated to expand by more than 21 percent from 2022 to 2030.[17] However, it has become evident that virtual events will complement rather than replace the opportunities for networking, business generation, and the euphoria and communal experience that come from being there in person with an energetic crowd, possibly witnessing something spectacular that's never been seen before.

The technology for hybrid events is evolving rapidly, so we can expect to have an even better experience once the use of virtual reality and augmented reality becomes widespread; however, this trend will erode some of the benefits (including environmental benefits) that come with virtual events.[18] The tools we use are only as good as the purpose they serve, so make sure the technology you employ serves yours.

Despite the important role that digital and hybrid events can play, they are not proposed as a silver bullet solution for the events industry to decarbonize, eliminate waste, and become more inclusive.

Conclusion

I do have reasons for hope: our clever brains, the resilience of nature,
the indomitable human spirit, and above all, the commitment of
young people when they're empowered to take action.

— Jane Goodall

Now it's time for you to act. Start right away with your next event. Don't wait for the perfect moment or the perfect plan. Don't wait for someone else to do it for you or ask you to. Don't wait for the industry to catch up or the regulations to change. As Mahatma Gandhi famously said, "Be the change you want to see in the world."

When events are at their best, they connect us to our community and expose us to new ideas, perspectives, and cultures. Events can enrich our lives, empower people to live their true values, and meaningfully contribute to a more inclusive, waste- and emissions-free society.

Take good care of your team and embrace diversity to unlock new perspectives and solutions. The deadline-driven nature of events can lead to burnout and prevent the kind of proactive, creative thinking required to plan purposeful events that have a positive impact.

So much of your impact as an event organizer will result from your procurement decisions. Therefore, it's important to engage your suppliers and work with those that are aligned with your purpose.

You have the power and the responsibility to make a difference with your events. You have the potential to create events that are not only sustainable but also regenerative, restorative, and transformative.

This is not a dream. It's a reality within your reach. But you need courage, creativity, and commitment. Know that you're not alone. There are many others who share your vision and passion for sustainable events. You can learn from them, collaborate with them, and support them. You can also refer to and contribute to my growing list of resources on my website at leor.ca.

This book was designed as an invitation for you to join this movement of sustainable event creators. It's a movement that's growing every day and making a positive impact—one event at a time. It's a movement that needs you and welcomes you.

So, what are you waiting for? Start planning your next event to grow your audience, shrink your footprint, and change the world.

Tools and Resources

The right tools can open doors you never thought possible.

— Tim Ferris

The following is a summary of the tools and resources mentioned throughout the book as well as some additional recommendations. This list is always growing, and you can visit my website on leor.ca for updates to this section.

I hope this resource section and the book in general can be helpful for you to plan more purposeful, inclusive, sustainable, memorable, and super fun events.

Purpose Resources

The British Academy—Future of the Corporation program:
    thebritishacademy.ac.uk/programmes/future-of-the-corporation
Canadian Purpose Economy Project: purposeeconomy.ca
Coro Strandberg Consulting: corostrandberg.com
Good Is the New Cool: goodisthenewcool.org and goodisthenewcool.com
Junxion Strategy: junxion.com
Kin & Co: kinandco.com
Prosper—formerly the Scottish Council for Development and Industry: prosper.scot
Simon Sinek—Start With Why: simonsinek.com/books/start-with-why
Social Purpose Institute (United Way)—Social Purpose Assessment:
    socialpurpose.ca/sp-assessment

Justice, Equity, Diversity, and Inclusion

AccessNow: accessnow.com
American Psychological Association—Brief Guide to Inclusive Language:
    tinyurl.com/ycxzjeax
AVoice4All: avoice4all.org
Black Lives Matter: blacklivesmatter.com
Calgary Folk Music Festival—Safer Spaces Disclosure Form: tinyurl.com/37z484tu

Canadian Broadcasting Corporation—Beyond 94 (progress on the 94 Calls to Action): cbc.ca/newsinteractives/beyond-94

Canadian Council for Aboriginal Business—Progressive Aboriginal Relations certification: ccab.com/programs/progressive-aboriginal-relations-par

Centre for Newcomers (Calgary): centrefornewcomers.ca

Centre for Sport and Human Rights: sporthumanrights.org

Coalition for Environmentally Responsible Economies—Just and Inclusive Economy by 2030: roadmap2030.ceres.org/ai-expectation/equity-diversity-and-inclusion

First Nations University Canada: reconciliationeducation.ca

Gender and the Economy—Increasing Supplier Diversity in Canada: gendereconomy.org/increasing-supplier-diversity-in-canada

Golin's Social Impact + Inclusion—Justice for All survey: golin.com/2022/09/07/justice-for-all-survey

Harvard Business Review—10 Commitments Companies Must Make to Advance Racial Justice: hbr.org/2020/06/the-10-commitments-companies-must-make-to-advance-racial-justice

Indigenomics: indigenomicsinstitute.com

Indspire: indspire.ca

Kairos Blanket Exercise: kairosblanketexercise.org

Minority and Women Owned Business Enterprise—Certification: mwbe-enterprises.com

Native Land—mapping Indigenous territories, treaties, and languages: native-land.ca

Pedesting: pedesting.com

Rick Hansen Foundation: rickhansen.com

Seatrac Mobility Solution: seatracusa.com

Stop Gap Foundation: stopgap.ca

The Secret Marathon: thesecretmarathon.com

Tourism Diversity Matters: tourismdiversitymatters.org

Truth and Reconciliation 94 Calls to Action: www2.gov.bc.ca/assets/gov/british-columbians-our-governments/indigenous-people/aboriginal-peoples-documents/-calls_to_action_english2.pdf

University of Alberta—Indigenous Canada Massive Open Online Course: ualberta.ca/admissions-programs/online-courses/indigenous-canada/index.html

University of British Columbia—Inclusive Language Resources: equity.ubc.ca/resources/inclusive-language-resources

Women's Business Enterprise National Council : wbenc.org

World Travel and Tourism Council—diversity, equity, inclusion and belonging report wttc.org/news-article/wttc-first-of-a-kind-report-reveals-deib-efforts-in-travel-and-tourism

Climate Change Resources

11th Hour Racing—Climate Action Plan:
    11thhourracing.org/app/uploads/2022/12/11hr-climate-action-plan-v3.pdf

Canadian Climate Institute: climateinstitute.ca

Climate Outreach—Alberta Narratives Project:
    climateoutreach.org/reports/alberta-narratives-project-core-narratives

Climate Reality Project: climaterealityproject.org

United Nations Framework Convention on Climate Change:
    greeneventstool.com
    racetozero.unfccc.int/system/criteria
    unfccc.int/documents/271269
    unfccc.int/climate-action/united-nations-carbon-offset-platform
    unfccc.int/climate-action/climate-neutral-now
    unfccc.int/process-and-meetings/the-paris-agreement

Carbon Offsets

Avondale Foundation—offsets education: avondalefoundation.org

Avondale Private Capital—offsets investor, insurance provider:
    avondaleprivatecapital.com

California Air Resources Board—Cap-and-Trade Program:
    ww2.arb.ca.gov/our-work/programs/cap-and-trade-program

Climate Trust: climatetrust.org

Environmental Protection Agency: GHG Inventory Guidance—Indirect Emissions
    from Events and Conferences: epa.gov/sites/default/files/2018-12/documents
    /indirectemissions_draft2_12212018_b_508pass_3.pdf

GHG Management Institute and the Stockholm Environment Institute—Carbon Guide:
    offsetguide.org/understanding-carbon-offsets/carbon-offset-programs/voluntary
    -offset-programs

Global Carbon Council: globalcarboncouncil.com

Gold Standard: goldstandard.org

Intergovernmental Panel on Climate Change (IPCC)—Assessment Report 6:
    ipcc.ch/assessment-report/ar6

International Emissions Trading Association: ieta.org

Ostrom Climate: ostromclimate.com

South Pole: southpole.com

UK Government—Participating in the UK Emissions Trading System:
    gov.uk/government/publications/participating-in-the-uk-ets/participating
    -in-the-uk-ets

Verra—Voluntary Carbon Standard: verra.org/programs/verified-carbon-standard
World Wildlife Fund—comparison of offset standards : panda.org/wwf_news/?126700
/A-Comparison-of-Carbon-Offset-Standards-Making-Sense-of-the-Voluntary
-Carbon-Market

Carbon Removal
Carbon Cure: carboncure.com
Carbon Engineering: carbonengineering.com
Carbon Upcycling Technologies: carbonupcycling.com
Clean O2: clean02.ca
TerraFixing: terrafixing.com

Greenhouse Gas Measurement
Carbon Footprint—calculator for small business : carbonfootprint.com/small_business
_calculator.html
Greenhouse Gases Protocol: ghgprotocol.org/calculation-tools
ghgprotocol.org/standards/scope-3-standard
isla:
traceyour.events
weareisla.co.uk
My Event Footprint: myeventfootprint.com
UK Government—MacKay Carbon Calculator: gov.uk/guidance/carbon-calculator

Net Zero
Canadian Business for Social Responsibility (CBSR)—Net-zero Climate Leaderboard:
cbsr.ca/net-zero-leaderboard
Carbon Disclosure Project: cdp.net
Climate Action 100+: climateaction100.org
Climate Action Tracker: climateactiontracker.org
Hawkins/Brown—net-zero design:
hawkinsbrown.com/conversation/net-zero-a-design-outcome
Net Zero Carbon Events: netzerocarbonevents.org/the-pledge
netzerocarbonevents.org/wp-content/uploads/NZCE_Roadmap2022
_Executive-Summary-1.pdf
netzerocarbonevents.org/wp-content/uploads/NZCE_Roadmap2022
_Full-Report-1.pdf
netzerocarbonevents.org/signatories-supporters
Project Drawdown: drawdown.org
Purpose Net Zero: purposenetzero.com
Rise Consulting: riseconsultingltd.ca

Small and Medium Enterprise Climate Hub:
    smeclimatehub.org
The Climate Group: theclimategroup.org
The Sustainable Advantage—Net-Zero Assessment Tool:
    sustainabilityadvantage.com/documents/NZAT%20v10.xlsx
UN High-Level Expert Group on Net-Zero:
    un.org/en/climatechange/high-level-expert-group
Yale Program on Climate Change Communication:
    climatecommunication.yale.edu

Nature and Biodiversity

Act4nature: act4nature.com/en/
Climate, Community, and Biodiversity Standards: climate-standards.org/ccb-standards/
Convention on Biological Diversity—Global Biodiversity Framework:
    cbd.int/conferences/post2020
Finance for Biodiversity Pledge: www.financeforbiodiversity.org/
Forest Stewardship Council: fsc.org
Global Goal for Nature: naturepositive.org
Kunming-Montreal Global Biodiversity Framework:
    cbd.int/article/cop15-final-text-kunming-montreal-gbf-221222
Pembina Institute—Nature Based Climate Solutions:
    pembina.org/pub/nature-based-climate-solutions
Reducing Emissions from Deforestation and Forest Degradation: un-redd.org
Science Based Targets for Nature:
    sciencebasedtargetsnetwork.org/wp-content/uploads/2020/09/SBTN-initial
    -guidance-for-business.pdf
Taskforce on Nature-related Financial Disclosure: tnfd.global
The Delphi Group—Nature Positive Ecosystem Guide: delphi.ca/wp-content/uploads
    /2022/12/MIM-the-nature-positive-ecosystem-interactive.pdf
The Nature Conservancy—Natural Climate Solutions Handbook:
    nature.org/content/dam/tnc/nature/en/documents/TNC_NCSHandbook
    -ENGLISH.pdf
We Value Nature—Natural Capital Journey: journey.wevaluenature.eu

Zero Waste and Circular Economy Resources

Alberta Bottle Depot Association: abda.ca
Bettercup: the-bettercompany.com/bettercup
The Better Future Factory: betterfuturefactory.com
Canada Plastics Pact: plasticspact.ca
Circularity Gap Report Initiative: circularity-gap.world

Circular Innovation Council: circularinnovation.ca
Cup Zero: cupzero.com
Disney—PlanetPossible: impact.disney.com/impact-stories/environment/disney-planet
    -possible-sharing-the-actions-were-taken-to-protect-the-planet
Earthware: earthware.me
Ellen MacArthur Foundation: ellenmacarthurfoundation.org
Fortum HorsePower: fortum.com/media/2017/11/horsepower-stable-energy-resource
HP Sustainable IT Purchasing Guide: h20195.www2.hp.com/v2/GetDocument
    .aspx?docname=c07023857
Incredible Eats: incredibleeats.com
Lanyard Library: lanyard-library.myshopify.com
ShareWares: sharewares.ca
TerraCycle: terracycle.com
Vecova: vecova.ca/recycling
Zero Waste Canada: zerowastecanada.ca
Zero Waste International Alliance: zwia.org
Zero Waste USA: zerowasteusa.org

Giveaways and Speaker Gifts
Do Better Marketing: promo.dobettermarketing.com
Fairware: fairware.com
Future Forest Company—Trees Not Tees: treesnottees.com

Printing
Paper: epa.vic.gov.au/about-epa/publications/1374-1
Printrelief—offsetting print impact: printreleaf.com
Stone Paper: kamp.solutions/stonepaper

Waste Bins
Busch Systems: buschsystems.com
Clear Stream: clearstreamrecycling.com
Nifty Bins: niftybins.com

Water
CAWST: cawst.org
Earth Group: earthgroup.org
Fill It Forward: fillitforward.com
Hiccup Earth: hiccupearth.com
Quench Buggy: quenchbuggy.com

Venues and Infrastructure

Global Association of the Exhibition Industry—Finding the Future, Together:
Towards a More Sustainable B2B Trade Show Industry in the US and Canada
ufi.org/wp-content/uploads/2022/09/ Finding_the_Future-Final_Report.pdf

Greenview hotel foot-printing tool: hotelfootprints.org

Interface Flooring: interface.com

International Association of Conference Centers—Meeting Room
of the Future Barometer: iacconline.org/iacc-meeting-room-of-the-future

International Energy Agency—data center impacts:
iea.org/reports/data-centres-and-data-transmission-networks

International Labour Organization—One Is Too Many:
ilo.org/wcmsp5/groups/public/---arabstates/---ro-beirut/---iloqatar/documents
/publication/wcms_ 828395.pdf

Manufacture 2030: manufacture2030.com

Qatar—Workers' Welfare Standards: workerswelfare.qa/en/our-legacy/our-standards

Tilos—world's first zero-waste island: justgozero.com/en/tilos-the-first-island-in
-the-world-to-achieve-zero-waste-to-landfill

Tracker Plus: tracker-plus.co.uk

UK Green Building Council—Guide to Scope 3 Reporting in Commercial Real Estate
ukgbc.org/resources/guide-to-scope-3-reporting-in-commercial-real-estate

US Green Building Council—Leadership in Energy and Environmental Design:
usgbc.org/leed

Vancouver Convention Centre—sustainability initiatives:
vancouverconventioncentre.com/about-us/sustainability

World Economic Forum—Green Building Principles: The Action Plan for Net Zero Carbon
Buildings: weforum.org/publications/green-building-principles-the
-action-plan-for-net-zero-carbon-buildings

World Green Building Council: worldgbc.org

Embodied Carbon

American Institute of Architects—Building Life Cycle Assessment in Practice Guide:
aia.org/resources/7961-building-life-cycle-assessment-inpractice

Building Transparency—Embodied Carbon in Construction Calculator:
buildingtransparency.org

Carbon Leadership Forum—Material Baseline for North America:
carbonleadershipforum.org/clf-material-baselines-2023

Circular Ecology—Inventory of Carbon and Energy Database:
circularecology.com/embodied-carbon-footprint-database.html

Getting to Zero Embodied Carbon resources: gettingtozeroforum.org/embodiedcarbon

Royal Institution of Chartered Surveyors—whole life carbon assessment standard:
rics.org/profession-standards/rics-standards-and-guidance/sector-standards
/construction-standards/whole-life-carbon-assessment
International Living Future Institute—Embodied Carbon Guidance:
www2.living-future.org/l/464132/2019-12-16/lt76zg?RD_Scheduler=EC
University of British Columbia—Embodied Carbon Pilot: strategicplan.ubc.ca
/embodied-carbon-pilot-helps-building-industry-address-climate-change

Food and Beverage

Beyond Burger: beyondmeat.com
Climate Change on Your Plate (2012, p. 27) by WWF Germany: wwf.de/ fileadmin
/fm-wwf/Publikationen-PDF/Climate_change_on_your_plate.pdf
Edmonton Convention Centre—plant based menu:
edmontonconventioncentre.com/wp-content/uploads/2022/10/ECC-Plant-Based
-Menu-2022.pdf
Ethnicity Catering: centrefornewcomers.ca/menu
Food Finders: foodfinders.org
Food Rescue: foodrescue.us
Fresh Routes: freshroutes.ca
Good Samaritan Food Donation Act:
usda.gov/media/blog/2020/08/13/good-samaritan-act-provides-liability
-protection-food-donations
IPCC—emissions factors for food and beverage:
ipcc-nggip.iges.or.jp/public/gl/guidelin/ch2ref3.pdf
Knead Technologies—platform connecting food waste with food reuse agencies:
kneadtech.com
Leftovers: rescuefood.ca
National Zero Waste Council—food donor protection laws in Canada:
nzwc.ca/Documents/FoodDonation-LiabilityDoc.pdf
Partake Brewing: drinkpartake.com
Second Harvest: secondharvest.ca
The Good Food Institute: gfi.org
Thrive Meetings: thrivemeetings.com
Trendi: trendi.com
United Nations Environment Program—Food Waste Index Report:
unep.org/resources/report/unep-food-waste-index-report-2021
Village Brewery: villagebrewery.com

Travel

Canadian Sustainable Aviation Fuel: c-saf.ca
Doogal: doogal.co.uk

ecolibrium: ecolibrium.earth/ecolibrium-launch-travel-carbon-app/
    ecolibrium.earth/wp-content/uploads/2023/05/Ecolibrium-Green-Travel
    -Transport-Guide-for-Events-2023_webFINAL.pdf
Ecolibrium—Travel Carbon Calculator: ecolibrium.earth/travel-carboncalculator
Global Destination Sustainability Movement: GDS.earth
Global Sustainable Tourism Council: gstcouncil.org
Goodwings: portal.goodwings.com
ICAO—Carbon Offsetting Scheme for International Aviation:
    icao.int/environmental-protection/CORSIA/pages/default.aspx
International Air Transport Association—Sustainable Aviation Fuel:
    iata.org/en/programs/environment/sustainable-aviation-fuels/
International Civil Aviation Organization (ICAO):
    icao.int/environmental-protection/Carbonoffset/Pages/default.aspx
Jet Zero Council: gov.uk/government/groups/jet-zero-council
Red Fox Cycling: redfoxcycling.co.uk
Sustainable Aviation Buyer's Alliance: flysaba.org
Transport and Environment: transportenvironment.org
The Vision: 2025 Industry Green Survey 2022 on Travel Practices:
    vision2025.org.uk/vision-themes/travel
United Nations Environment, Scientific, and Cultural Organization—
    Sustainable Travel Pledge: core.unesco.org/en/project/570RAS4004
You.Smart.Thing: yousmartthing.com

Sustainable Procurement

Buy Social Canada: buysocialcanada.com/learn/community-benefit-agreement
    buysocialcanada.com/directories/certified-social-enterprises/?location=null
    &product=null&value=null
Canadian Council for Aboriginal Business—SupplyChange: www.ccab.com/supply-change
Canadian Collaboration for Sustainable Procurement: reeveconsulting.com/about-ccsp/
EcoVadis: ecovadis.com
Espace québécois de concertation sur les pratiques d'approvisionnement responsable:
    ecpar.org
Exponential Roadmap Initiative: exponentialroadmap.org/supplier-engagement-guide
Global Green Events—Sustainable Suppliers:
    globalgreenevents.org/sustainable-supplier-list
Government of Canada—Bill S-211 An Act to enact the Fighting Against
    Forced Labour and Child Labour in Supply Chains:
    publicsafety.gc.ca/cnt/cntrng-crm/frcd-lbr-cndn-spply-chns/index-en.aspx
Green Economy Canada—IT Self Assessment tool:
    greeneconomy.ca/wp-content/uploads/2022/07/Buying-a-Better-Future
    _Insights-from-a-Sustainable-IT-Procurement-Project_GEC.pdf

Materials Impact Explorer: materialsimpactexplorer.com
National Aboriginal Capital Corporations Association: nacca.ca/procurement/
Shift and Build: shiftandbuild.ca
Sourcing Industry Group—Resources for Supplier Diversity Programs:
    sig.org/blog/resources-supplier-diversity-programs
Supplier IO—Supplier Diversity: supplier.io
Sustainable Purchasing Leadership Council: sustainablepurchasing.org
The Sustainability Advantage—Sustainable Procurement Toolkit:
    sustainabilityadvantage.com/sp/toolkit
Ulula: ulula.com
The Vendry—20+ Best Black-Owned Vendors:
    thevendry.com/pros/all/black-owned?dp=black-owned
The Vision: 2025—Green Suppliers: vision2025.org.uk/green-suppliers

More Sustainable Event Resources
Arup: arup.com
Clean Vibes: cleanvibes.com
Council for Responsible Sport: councilforresponsiblesport.org
Ecosystem Events: ecosystemevents.com
Explore Edmonton—Responsible Events Program:
    exploreedmonton.com/responsible-events-program
Future Festival Tools: futurefestivaltools.eu
Global Green Events: globalgreenevents.org
Green Deal Circular Festivals: circularfestivals.nl
Green Festivals: greenfestivals.ca
Impactt: impacttlimited.com
Institute for Sustainable Events: ise.world
Julia Spangler: juliaspangler.com
Julie's Bicycle: juliesbicycle.com
Leave No Trace—outdoor ethics: lnt.org
#Meet4Impact: meet4impact.global
MeetGreen: meetgreen.com
Members United for Sustainable Events: museusa.org
Music Declares Emergency: musicdeclares.net
The Ocean Race—Sustainability Knowledge Centre: theoceanrace.com/en
    /racing-with-purpose/sustainable-sports-and-innovation
Ovation Global Destination Management Company: ovationdmc.com
Positive Impact Events: positiveimpactevents.com
Priya Parker—The Art of Gathering: priyaparker.com
Quebec Council for Sustainable Events: evenementecoresponsable.com

Racing to Zero: racingtozero.ca
REVERB: reverb.org
Sustainable Events Network Florida and Caribbean: senfc.org
The Sustainable Events Forum: tsef.ca
Sustainable Event Supplier Database: suppliers.greeneventbook.com
Sustainaval: sustainival.com
University of British Columbia—Green Your Events:
    sustain.ubc.ca/get-involved/take-action-tips/green-your-events
Viridescent: linktr.ee/VIRIDESCENT

Media
Association Meetings International: amimagazine.global
Corporate Knights: corporateknights.com
Eventcellany—Shawna McKinley blog: eventcellany.com
Event Industry News: eventindustrynews.com
Green Biz: greenbiz.com
Prevue Meetings + Incentives: prevuemeetings.com
Professional Convention Management Association—Convene: pcmaconvene.org
Skift: skift.com
Talking Climate—Katherine Hayhoe newsletter: talkingclimate.com
Trade Show News Network: tsnn.com

Power
Bullfrog Power: bullfrogpower.com/events-and-sponsorships
International Renewable Energy Agency: irena.org
Portable Electric: portable-electric.com
Showpower: showpower.com

Research
Centre for Climate Change and Social Transformations—Cardiff University:
    cardiff.ac.uk/psychology/research/themes/social-and-environmental
    /centre-for-climate-change-and-social-transformations-cast
Cornell Hotel Sustainability Benchmarking: greenview.sg/chsb-index
Network for Business Sustainability: nbs.net
Tyndall Centre for Climate Change: tyndall.ac.uk

Standards and Certifications
A Greener Future: agreenerfuture.com
American Society of Heating, Refrigerating and Air-Conditioning
    Engineers—90.1 Energy: ashrae.org/technical-resources/bookstore/standard-90-1

B Lab—B Corporation: bcorporation.net

British Standards Institution—PAS 2060:
    bsigroup.com/en-GB/PAS-2060-Carbon-Neutrality

Ecochain—Environmental Product Declarations:
    ecochain.com/blog/environmental-product-declaration-epd-overview

Energy Star: energystar.gov

European Advertising Alliance: easa-alliance.org

Events Industry Council—Sustainable Events Standard:
    insights.eventscouncil.org/Sustainability/Sustainability-Standards-and-Registry

Fair Trade: fairtrade.net

Global Sustainability Assessment System: gsas.gord.qa

International Standards Organization: iso.org/iso-20121-sustainableevents.html
    iso.org/netzero
    iso.org/standard/66455.html
    iso.org/standard/74257.html

International Sustainability Standards Board:
    ifrs.org/groups/international-sustainability-standards-board

Science Based Targets Initiative—Net Zero Standard:
    sciencebasedtargets.org/resources/files/Net-Zero-Standard.pdf

Sustainable Development Goals: sdgs.un.org/goals

Swiss Commission for Fairness in Commercial Communication: faire-werbung.ch

Virtual Resources

Bizzabo: bizzabo.com

Burning Man in the Multiverse: burningman.org/about/history
    /brc-history/event-archives/2020-event-archive/virtual-brc-2020

GreenShows: dobettermarketing.com/virtual-and-hybrid-events

Miro: miro.com

Side Door: sidedooraccess.com

Slido: slido.com

Streamyard: streamyard.com

Events Mentioned in the Book

5 Peaks Trail Running Series: 5peaks.com

Bass Coast: basscoast.ca

Burning Man—Sustainability: burningman.org/about/about-us/sustainability

Calgary Folk Music Festival: calgaryfolkfest.com

Calgary Justice Film Festival—Our Story: justicefilmfestival.ca/our-story-1

Calgary Marathon—Sustainability: calgarymarathon.com/about/sustainability

Calgary Stampede—Safety and Sustainability:
   corporate.calgarystampede.com/about-us/who-we-are/safety-sustainability
California International Marathon—Sustainability:
   runsra.org/california-international-marathon/sustainability
Canadian Rockies 24: canadianrockies24.com
COP15—UN Convention on Biological Diversity: cbd.int/cop
COP26—Sustainability Report: unfccc.int/sites/default/files/resource/COP26
   -Sustainability-Report_Final.pdf
Energy Futures Lab: https://energyfutureslab.com
FIFA World Cup Qatar 2022—Sustainability: fifa.com/fifa-world-cup-qatar-2022
   -sustainability
GLOBE Series: globeseries.com
Greenbelt Festival—A Greener Festival: greenbelt.org.uk/info/a-greener-festival
Heritage Park—Innovation Crossing: heritagepark.ca/exhibits/innovation-crossing
High Lonesome 100—Community and Equity Policies:
   highlonesome100.com/community-and-equity
IMEX America—Net Zero Roadmap: imexexhibitions.com/initiatives
   /imex-net-zero-strategy.html
IMEX Frankfurt: imex-frankfurt.com
International Federation for Equestrian Sports: fei.org
Ismaili Stampede Breakfast: ismailimail.blog/?s=stampede+breakfast
Live Nation—Green Nation:
   livenationentertainment.com/2021/04/live-nation-announces-green-nation-
   touring-program-giving-artists-tools-to-reduce-the-environmental-impact-of-tours
Olympic and Paralympic Games—Sustainability Essentials:
   olympics.com/ioc/sustainability/essentials
OpenAir St. Gallen—Sustainability: openairsg.ch/nachhaltigkeit
Run With Maud: ahmaudarberyfoundation.org
Secret 3K—Purpose and Values: secret3k.com/values
Social Next, Social West: socialnext.ca
St. Pete Run Fest: stpeterunfest.org
TED: ted.com; ted.com/tedx/events; tedxyyc.ca
Vancouver Marathon—Sustainability: bmovanmarathon.ca/sustainability
World Petroleum Congress: 24wpc.com

Notes

Introduction

1. Michele Parmelee, "A Generation Disrupted: Highlights from the 2019 Deloitte Global Millennial Survey," Deloitte, 2019, www2.deloitte.com
2. "Event Industry Statistics," Truelist, updated July 1, 2023, https://truelist.co
3. "Home," A Greener Future, accessed May 14, 2023, https://agreenerfuture.com
4. "Net Zero Carbon Events," Net Zero Carbon Events, accessed May 14, 2023, www.netzerocarbonevents.org
5. "Vision 2025," Vision 2025, modified March 23, 2023, www.vision2025.org.uk
6. "Home," Events Industry Council, accessed May 14, 2023, www.eventscouncil.org
7. Natalie Lowe, Sustainable Events Forum, interviewed February 2, 2023.
8. Suzanne Morrell, interviewed February 2023.
9. Mercedes Hunt, Marriott, interviewed February 17, 2023.
10. Mark Bannister, COP26, interviewed May 14, 2023.

Chapter 1: Start with Purpose

1. Drew Weisholtz, "Taylor Swift Gives $100,000 Bonuses and Handwritten Letters to Thank Truck Drivers on Her Eras Tour," *Today*, August 2, 2023, www.today.com
2. Kimberley J. Smith, et al., "The Association Between Loneliness, Social Isolation and Inflammation: A Systematic Review and Meta-analysis," *Neuroscience & Biobehavioral Reviews*, 112, May 2020: 519–41.
3. Géza Gergely Ambrus et al., "Getting to Know You: Emerging Neural Representations During Face Familiarization," *Journal of Neuroscience*, 41(26), June 2021: 5687–98.
4. Priya Parker, *The Art of Gathering: How We Meet and Why It Matters*, April 14, 2020.
5. "Energy Futures Lab," The Natural Step Canada, accessed May 14, 2023, https://energyfutureslab.com
6. "Home: GLOBE Forum 2022," GLOBE Forum 2022, accessed May 14, 2023, https://forum.globeseries.com
7. "The 44th Annual Calgary Folk Fest Returns July 27–30, Powered by ATB," Globe Forum, accessed May 14, 2023, www.calgaryfolkfest.com
8. "Heritage Park Historical Village," Calgary Folk Festival, modified May 15, 2023, https://heritagepark.ca
9. "Calgary Justice Film Festival," Calgary Justice Film Festival, accessed May 14, 2023, https://justicefilmfestival.ca

10. "Calgary Stampede," The Calgary Stampede, accessed May 14, 2023, www.calgary stampede.com

11. "Burning Man," Burning Man Foundation, accessed May 14, 2023, https://burningman.org

12. "The 17 Goals," United Nations, accessed May 15, 2023, https://sdgs.un.org/goals

13. "Social Purpose Assessment," United Way British Columbia, modified March 3, 2023, https://socialpurpose.ca/sp-assessment

Chapter 2: Grow Your Audience through Inclusion

1. Priya Parker, *The Art of Gathering: How We Meet and Why It Matters*, April 14, 2020.

2. Richard Rothstein, *The Color of Law: A Forgotten History of How our Government Segregated America*, New York, Liveright, 2017.

3. Rodney P. Joseph et al., "Barriers to Physical Activity Among African American Women: An Integrative Review of the Literature," *Taylor & Francis Online*, 55(6), June 2015: 679–99.

4. Kate Dashper, "Will the Lack of Diversity in the Events Industry Be Addressed in 2018?", *Leeds Beckett University* (blog), January 3, 2018, www.leedsbeckett.ac.uk/blogs/expert-opinion/2018/01.

5. Barbara Scofidio, "#MeToo: Majority of Women Meeting Planners Have Been Sexually Harassed," Prevue Meetings + Incentives, modified October 25, 2019, www.prevuemeetings.com

6. "#MeToo Meets Meetings," Prevue Meetings + Incentives.

7. Scofidio, "#MeToo."

8. "Men Only: Inside the Charity Fundraiser Where Hostesses Are Put on Show," *Financial Times*, modified January 23, 2018, www.ft.com

9. Rob Davies, "Gambling Firms Defy Calls to Stamp Out Sexist Behaviour at Event," Guardian, February 7, 2018.

10. David Betke, Greenshows/Do Better Marketing, interview June 18, 2020.

11. "Booth Babes Don't Work," TechCrunch, modified January 13, 2014, https://techcrunch .com

12. Betke, 2020.

13. Natalka Antoniuk, "Are We Really Still Talking About Booth Babes?", Quandrant2-Design, Medium, January 30, 2020, https://medium.com/quadrant2design

14. Ben Snider-McGrath, "Calgary Marathon Introduces Pregnancy Deferral, Child Care for 2023," *Running Magazine*, March 20, 2023, https://runningmagazine.ca/sections/runs-races

15. Christie Smith and Stephanie Turner, *The Radical Transformation of Diversity and Notes 241 Inclusion: The Millennial Influence*, Deloitte Consulting LLP, 2015, www2.deloitte.com/content/dam/Deloitte/us/Documents/human-capital/us-deloitte-diversity-inclusion-the-radical-transformation.pdf

16. Greggor Mattson, "Are Gay Bars Closing? Using Business Listings to Infer Rates of Gay Bar Closure in the United States, 1977–2019," *Socius: Sociological Research for a Dynamic World*, 5(1), 2019.

17. How to Be an Antiracist. Goodreads, accessed May 15, 2023, www.goodreads.com

18. "On-Demand Survey to Assess Workplace Diversity," *Engagement Multiplier*, modified April 1, 2022, www.engagementmultiplier.com

19. "Safer Spaces Policy," Calgary Folk Music Festival, accessed May 15, 2023, https://calgaryfolkfest.com

20. "Diversity and Inclusion in the Event Agency World," inVOYAGE.net, modified May 14, 2021.

21. "Recruiting a Diverse Workforce," *Glassdoor*, modified July 19, 2021, www.glassdoor.com

22. "GLOBE Series," accessed May 15, 2023, www.globeseries.com

23. "Leading Change Canada," Leading Change, accessed May 15, 2023, https://leadingchangecanada.com

24. "New Research Finds That Event Speaker Panels Are Still Not Diverse," Skift Meetings, modified May 19, 2022, www.eventmanagerblog.com

25. Keneisha Williams, "New Research Finds That Event Speaker Panels Are Still Not Diverse," Skift Meetings, September 9, 2020, https://meetings.skift.com

26. "Kill Every Buffalo You Can! Every Buffalo Dead Is an Indian Gone," *Atlantic*, May 12, 2016, www.theatlantic.com

27. American Psychological Association, Inclusive Language Guidelines, 2021, www.apa.org

28. Anika Nishat, "How to Develop a Diversity & Inclusion Program from Scratch," *Remesh* (blog), April 22, 2022, https://blog.remesh.ai/diversity-inclusion-programs

29. Katerina Bezrukova et al., "A Meta-analytical Integration of Over 40 Years of Research on Diversity Training Evaluation," eCommons, accessed May 15, 2023, https://ecommons.cornell.edu

30. "Diversity Event Ideas in the Workplace: 7 Fun Events That Work," *Impactly*, modified April 10, 2023, www.getimpactly.com

31. "Ethnicity Catering Training Program" Centre for Newcomers, accessed May 15, 2023. https://www.centrefornewcomers.ca

32. "Ethnicity Catering" Centre for Newcomers, accessed May 15, 2023, https://www.centrefornewcomers.ca

33. "Land Acknowledgment to Be Part of Flames' 1st Indigenous Celebration Game," CBC, modified March 3, 2023, www.cbc.ca/news

34. "Diversity and Inclusion: Best Practices and Case Studies," *Draup*, modified September 23, 2020, https://draup.com

Chapter 3: Produce Zero Waste

1. "How Much Waste Will Your Event Generate? Event Waste Estimate Formula," Ecosystem Events, modified April 5, 2019, www.ecosystemevents.com

2. "Trends in Solid Waste Management," World Bank, accessed May 17, 2023, https://datatopics.worldbank.org

3. *AR5 Synthesis Report: Climate Change 2014*, IPCC, accessed May 17, 2023, www.ipcc.ch/report/ar5/syr

4. "New UN Report Finds Marine Debris Harming More Than 800 Species, Costing Countries Millions," United Nations, modified December 5, 2016, https://news.un.org

5. Simon Reddy, "Plastic Pollution Affects Sea Life Throughout the Ocean," Pew Charitable Trusts, September 24, 2018, accessed May 18, 2023, www.pewtrusts.org

6. "A Whopping 91 Percent of Plastic Isn't Recycled," National Geographic Society, December 20, 2018, modified May 20, 2022, https://education.nationalgeographic.org

7. Damian Carrington, "People Eat at Least 50,000 Plastic Particles a Year, Study Finds," *Guardian*, June 5, 2019.

8. Damian Carrington, "Plastic Fibres Found in Tap Water Around the World, Study Reveals," *Guardian*, September, 6, 2017, modified October 22, 2018.

9. Damian Carrington, "Revealed: Microplastic Pollution Is Raining Down on City Dwellers," *Guardian*, December 27, 2019.

10. Sofia Quaglia, "More Microplastics in Babies' Faeces Than in Adults': Study," *Guardian* September 22, 2021, modified November 22, 2021.

11. Damian Carrington, "Microplastics Found in Human Blood for First Time," *Guardian*, March 24, 2022.

12. Damian Carrington, "Microplastics Cause Damage to Human Cells, Study Shows," *Guardian*, December 8, 2021.

13. Damian Carrington, "Revealed: Air Pollution May Be Damaging 'Every Organ in the Body,'" *Guardian*, May 17, 2019.

14. Syjil Ashraf, "Disney Park Secrets That Keep the Magic Alive (Gallery)," Daily Meal, September 21, 2017, www.thedailymeal.com

15. Sonny Rosenthal and Noah Linder, "Effects of Bin Proximity and Informational Prompts on Recycling and Contamination," *ScienceDirect*, 168, May 2021: 105430.

16. "These New Trash Cans in Disney World Have a SPECIAL Purpose," *Disney Food Blog*, February 2, 2021, www.disneyfoodblog.com

17. "Disney Planet Possible's Commitment to Reducing Food Waste," *Disney Parks Blog*, modified April 12, 2022.

18. Mercedes Hunt, Marriott, February 17, 2023.

19. Mary Johnson-Gerard, "What Are the Dangers of Accidentally Burning Styrofoam?," *Sciencing*, modified November 22, 2019, https://sciencing.com

20. "Leave No Trace—Home," Leave No Trace, modified May 18, 2023, https://lnt.org

21. "Home," Trees Not Tees, modified November 2, 2022, https://treesnottees.com

22. "Home," Future Forest Company, modified April 21, 2023, https://thefutureforestcompany.com

23. Lourdes Juan, Leftovers, Fresh Routes, Knead Tech, interviewed October 8, 2019.

24. Kalynn Krump, ReBLOOM, interviewed August 14, 2018.

Chapter 4: Ban Bottled Water without Causing a Meltdown

1. Diane Dragan, "10 Outrageous Markups You'd Never Guess You Were Paying," *Readers Digest*, June 21, 2012, updated March 16, 2022, www.rd.com

2. "Calgary Folk Music Fest Ditches Bottled Water," CBC, modified July 23, 2011, www.cbc.ca/news/canada/calgary

3. "Music News Live: Record Breaking Year for Greener Festival Award Scheme," *Music News Live*, October 14, 2014, accessed May 22, 2023, https://musicnewslive.blogspot.com

4. "Plastic Products Contain Toxic Chemicals," *Consumer Reports*, modified September 8, 2021, www.consumerreports.org

5. Martin Wagner and Jörg Oehlmann, "Endocrine Disruptors in Bottled Mineral Water: Total Estrogenic Burden and Migration from Plastic Bottles," *National Library of Medicine*, 16(3), May 2009: 278–86.

6. "Bottled Water Quality Investigation," Environmental Working Group, October 15, 2008, accessed May 24, 2023, www.ewg.org/research

7. Ana Ribeiro et al., "Fungi in Bottled Water: A Case Study of a Production Plant," *ResearchGate*, 23(3), October 2006: 139–44.

8. "Small Entity Compliance Guide: Bottled Water and Total Coliform and E. coli," FDA, modified September 20, 2019, www.fda.gov

9. Ryan Felton, "Arsenic in Some Bottled Water at Unsafe Levels," *Consumer Reports*, modified November 4, 2021, www.consumerreports.org

10. "St. Pete Run Fest: Half Marathon, 10K, 5K, Kid's Race: Nov 10–12," St. Pete Run Fest, modified May 21, 2023, https://stpeterunfest.org

11. "The Best Hydration Powders for Every Aspect of Your Training," *Runner's World*, modified August 10, 2022, www.runnersworld.com

12. Morgan Tilton, "How U.S. Road Races Can Be More Sustainable," *Runners World*, December 8, 2021.

13. "Athlinks," Athlinks, accessed May 24, 2023, athlinks.com

14. "Council for Responsible Sport," Council for Responsible Sport, accessed May 24, 2023, www.councilforresponsiblesport.org

15. Tilton, 2021.

16. Ibid.

Chapter 5: Go Net Zero

1. Mark Bannister, COP26, interviewed May 14, 2023.

2. "Meetings and Climate Change," PCMA, modified March 14, 2016, www.pcmaconvene.org

3. "Basic Information about Landfill Gas," EPA, modified April 21, 2023, www.epa.gov

4. Erika Welch, interviewed September 11, 2023.

5. "Sustainability," Burning Man Project, last updated October 2023, https://burningman .org/about/about-us/sustainability

6. "Climate Change in Data," *Climate Change 2021: The Physical Science Basis*, Intergovernmental Panel on Climate Change, accessed May 14, 2023, www.ipcc.ch/report/sixth -assessment-report-working-group

7. Bill Gates, *How to Avoid a Climate Disaster: The Solutions We Have and the Breakthroughs We Need*, Knopf, 2021.

6. "ISO: Net Zero Guidelines," ISO, accessed May 17, 2023, www.iso.org/netzero.

10. "Net Zero Carbon in Events Survey," Ovation Global DMC, July 12, 2023, https://ovationdmc.com

8. *Route to Net Zero Executive Summary November 2022*, Net Zero Carbon Events, accessed May 16, 2023, https://netzerocarbonevents.org

9. "ISO: Net Zero Guidelines," ISO, accessed May 17, 2023, www.iso.org/netzero.

10. "Net Zero Carbon in Events Survey," Ovation Global DMC, July 12, 2023, https://ovationdmc.com

11. "The Net Zero Carbon Events Pledge," Net Zero Carbon Events, accessed May 16, 2023, www.netzerocarbonevents.org

12. . "Net-Zero Assessment Tool."

13. "Net-Zero Leaderboard," CBSR, modified April 9, 2023, https://cbsr.ca

14. "My Event Footprint: An Attendee Engagement & Story Telling App, MeetGreen," My Event Footprint, modified June 8, 2022, https://myeventfootprint.com

15. "Calculation Tools and Guidance," Greenhouse Gas Protocol, accessed May 17, 2023, https://ghgprotocol.org

16. "Leor Rotchild," accessed May 17, 2023, www.leor.ca

17. *Explore Edmonton's Carbon Reduction Plan*, Explore Edmonton,2021, https://assets .exploreedmonton.com/images/Final-GHG-report-2021.pdf

18. Mark Rabin, Portable Electric, interviewed October 2, 2023.

19. Mark Bannister, COP26, interviewed May 14, 2023.

20. Melissa Radu, Explore Edmonton, interviewed December 2022.

21. Tom Dowdall, "Science-Based Net-Zero Targets: 'Less Net, More Zero,'" Science Based Targets Initiative, October 2021, https://sciencebasedtargets.org

22. "Avoidance and Removal Offsets Are Needed Equally," Climate Trust, modified February 16, 2021, https://climatetrust.org

23. Ibid.

24. "A Net Zero Roadmap for Travel and Tourism," World Travel and Tourism Council, November 20, 2021, https://wttc.org

Chapter 6: Be Proactive to Avoid Greenwashing

1. Dan Palmer, "FIFA's Claim of Carbon Neutral Qatar 2022 World Cup Branded 'Misleading' by Regulator," Inside the Games, June 8, 2023, www.insidethegames.biz/articles /1137721/fifa-world-cup-carbon-neutral

2. "Sustainability Progress Report," FIFA World Cup Qatar 2022, accessed September 15, https://publications.fifa.com/en/final-sustainability-report/sustainability-at-the-fifa -world-cup/sustainability-at-the-fifa-world-cup-2022

3. "Will Qatar Really Produce 'the First Carbon-neutral World Cup in History'?: World Cup 2022," *Guardian*, modified October 13, 2022.

4. "'Greenwashing' Mars Qatar's Carbon-neutral World Cup Promise," France 24, modified October 30, 2022, www.france24.com

5. Antoine De Spiegeleir, "The 2022 Qatar World Cup Was Greenwashed: The Swiss Fairness Commission Finds in Favour of Six NGOs Alleging Misleading and Unfair Advertisement by FIFA," Columbia Law School, July 3, 2023, https://blogs.law.columbia .edu/climatechange/2023/07/03

6. "World Cup in Qatar," DW, accessed May 30, 2023, www.dw.com

7. "Revealed: 6,500 Migrant Workers Have Died in Qatar Since World Cup Awarded: Workers' Rights," *Guardian*, modified December 13, 2022.

8. Lauren M. Baum, "It's Not Easy Being Green…Or Is It? A Content Analysis of Environmental Claims in Magazine Advertisements from the United States and United Kingdom," ResearchGate, 6(4), December 2012: 423–40.

9. Magali A. Delmas and Vanessa Cuerel Burbano, "The Drivers of Greenwashing," 2011, *SAGE Journals*, 54(1), accessed May 28, 2023.

10. "What Is Business Sustainability?," Network for Business Sustainability, modified March 8, 2023, https://nbs.net

11. "The Legal Risks of Greenwashing Are Real," Bloomberg Law, accessed May 28, 2023, https://news.bloomberglaw.com

12. "Circular Economy: Commission Proposes New Consumer Rights and a Ban on Greenwashing," European Commission, accessed May 30, 2023, https://ec.europa.eu

13. "France Introduces One of the World's First Greenwashing Laws," *Communicate*, accessed May 30, 2023, www.communicatemagazine.com

14. "Protecting Consumers from Greenwashing," Behavioural Insights Team, accessed May 30, 2023, www.bi.team/blogs

15. "What Is Sustainable Marketing?," Network for Business Sustainability, accessed May 30, 2023, https://nbs.net

16. "Procurement Is Missing in Supply Chain Sustainability," Network for Business Sustainability, accessed May 30, 2023, https://nbs.net

17. "Deny, Deceive, Delay: Documenting and Responding to Climate Disinformation at COP26 & Beyond: Summary," Institute for Strategic Dialogue, modified June 16, 2022, www.isdglobal.org/isd-publications

18. "From Ambition to Action: Your Climate Journey Starts Here with South Pole," South Pole, accessed May 30, 2023, www.southpole.com

19. "Beyond the Games: Promoting Sport and the Olympic Values in Society," International Olympic Committee, modified May 10, 2023, https://olympics.com

20. Natalie Lowe, Sustainable Events Forum, interview February 2, 2023.

21. "Centre for Sport and Human Rights," LinkedIn, accessed May 31, 2023, www.linkedin.com

22. *One Is Too Many*, International Labour Organization, November 2021, www.ilo.org

23. *Fifth Annual Workers' Welfare Progress Report*, Wayback Machine, accessed May 18, 2023, workerswelfare.qa

24. *Sustainability Strategy*, FIFA, accessed May 30, 2023, https://digitalhub.fifa.com

25. "VCM Reaches Toward $2 Billion in 2021: New Market Analysis Published from Ecosystem Marketplace," Ecosystem Marketplace, modified August 3, 2022, www.ecosystemmarketplace.com

26. "Evicted for Carbon Credits: Norway, Sweden, and Finland Displace Ugandan Farmers for Carbon Trading," Oakland Institute, modified October 13, 2020, www.oaklandinstitute.org

27. "Green Resources Is Africa's Largest Afforestation Company and a Leader in East African Wood Processing," Green Resources, accessed May 31, 2023, www.greenresources.no

28. "Voluntary v. Mandatory Carbon Credit Market," ClimateTrade, modified May 02, 2023, https://climatetrade.com

29. "Voluntary Offset Programs," Carbon Offset Guide, modified December 29, 2020, www.offsetguide.org

30. "Cap-and-Trade Program," California Air Resources Board, accessed May 31, 2023, https://ww2.arb.ca.gov

31. "Participating in the EU Emissions Trading System (EU ETS)," GOV.UK, modified July 23, 2020, www.gov.uk

32. "A User's Guide to the CDM (Clean Development Mechanism), Second Edition," Pembina Institute, accessed May 31, 2023, www.pembina.org

33. *Corporate Net-Zero Pledges: The Bad and the Ugly*, Columbia Center on Sustainable Investment, accessed May 31, 2023, https://ccsi.columbia.edu

34. "A Comparison of Carbon Offset Standards: Making Sense of the Voluntary Carbon Market," WWF, accessed May 31, 2023, https://wwf.panda.org/wwf_news

35. Natalie Lowe, 2023.

36. "Leading Providers of Carbon Management Solutions," Ostrom Climate, modified November 4, 2022, https://ostromclimate.com

37. "Home," Verra, modified April 28, 2023, https://verra.org

38. "Turkey: News, Videos, Reports and Analysis," France 24, accessed May 31, 2023, www.france24.com

39. Ibid.

40. Jules Boykoff and Christopher Gaffney, "The Tokyo 2020 Games and the End of Olympic History," *Taylor & Francis Online*, 31(2), April 2020: 1–19.

41. Martin Müller et al., "Peak Event: The Rise, Crisis and Potential Decline of the Olympic Games and the World Cup," *ScienceDirect*, 95, April 2023: 104657.

Chapter 7: Change the Venue without Changing the Venue

1. IACC, *Meeting Room of the Future Barometer*, IACC, modified November 23, 2022, www.iacconline.org

2. Sue Pelletier, "Sustainability: A Growing Planner Priority," Prevue Meetings and Incentives, June 29, 2022, www.prevuemeetings.com

3. *A Net Zero Roadmap for Travel and Tourism*, World Travel and Tourism Council, November 20, 2021, https://wttc.org

4. "Race to Net Zero," United Nations Framework Convention on Climate Change, accessed May 25, 2023, https://unfccc.int

5. *A Net Zero Roadmap for Travel and Tourism.*

6. *Meeting Room of the Future.*

7. Pelletier, "Sustainability."

8. Ibid.

9. "Ethnicity Catering," Centre for Newcomers, accessed May 25, 2023, www.centrefornewcomers.ca

10. "Kitchen Training," Centre for Newcomers, accessed May 26, 2023.

11. Oliver Milman, "Meat Accounts for Nearly 60% of All Greenhouse Gases from Food Production, Study Finds: Meat Industry," *Guardian*, September 13, 2021.

12. *ECC Plant Based Menu 2019*, Edmonton Convention Centre, accessed May 18, 2023, www.edmontonconventioncentre.com

13. Chris St. Prince, "Vegan Restaurateurs Are Putting the Fast Food Industry on Notice," Corporate Knights, April 11, 2023, www.corporateknights.com

14. "LEED Rating System," U.S. Green Building Council, accessed May 26, 2023, www.usgbc.org

15. "Vancouver Convention Centre," accessed May 26, 2023, www.vancouverconvention centre.com

16. "Calgary Stampede," *Wikipedia*, accessed May 26, 2023, https://en.wikipedia.org

17. "Scotiabank Saddledome," *Wikipedia*, accessed May 26, 2023, https://en.wikipedia.org

18. "10 Key Facts about Qatar 2022's Sustainable FIFA World Cup™ Stadiums," FIFA World Cup Qatar 2022, accessed May 26, 2023, workerswelfare.qa

19. "Status of Sustainability in the Exhibition Industry," UFI, the Global Association of the Exhibition Industry, Media Release, July 29, 2021, www.ufi.org

20. David Betke, GreenShows/Do Better Marketing, interview June 18, 2020.

21. "Home," Fill It Forward, modified March 28, 2023, www.fillitforward.com

Chapter 8: Make Mobility More Sustainable

1. Robert Thomson and Roland Berger, "Hydrogen: A Future Fuel for Aviation?," March 11, 2020, www.rolandberger.com

2. *A Net Zero Roadmap for the Events Industry*, Net Zero Carbon Events, November 2022, www.netzerocarbonevents.org/wp-content/uploads/NZCE_Roadmap2022_Full -Report-updated-26Jan2023.pdf

3. Lottie Limb, "It's Official: France Bans Short-Haul Domestic Flights in Favour of Train Travel," Euronews, updated May 5, 2023, www.euronews.com/green/2022/12/02

4. Calum Maclaren, "How a New Wave of Lawsuits Is Targeting Airline 'Greenwashing,'" Corporate Knights, October 5, 2023, www.corporateknights.com

5. Joanna Plucinska, Toby Sterling, and Rajesh Kumar Singh, "Greenwashing Cases Against Airlines in Europe, US," Reuters, September 13, 2023, www.reuters.com

6. "What Is Sustainable Aviation Fuel?" Aviation Benefits Beyond Borders, accessed May 27, 2023, https://aviationbenefits.org

7. "UK Net Zero Aviation Ambitions Must Resolve Resource and Research Questions Around Alternatives to Jet Fuel," Royal Society, February 28, 2023, https://royalsociety.org

8. Leigh Collins, "A Wake-up Call on Green Hydrogen: The Amount of Wind and Solar Needed Is Immense," Recharge, March 19, 2020, www.rechargenews.com

9. Ibid.

10. Mark Bannister, COP26, interview May 14, 2023.

11. *Jet Zero Strategy Delivering Net Zero Aviation by 2050*, UK Department of Transport, July 2022, https://assets.publishing.service.gov.uk

12. *"Greenbelt Festival: Case Study from the Green Travel and Transport Guide for Festivals and Events 2023,"* ecolibrium, May 18, 2023, accessed May 27, 2023, https://ecolibrium.earth

13. C. Jones, L. Pennington, and C. McLachlan, *Car Use, Carbon and Festivals*, February 28, 2023, Tyndall Centre for Climate Change Research, University of Manchester, UK, https://pure.manchester.ac.uk

14. "OpenAir St. Gallen," Future Festival Tools, accessed May 27, 2023, www.futurefestivaltools.eu

15. Emine Saner, "Flying Shame: The Scandalous Rise of Private Jets," *Guardian News*, January 26, 2023, www.theguardian.com

16. Bethan Riach, "Vision: 2025 Green Industry Survey Results 2022," January 26, 2023, www.vision2025.org.uk

17. *A Net Zero Roadmap for the Events Industry*, November 2022, Net Zero Carbon Events, accessed May 16, 2023, https://netzerocarbonevents.org

18. Chrisopher Severen, "Why Are Young People Driving Less? Evidence Points to Economics, Not Preferences," Brookings Institution, March 24, 2023, www.brookings.edu /articles

Chapter 9: Leverage Procurement to Build a Circular Economy

1. "The Circularity Gap Report 2023," Circularity Gap Report Initiative, accessed May 28, 2023, www.circularity-gap.world/2023

2. "Sustainable Purchasing Leadership Council," Sustainable Purchasing Leadership Council, accessed May 26, 2023, www.sustainablepurchasing.org

3. Monica Da Ponte, Megan Foley and Charles H. Cho, "Assessing the Degree of Sustainability Integration in Canadian Public Sector Procurement," *Sustainability*, July 2020, 12(14): 5550.

4. Peter Spiller, "Making Supply-chain Decarbonization Happen," McKinsey and Company, June 24, 2021, www.mckinsey.com

5. *Transparency to Transformation: A Chain Reaction, Global Supply Chain Report 2020*, Climate Disclosure Project, accessed May 28, 2023, www.cdp.net

6. Mark Bannister, COP26, interview May 14, 2023.

7. "Sustainable Procurement," Reeve Consulting, 2023, www.reeveconsulting.com

8. Steve Chase, "Canada Seizes Goods Made with Forced Labour from China; MPs Urge More Action for Uyghurs," *Globe and Mail*, November 15, 2021.

9. "All Resources," Buy Social Canada, accessed May 28, 2023, www.buysocialcanada.com

10. James Dunne, "Indigenous Entrepreneurship: Making a Business Case for Reconciliation," CBC, September 30, 2022, www.cbc.ca/news

11. "Census Bureau Releases New Data on Minority-Owned, Veteran-Owned and Women-Owned Businesses," US Census Bureau, Press Release, October 28, 2021, www.census.gov/newsroom

12. Jessica Davis Pluess, "What Total Cost of Ownership Offers Sustainable Procurement," Business for Social Responsibility, September 11, 2012, accessed May 28, 2023, www.bsr.org

13. "Sustainable Purchasing Leadership Council," accessed May 28, 2023, www.sustainablepurchasing.org

14. "Sustainable Event Supplier Database," Jones, Meegan and Rotchild, Leor, last updated February, 2024, https://suppliers.greeneventbook.com.

15. "20+ Best Black-owned Vendors," The Vendry, modified January 12, 2023, https://thevendry.com

16. "Certified Social Enterprises" Buy Social Canada, accessed May 2023, https://www.buysocialcanada.com

17. Mark Bannister, 2023.

18. Ibid.

Chapter 10: Embrace Hybrid Events

1. "Zoom Stock Skyrockets Over 40% After Blowout Quarter, and It Expects to Keep Rising," *Forbes*, modified December 15, 2020, www.forbes.com

2. David Betke, GreenShows / Do Better Marketing, interview June 18, 2020.

3. Natalie Campisi and Korrena Bailie, "42 Million Americans Still Don't Have Access to Broadband Internet," *Forbes*, modified May 26, 2023, www.forbes.com

4. "Write Good Alt Text to Describe Images," Harvard University, Digital Accessibility Services, accessed May 31, 2023, https://accessibility.huit.harvard.edu

5. Amir Kosari, "Colorblind People Population! Statistics," Colorblind Guide, modified November 12, 2022, www.colorblindguide.com

6. *A Net Zero Roadmap for the Events Industry November 2022*, Net Zero Carbon Events, accessed May 16, 2023, https://netzerocarbonevents.org

7. Ibid.

8. Patricia Duchene, "The Future of Events through the Eyes of Industry Professionals," *Forbes*, modified March 2, 2023, www.forbes.com

9. "The Visual Collaboration Platform for Every Team," Miro, accessed May 31, 2023, https://miro.com

10. "Events: In-Person vs. Online after COVID-19 Worldwide 2021," Statista, modified May 27, 2021, www.statista.com/statistics

11. "Top Meetings Industry Statistics: GMID 2023 Edition," Skift Meetings, modified March 30, 2023, www.eventmanagerblog.com/event-statistics

12. "Juno Award Winner Dan Mangan Took His Side Door Project to the Dragons—and Got an Offer," CBC, last modified November 10, 2022, www.cbc.ca/news

13. "Memorable Shows in Any Space," Side Door, accessed May 31, 2023, https://sidedooraccess.com/home

14. "Top Meetings Industry Statistics."

15. Elizabeth Shirt, GLOBE Series, interview May 2023.

16. "Find Meeting Venues and Event Spaces," Cvent, accessed May 31, 2023, www.cvent.com

17. *Global Virtual Events Market Size & Share Report, 2023–2030*, Grand View Research, accessed May 31, 2023, www.grandviewresearch.com

18. "The Ultimate Guide to Virtual Reality Marketing in 2023," Influencer Marketing Hub, modified December 23, 2022, https://influencermarketinghub.com

Index

About the Author

LEOR ROTCHILD is a nationally-recognized speaker, author, podcaster, and consultant with 20 years of sustainable business experience. He currently serves as the Senior Director at Upswing Solutions, a B Corp certified, boutique sustainability consulting firm.

Leor founded an environmental events company called Do It Green, which supported hundreds of events in Canada. He also served as Executive Director of Canadian Business for Social Responsibility, a national hub for sustainability leaders across all sectors.

Leor's writing has appeared in *The Globe and Mail* and CBC. His podcast—Pipelines and Turbines can be found on most major platforms and he delivered keynote presentations at events including The Sustainable Events Forum, The Walrus Talks, and the World Forum for a Responsible Economy.

He lives in Calgary, Alberta with his partner and two children.

Website: leor.ca

ABOUT NEW SOCIETY PUBLISHERS

New Society Publishers is an activist, solutions-oriented publisher focused on publishing books to build a more just and sustainable future. Our books offer tips, tools, and insights from leading experts in a wide range of areas.

We're proud to hold to the highest environmental and social standards of any publisher in North America. When you buy New Society books, you are part of the solution!

At New Society Publishers, we care deeply about *what* we publish—but also about *how* we do business.

- This book is printed on 100% **post-consumer recycled paper**, processed chlorine-free, with low-VOC vegetable-based inks (since 2002)

- Our corporate structure is an innovative employee shareholder agreement, so we're one-third employee-owned (since 2015)

- We've created a Statement of Ethics (2021). The intent of this Statement is to act as a framework to guide our actions and facilitate feedback for continuous improvement of our work

- We're carbon-neutral (since 2006)

- We're certified as a B Corporation (since 2016)

- We're Signatories to the UN's Sustainable Development Goals (SDG) Publishers Compact (2020–2030, the Decade of Action)

To download our full catalog, sign up for our quarterly newsletter, and to learn more about New Society Publishers, please visit newsociety.com.

ENVIRONMENTAL BENEFITS STATEMENT

New Society Publishers saved the following resources by printing the pages of this book on chlorine free paper made with 100% post-consumer waste.

TREES	WATER	ENERGY	SOLID WASTE	GREENHOUSE GASES
49	3,900	20	170	21,100
FULLY GROWN	GALLONS	MILLION BTUs	POUNDS	POUNDS

Environmental impact estimates were made using the Environmental Paper Network Paper Calculator 4.0. For more information visit www.papercalculator.org